WHY THE FRENCH DON'T LIKE HEADSCARVES

JOHN R. BOWEN

WHY THE FRENCH DON'T LIKE HEADSCARVES

Islam, the State, and Public Space

PRINCETON UNIVERSITY PRESS

PRINCETON AND OXFORD

Copyright © 2007 by Princeton University Press
Published by Princeton University Press, 41 William Street,
Princeton, New Jersey 08540
In the United Kingdom: Princeton University Press, 6 Oxford Street,
Woodstock, Oxfordshire OX20 1TW

Fifth printing, and first paperback printing, 2008
Paperback ISBN: 978-0-691-13839-8

The Library of Congress has cataloged the cloth edition of this book as follows

Bowen, John Richard, 1951–
Why the French don't like headscarves : Islam, the State, and
public space / John R. Bowen
p. cm.
Includes bibliographical references and index.
ISBN-13: 978-0-691–12506–0 (cloth : alk. paper)
ISBN-10: 0–691–12506–6 (cloth : alk. paper)
1. Hijab (Islamic clothing)—France. 2. Velis—Social aspects—France.
3. Muslim women—France—Clothing. 4. Clothing and dress—Religious
aspects—Islam. 5. Clothing and dress—Political aspects—France.
6. Islam and secularism—France. 7. France—Race relations. I. Title.
GT2212.B69 2006
391.4′30944—dc22   2006005111

British Library Cataloging-in-Publication Data is available
This book has been composed in Bembo Typeface
Printed on acid-free paper. ∞
press.princeton.edu

Printed in the United States of America

10 9 8 7 6 5

To my parents, *for a lifetime of love and support*

Contents

Acknowledgments

IN the introduction I acknowledge my intellectual debts, but here I wish to thank those who have shared their time, their thoughts, their experiences, their friendship; they include Marc Abélès, Fariba Adelkhah, Valérie Amiraux, Jean Baubérot, Didier Bourg, Saïd Branine, Jocelyne Cesari, Hanifa Chérifi, Jacques Commaille, Catherine Coroller, Hichem El Arafa, Hakim El Ghissassi, Claire de Galembert, Virginie Giraudon, Ghislaine Hudson, Christophe Jaffrelot, Riva Kastoryano, Larbi Kechat, Gilles Kepel, Farhad Khosrokhavar, Dhaou Meskine, Olivier Roy, Patrick Simon, Samia Taouati, Xavier Ternissien, Patrick Weil, Jean-Paul Willaime, and all those, cited in the text, who taught me about France. Fariba Adelkhah, Christophe Jaffrelot, Jean-François Bayart, and Gilles Kepel made possible a visiting professorship at the Institut des Sciences Politique in 2001 that allowed me to begin work on these questions, and they along with Riva Kastoryano have continued to make it possible for me to work in Paris, as has a more recent collaboration with the École Pratiques des Hautes Études through the good graces of Jean-Paul Willaime.

In France, however, it is above all Martine and Robert Bentaboulet who, by inviting me to join their family and engaging in endless discussions on the issues covered here, have made fieldwork both possible and much more than fieldwork. Such are the joys of anthropology, the continuing friendships of those whom we come to know as well as we do anyone in our "home" countries.

At Washington University I benefit from a wonderful and supportive scholarly environment and from the support of Georgia Dunbar Van Cleve and her late husband Bill. These traditions of beneficence for scholarship are one of our society's strengths. Many of my colleagues, too numerous to name, have given me comments and suggestions over the years. I have benefited from the opportunity to present portions of this book during 2004–2005 at Cornell University's Law School, at Stanford University's Department of Cultural and Social Anthropology, at Georgetown University's French Department, at Amsterdam University to members of the EU IMISCOE network, and in Paris to the International Congress of the Sociology of Law. I learned a lot from comments by anonymous readers of the manuscript and by my dedicated and perceptive editor at Princeton University Press, Fred Appel. The manuscript benefited enormously from conscientious and professional editing by Madeleine B. Adams and production editing by Meera Vaidyanathan.

My wife, Vicki Carlson, and sons, Jeff and Greg, have graciously understood my absences and, joyfully for me, accompanied me for some travel to France. Their love sustains me.

My parents made it possible for me to grow, learn, live, and, eventually, teach and write. To them this book is dedicated.

WHY THE FRENCH DON'T LIKE HEADSCARVES

ONE

Introduction

IN EARLY 2004, the French government passed a law prohibiting from public schools any clothing that clearly indicated a pupil's religious affiliation. Although worded in a religion-neutral way, everyone understood the law to be aimed at keeping Muslim girls from wearing headscarves in school. The law was based on recommendations issued in late 2003 by two prestigious commissions, one formed by the Parliament, the other appointed by President Jacques Chirac (the Stasi Commission). Their hearings and the media coverage of the issue depicted grave dangers to French society and its tradition of secularism (*laïcité*) presented by Islamic radicalism, a trend toward "communalism," and the oppression of women in the poor suburbs. Although some Muslims objected that the proposed law would violate their right to express religious beliefs and many observers doubted that a law banning scarves would seriously address the severe problems of integration in French society, the two commissions voted with near-unanimity for the law, and the measure passed with large majorities in the National Assembly and in the Senate. It went into effect in September 2004.

The debate and votes perplexed many observers. French public figures seemed to blame the headscarves for a surprising range of France's problems, including anti-Semitism, Islamic fundamentalism, growing ghetto-ization in the poor suburbs, and the breakdown of order in the classroom. A vote against headscarves would, we heard, support women battling for freedom in Afghanistan, schoolteachers trying to teach history in Lyon, and all those who wished to reinforce the principles of liberty, equality, and fraternity.

Given that relatively few disputes over scarf-wearing ever went beyond the classroom and that virtually no one accused scarf-wearing girls of presenting a serious danger to French society, why was a law that would force them to choose between leaving their scarves at home or leaving school be seen as such a broad palliative for France's social ills and such an important step for women everywhere? Why focus on this issue above all others? The French actions puzzled most of the world; many people saw it as at best a misplaced concern and at worst a violation of religious freedom.

It seemed to me that the law, and its broad support, should be explained. I realized that doing so would require unpacking a great deal about France, including France's very particular history of religion and the state, the great hopes placed in the public schools, ideas about citizens and integration (and the challenge posed by Muslims and by Islam to those ideas), the continued weight of the colonial past, the role of television in shaping public opinion, and the tendency to think that passing a law will resolve a social problem. I would then need to show how all these dimensions of French memory, society, and ways of thinking combined to move the political machinery toward passage of a law during 2003–2004. But I also wished to see what we could learn about France from the debates over the law. It seemed to me that its passage was one of those key moments in a country's life at which certain anxieties and assumptions come to the surface, when people take stock of who they are and of what kind of social life they wish to have.

I begin this volume by examining the long-term institutional arrangements that govern relations among the state, religion, and the individual in France. The key term in the debates about the law has been *laïcité*, a word that is particularly difficult to translate and that I leave in French throughout the book. As a philosophy about religion's place in politics and society, it can be translated as "secularism." But the word came late to the French language, and it does not appear in the major law (of 1905) regulating the status of religions. That law only restrains the state from subsidizing or extending special recognition to any one religion. In France's very recent history, laïcité has become one of those "essentially contested concepts," such as "freedom" and "equality," that provide resources for arguments, not starting points of agreement.[1]

Laïcité does not, therefore, serve as a useful analytical tool. It makes no sense for a social scientist or historian to ask, "Does this policy reinforce

laïcité?"—although it makes great sense for a politician to do so.² I prefer
to ask how French public figures understand the proper relationships
among religion, the state, and the individual, and how they justify their
arguments and policies in terms of concepts such as laïcité, Republicanism, and equality. Here I practice an "anthropology of public reasoning,"
which allows us to see connections among political philosophy, public
policy, and common sense by studying how people deliberate about an
important social issue.³

Indeed, throughout this volume I draw on French works of philosophy and sociology as guides to more widely distributed ways of thinking
about religion and society in France. Making this connection may seem
tendentious. I find, however, that French politicians, writers about public affairs, television "talking heads," and philosophers are much more
likely to read one another's work, be related to one another, or indeed
be the same person than is the case in most in other countries. Academics
strive to write newspaper columns, politicians cite current best-sellers
on domestic policy, and television producers have their newest books
reviewed by academics. The mechanisms of promotion and review in
France help to explain a phenomenon that everyone denounces but in
which everyone participates: *la pensée unique*, a single way of thinking.
Public intellectuals, editors, and producers are caught up in webs of re-
ciprocal promotion; it would be an unusually independent thinker who
could free her- or himself. Because these intellectuals aspire to become
well known in the public arena as well as (or sometimes instead of) being
respected as humanists or social scientists, they are subject to unusually
strong channeling forces.⁴ Whatever the strengths or weaknesses of this
sort of public intellectual life, it means that intellectual writings provide
relatively well-organized versions of orientations that one finds in popular writings, television programs, and political speeches.

But the philosophies, laws, histories, and attitudes about the role of
the state in religious life do not explain why the appearance of Muslim
schoolgirls wearing headscarves became a recurrently divisive issue. It is
not exactly right, for example, to say that religion remains entirely "private" in France. Leaving aside the legacies of Catholicism, we note that
the French state and municipal governments have endeavored to aid
Muslims in building mosques, to provide graveyard space for Muslim

burials, and to create a highly public quasi-state Muslim council. In doing so, they give official recognition to Islamic bodies. The state will certainly recognize and subsidize Islamic private schools by the end of the first decade of the twenty-first century. As we shall see in the next two chapters, this degree of state involvement in religious affairs is part of the French tradition. Why, then, did scarves in schools create a scandal?

It was not, of course, the scarves in and of themselves. This book's title is intended to be provocative, not sociologically precise. Many French women wear some sort of scarf, and many Muslims wearing Islamic dress are French. But these bits of cloth came to stand for certain fears and threats at several specific moments and because of several historical processes and events. In the second section of this book, I trace the gradually developing public presence of Islam in France. The story begins with colonial rule in North Africa, picks up the pace in 1989 with the first "headscarf affair," and moves to a still higher velocity in early 2003, when a bandwagon (or steamroller) heads toward passage of the law. This part of the story is largely about politics: about how anxieties over domestic and international threats combined at certain times to produce a set of opportunities for politicians. At three such moments, in 1989, 1993–1994, and 2003–2004, the headscarf became a convenient, and prominent, symbol of external and internal dangers to France.

The story is also about the lives of the women and girls who wear Islamic headscarves and who confront fluctuating public opinion about who they are and what their headscarves mean. The story is only incidentally about Islam, however. Although elsewhere I examine Muslims' debates about the proper understandings of Islam in France, this volume is an anthropology of French reasoning about Islam, politics, and public life, designed to understand broad French responses to what became (for better or worse) a symbol of Islam.[5]

In the final section, this quest takes us to three major anxieties in France, each linked to the headscarves by politicians, intellectuals, and media producers. It is a particularly intriguing feature of the headscarf debates that although "defending laïcité" was cited as the major justification of the law on religious signs, the arguments carried out in the media linked the scarves to more concrete social concerns. I highlight three such concerns: the growth in "communalism" at the expense of social mixing, the increasing influence of international "Islamism" in France, and the denigration of women in the poor suburbs.

During the early 2000s, public actors linked each of these concerns to the public presence of Islamic headscarves. In doing so, they drew on deep-seated philosophical assumptions about what French society ought to be and equally deep-seated fears about what it had become. I examine both the assumptions and the fears as they have become part of public reasoning. I draw on French works of sociology or political theory to interpret televised exposés about Muslim threats, and I learn from those exposés about the emotions lying under the surface of the philosophy.

My approach has been that of an anthropologist, or at least of the kind of social anthropologist that I have become. I prefer to look for naturally occurring arguments, presentations, and debates, and to draw out of those events certain ways of acting and reasoning that can help account for other actions. I also interview those who are involved in these debates and events, and I read their works. For these purposes, I think about interviews as approximations to naturally occurring events (rather than as windows into attitudes, for example). I try to prompt someone to speak on a familiar topic, on the assumption that the response will include ways of speaking that the speaker also uses in more natural settings. But I prefer conversations to interviews, events that occur because of a social connection already established, which include casual chats and dinnertime conversations but also arranged conversations such as the extended interview about headscarves included in chapter 4.[6]

These interviews and conversations highlight collective narrative habits, which shape the ways in which members of a society attempt to resolve problems.[7] For example, I am often struck by the tendency of French public figures to frame the discussion of nearly any important social issue in terms of its long-term history. You must look back to Philippe Auguste or Henri IV, Robespierre or Rousseau, they say, before you can understand our society and our values. The current French ambassador to the United States, Jean-David Levitte, once told me that the difficulty in explaining the new French law to Americans was that to do so he had to retell, each time, so much of French history.

This collective habit leads public figures to emphasize (or invent) continuity over rupture. By framing the many concerns surrounding head-

scarves in terms of the history of laïcité, for example, French public figures can claim to speak for a France of long-term structures to which
newcomers must adapt. Furthermore, nearly all French public figures
claim that the French share certain basic Republican values, including
the equality of men and women and the removal of religion from the
public sphere. To argue that these values be shared is a valid political
project; to argue that they have been shared by all French for a long time
is to occlude some very recent debates about women's rights and the
public role of the Church, not to mention the intense divisions in post-
war French public life over politics, religion, and social equality.[8]

I began research in Paris in early 2001. My research has continued
through world-shaking events directly implicating Muslims and the
United States: 9/11, the attack on Afghanistan, the invasion of Iraq.
These changes have affected how people have reacted to me as an American. Whereas at the beginning of my research, Muslims would be more
likely to speak with me than with a French researcher (I was less likely to
be a police agent, and I shared with many of them the status of outsider), I
am sure that some Muslims in Paris looked on me with greater suspicion
after the Iraq invasion. Two things helped me: that I had begun research
prior to those events, and that I already was credentialed as a scholar of
Islam. Muslims in France were and are very interested in learning about
Indonesia, where I had done my previous fieldwork, and I could give
lectures and classes on Indonesia and on Islam in the United States. I
continue to give public talks as part of my research; among other benefits,
it makes the research more a joint effort to learn about Islam in pluralistic
societies than a one-way relationship between researcher and subjects.

My relationships with non-Muslim French scholars, officials, and
friends have perhaps been less directly affected by these recent events. I
have had little difficulty calling on people to talk about the issues discussed here; indeed, public figures have valued the project of trying to
explain to a wider audience how and why the French have taken the
steps they have taken. At times in this book, I refer to the works of
colleagues both as sources of knowledge and as indicators of French ways
of approaching these complex topics. I do not think that this dual appreciation of their work in any way lowers its scholarly value or lessens
my appreciation of its perspicacity. We all write from within our back-

grounds and our circles of reference and readership. I hope that these excursions into their work are taken in that way.

Many books and articles have been written about the headscarves, about Islam and Muslims in France, and about laïcité at the beginning of the twenty-first century. I mention many of these works in the chapters that follow, but in particular I draw on studies of Muslims in France by Jocelyne Cesari (1994, 1998), Nacira Guénif-Souilamas (2000), Gilles Kepel (1987), Farhad Khosrokhavar (1997), Paul Silverstein (2004), and Nancy Venel (2004); studies of laïcité by Jean Baubérot (2000, 2004), Émile Poulat (2003), and Olivier Roy (2005); Alain Gresh's (2004) treatment of the headscarf issue; and comparative studies by Jocelyne Cesari (2004), Adrian Favel (2001), Joel Fetzer and Christopher Soper (2005), Riva Kastoryano (2002), Gilles Kepel (1997), Michèle Lamont (1992), and Nikola Tietze (2002). I am immensely grateful to have been able to rely on this scholarship and that of many others. The present work seeks to do something a bit different, however, which is to focus on French ideas and concerns in the light of new challenges.[9]

I am often asked what I think about the law of March 15, 2004 (as it sometimes is referred to, rather officiously, in France). I am gratified when, after I have talked about why and how the law came to be passed, people are still unsure what I think. I see my role as a friendly critic. On the one hand, I wish to show how the law's advocates have drawn on long-term ways of thinking about the state, religion, and the individual in France, and how they have responded to very real concerns about how a newly diverse population can live together in one country. On the other hand, I underscore the political pressures to "do something" and do it quickly that rose to new heights in late 2003, the ways in which televised and print coverage played to popular fears, and the extraordinary symbolic weight given to a scarf worn on the head by a small number of schoolgirls. My interest lies in explicating the reasons and the mechanisms more than in rendering a simple judgment "for or against." In juxtaposing reasons and fears, debate and exposés, I would hope that the reader finishes this volume with a sharper sense of how publicity, philosophy, and politics can combine to produce a law, and that he or she remains, as I hope to remain, an informed skeptic.

PART 1

STATE AND RELIGION IN THE LONG RUN

TWO

Remembering Laïcité

LET ME begin by characterizing a way of thinking about the individual, the state, and society that strongly shapes public discourse and decisions in France, a way of thinking often called Republicanism. Of course, France has a wealth of competing ideas on these topics, and to claim (as many do) that the French once agreed on certain values (left unsaid: "before the immigrants came") is to ignore those competitions. Communists, hard-line Catholics, National Front supporters, and free-market "liberals" (in the European sense) all have their distinct views of things.[1] But some in each of these categories, and most of those who generally vote for the moderate Left or Right, come together, at certain key moments, around French Republican ideals.[2] And even more important for the purpose of this book, those in the government and the media find Republicanism to be the safest place to anchor their particular policies, attacks, and analyses, *especially* when these are under siege.

According to the Republican way of thinking, living together in a society requires agreement on basic values. People in many countries would agree with this claim, but French Republicans seek to rigorously and consistently justify policies according to this idea. To do so means adhering to a certain brand of political philosophy, one that emphasizes general interests and shared values over individual interests and pluralism. That philosophy is, roughly, that of Jean-Jacques Rousseau.[3] It requires the state to construct institutions and policies designed to integrate newborns and newcomers into French society by teaching them certain ways of acting and thinking.[4] If the society has the right mechanisms to integrate people, to make them into citizens, then the state can be quite generous in welcoming immigrants, extending borders, even conceiving of a European Empire or a transoceanic one. But these mechanisms require immigrants to take on the values and the behaviors that signify that one has become French.

The institutions of integration must be centrally designed and controlled to ensure uniformity, which implies an important role for the state.[5] (*State* in France always means the central state and its own employees, not regions or cities or "government" in general.) The state sets itself the task of creating citizens who are properly prepared to participate in public life. State officials do this by educating them in schools and by exemplifying what it means to be a French citizen. This dual function of state institutions, to instruct and to exemplify, helps explain the concern over divergent and pluralistic appearances in the public schools.

Indeed, the schools are central for both conceptual and historical reasons. Conceptually, they play the role of public socializing agent. Historically, they provided the central mechanism to produce citizens over and against two cleavages: regional and religious. Schoolteachers were the designated agents to make "peasants into Frenchmen," meaning to increase the capacity of people living within French state boundaries to participate in a national public life, one that was lived in the French language and understood as part of a long-term French history. Teachers also served the Republican state by fighting against the Church's efforts to control the minds of primary school pupils. From the mid-1880s to the mid-1920s, the Third Republic succeeded, through a series of decrees, laws, and negotiations, in removing the Church from the public schools and depriving the Church of its public status, a dual victory that *later* was to be summed up with the single word *laïcité*.[6]

In the Republican way of understanding French history, integration and laïcité are twin signposts on the road to realizing the French political model. They point to historical processes, often aggressive ones, by which the state asserted its supremacy over alternative sources of power and truth. These processes have required the active work of the public school in forming the minds of the young in Republican ways. The idea of the private school thus ought to trouble the Republican consciousness. A concession to its Catholic and Jewish citizens, the state-subsidized private school offers an alternative to those who would prefer not follow all dictates of public schools or those who would rather socialize with people of their own faith. But even though in theory those private schools that receive state subsidies provide the same curriculum as do public schools, limit their religious instruction, and admit students of all confessions, they also reinforce the "communalist" division of society that Republicans denounce. Thus, some public officials find themselves in the awkward (at least logically awkward) position of saying that girls must attend class bareheaded so that all citizens will learn to live together, and then saying that those girls not wishing to do so could always make use of Muslim schools (were such schools to exist).[7]

Thus one finds a general embarrassment even among some people who support the new law. Rather than arguing that the law would have its intended effect, many of its proponents instead argued that France had to send a message that was consistent with its principles and its history. Indeed, when intellectuals and officials (the two categories densely interpenetrate) explain and justify policies regarding religion and society, they often begin by talking about history. The history they appeal to depends on the precise point they wish to make.

How to Think about State and Religion in France

I now offer two vignettes that illustrate this way of justifying the contemporary by reference to the past. These two stories also will clarify the ways in which Republicanism, inflected through the key notions of integration and laïcité, shape contemporary French policy about the place of religions in public life.

Learning the Common Good through the State

Brilliant, resolute, and difficult, the political philosopher Blandine Kriegel began her career by working with Michel Foucault and espousing Maoism before rising into the ranks of conservative governments.[8] She became an advisor to President Jacques Chirac, the chairperson of the High Council on Integration, and a frequent member of commissions to address important social issues. Mme. Kriegel works from a small office with a window, a large picture of the president, a television, and a computer, all packed into an apartment-style building across from the Elysée Palace. Gendarmes take turns manning the front desk. She is a small woman with dark blonde hair, animated, very demanding on all around her.

To my questions in October 2003 about Muslims in France, she emphasized France's distinctive approach to society. "We hold strongly to the principle of laïcité. We have to place ourselves in the public space, by abstracting from our individual characteristics, from where we came from, our roots. This is the idea of the social contract." Although a proponent of Rousseau's idea that citizens should be presumed to agree, in the social contract, to abide by general principles, Mme. Kriegel admitted that Rousseau's critics are correct in observing that individuals do not just come together to make such an agreement; they come with their particular traditions and histories. "All this is true," she said, "but here in France each individual has to abstract her/himself from those traditions and accept the transfer of certain rights to the Law. That is the contract: we move from pluralism to unity through consent." Here she followed word for word Rousseau's insistence in *The Social Contract* that the law concerns the individual in the abstract, not the particular circumstance of each citizen's life.

Does the acceptance of unity mean rejecting diverse traditions? Not entirely: "We accept cultural diversity; we ought to teach about the history of religions and appreciate that diversity, from cuisine to art, but we have to draw the line at personal rights, which are universal rights of every individual. These are human rights."

Finally, she explained to me how laïcité was not the same as the "Anglo-Saxon" idea of freedom of religion. "In Anglo-Saxon thinking, in Locke or Spinoza, it is the concrete individual who has rights; freedom of conscience is the foundation. In our tradition these liberties are guaranteed through political power, which guarantees a public space that is neutral with respect to religion. You see this with Henri IV, where Protestants were in state positions." She then explained that *public* means all that has to do with the state. "The public school is part of the public because it is where civic education takes place. And so is public administration. There will never be Sikh civil servants in France!"

Kriegel's final emphatic promise referred to the much-publicized British cases in which Sikhs, whose religious norms require them to keep their hair uncut and covered, had won the right to keep their turbans on even while working for the government. Her declaration summed up the contrast between French Republicanism and that curious amalgam that is the constant foil for French theorists, the "Anglo-Saxon" way of thinking. Here Rousseau stands against Locke, freedom through the state against freedom from the state, society as a "coming together" and "living together" against society as isolated rights-bearing individuals or (worse) as isolated communities defined by religion, race, or ethnicity. In the Anglo-Saxon mirror image of France, agents of the state display their separateness in their turbans or their headscarves, and the people follow suit.

In her many books on the state, Kriegel has discovered the roots of the French state-society relationship in an even older history of political thought. For her, the key French idea is the "Republican polis" (*la cité républicaine*), the title of a 1998 monograph in which she traces the genealogy of the idea of citizenship—a method signaling her own intellectual origins with Foucault. She locates its origins in the Greek idea that the citizens *were* the state. In Sparta, it was only after finishing public education and partaking of a public meal that one became a full citizen.[9] Kriegel's intellectual career has been devoted to rehabilitating the sovereignty of the state against the antistate heritage of May 1968. In her effort to understand state power she shows herself the student of Foucault; in her political journey from Maoism to the Right she maintained her faith in the state's transformative role. In her dual intellectual-political career she embodies both the importance of situating and justifying politics through long-term historical accounting and the value given to the state as the domain in which citizens realize their freedom.

The intimate relationship of the common good and the state has a long lineage. One source is in the premodern efforts to develop a legal base for the king to give away what belonged to others. At the top of the feudal pyramid of protection and obligation the king found himself obliged to give lavishly—a practice that long outlived the feudal period. To do so he had to appropriate others' property. Legal scholars invented the principle of "public utility" to justify this practice. This idea became closely linked to the idea of the "common good," which long predates the philosophy of Rousseau. In the medieval period, the common good was moral good derived from God. Gradually, both public utility and the common good came to be understood as referring to the good of society rather than the good of God, and by the sixteenth century the two notions provided a rationale for the power of the state.

After the Revolution, the state continued to be responsible for implementing the common good, now outlined in constitutions and including economics and welfare (*bienfaisance*) as well as law and justice. One of the contributors to the quasi-official musings on the key "sites of memory" in France expressed the post-Revolutionary conception thus: "It is in the daily relationship between citizens and public servants that the common good expresses itself most directly. . . . The originality of the French is to have made the common good into an attribute of the state."[10] The editor of this "sites of memory" project, Pierre Nora, adds that "it is by means of the State—that is, by its history and politics—that France has remained aware of itself." It is thus the state rather than language, constitutions, or culture that unifies France. Nora adds that the French Civil Code, having survived through many different constitutions, "might be regarded as the true constitution of the French people."[11] Pierre Rosanvallon's claim that the development of the Code was a "veritable therapeutic enterprise" for those who participated gives us a clue as to the intended effects of passing the law against religious signs: social regeneration through legislative catharsis.[12]

The State as Guarantor of Organized Religion

If the state oversees the common good, does that mean that it monitors religion? And if so, what is meant by laïcité? To find out, I had a series of conversations with Vianney Sevaistre, who from early 2002 to late 2004 served as the Chief of the Central Office of Organized Religions (*Chef du Bureau Central des Cultes*) within the Ministry of the Interior. One might be surprised that supersecular France has a Bureau of Religions. Did not Mme. Kriegel just tell us that religion is supposed to be kept out of public administration?

I went to see M. Sevaistre to learn about how the French state regulates Islam, but I realized that first I needed to know what the state was doing regulating any religion. Sevaistre is a tall, lean man of military background who was eager to explain how he managed to learn the fine points of French policy. He pointed out that the relevant word was *culte*, which means, roughly, "organized religion," but which I will leave in French for the moment. "There is no legal definition of *culte*," he told me in his office in the Ministry in October 2003. "You know, the word 'religion' (*religion*) has no place in French law. Religion has to do with the relationship of the individual to God. *Le culte* is the outward expression of that relationship." He had asked for an explanation of *le culte* from a member of the State Council (*Conseil d'État*). The State Council, created as an advisory body to the king, serves as the highest administrative tribunal in France. It hears appeals from state institutions (including schools) and has been the ultimate arbiter in headscarf disputes.

Sevaistre gave me a photocopy of his handwritten notes of his conversation and summarized the contents. "*Le culte* involves three elements: the celebration of the *culte*, as in the mass; its buildings; and the teaching of its principles. That's all! Freedom of *culte* is limited to those three domains. This is because of history. In French history, we came out of the religious wars, both Catholics against Protestants and then the Catholic Church against secularists, and then we developed the system of laïcité. This limits the freedom of *culte* so as to prevent the reemergence of wars. Other things, such as selling peanuts or selling books, are not part of a *culte*, such that when Scientology comes here and sells a book that costs 10,000 euros, that goes against public order."[13]

He continued, now entering the field of recent combats. "I know well that in the United States you have a different history: the Pilgrims fled from constraints on their individual liberty, so, there, anything can be a religious practice. There are even racist religions. They could not be allowed to practice here because they would contravene public order. So the Scientologists complain that their religious freedom is limited, and even some Protestant [evangelical] ministers come here and complain of that, that 'the French are savages, and we used to be like you but then we learned more'—of course they also killed off all the savages, but I don't say that—'and so you ought to change your system of laïcité.' They do not understand French history. Even the French Scientologists with whom I meet, even if they understand that a bit, they say that they cannot explain it to their American colleagues. So are we supposed to change our laws because you have trouble explaining France? But we have wandered far from our topic."

In fact, we had not wandered at all; understanding the ideas behind government control of religion was central to our discussion about Islam and the French state. Organized religion, as I will now translate *le culte*, is supposed to remain just that: organized, bounded, orderly, contained in its buildings and defined by worship practices in those buildings. If it strays into the street, selling tracts or proselytizing, it is out of bounds, and even when it is tolerated it is no longer protected by the French constitution and can easily be quashed in the name of protecting public order.

In Sevaistre's discussion, as in Kriegel's, if you do not "understand French history" you cannot understand the current sense of key terms. His historical references are negative ones, to the times of disorder, the wars of religion, which the regime of laïcité was intended to prevent. (This use of history in fact resembles the rhetoric of classical Islamic political theory, which assigned to the ruler the task of avoiding disorder or *fitna*.) State control of organized religion is intended to guarantee public order. That is why the state must be active in defining, regulating, and observing the activities of religious leaders, and also, as we shall see, in protecting and guaranteeing the ability of practitioners to worship.

The state is restrained only insofar as the law forbids it from promoting or favoring a particular belief. This important legal restraint on the state is contained in the major law regulating the relationship of religion and state in France today, the law of 1905. Article 2 of this law stipulates that "the Republic will not recognize any religion." As Sevaistre explained it, "This second article should be understood in this way: the Republic does not decide to favor one religion or to favor one school of thought within a religion."[14]

In fact, the State Council (Conseil d'État) does "recognize religions." More precisely, it confers legal recognition on a religious association as complying with the requirements set out by the law of 1905. In considering an association's request for such recognition, the Council examines its claims that its followers come together in formal ceremonies, that the beliefs contain universal religious principles, that the group has had a long existence, and that its activities do not threaten public order. In some cases, the Council has changed its position, for example, when it recognized Jehovah's Witnesses as a legal *culte* after having rejected them on previous occasions because of their refusal to accept blood transfusions and their active proselytizing. Gaining this recognition by the State Council exempts an association from taxes, and it opens the door to assistance from municipal governments in building houses of worship or in gaining access to public spaces for special services. Recognition does also bring limitations. The 1905 law requires that a *culte* limit its activities to religious ones and not engage in "cultural activities" such as publishing or healing—a requirement that keeps Christian Scientists from obtaining recognition, and that some Protestant churches have tried to change to allow churches to benefit from publishing revenues. But the same people who organize a religion may also organize a cultural association to carry out such activities, and most religious associations do indeed have parallel cultural ones.[15]

Together, these two highly placed public officials illustrate three features of French ways of talking about issues of contemporary social life: the penchant for explaining an institution by giving its genealogy, the idea that one finds both liberty and order only through the intervention of the state, and the strong distinction between the public practice of organized religion and the private activities characteristic of one's personal religious belief.

The first feature, the ubiquity of genealogy, reinforces the tendency to look for continuities in French history in order to explain contemporary policies. In France, the historian, political theorist, or philosopher often plays an important role in defining public debates and public policy. Social scientists also may play that role, but only insofar as they also become normative theorists, advocating certain state policies. The sociologist Dominique Schnapper, a member of the Constitutional Council, is an example of someone whose writings are aimed at supporting French policies of promoting integration. By contrast, sociologists (such as the late Pierre Bourdieu) who criticize the system may become academic and media stars, but they will not play the same policy-defining role. If they bring empirical findings to bear on a policy decision without first theorizing those facts in Republican terms, their findings are ignored. Such was the case with the many sociologists who had studied schoolgirls in headscarves in the 1990s and who often were critical of efforts to ban these girls from the schools. The presidential commission charged with considering a law against religious signs (the Stasi Commission) took testimony from hundreds of experts, but they neglected to ask any of these sociologists to testify on their research.[16]

The second common feature is that the state is expected to regulate and protect both public order and the freedom of the individual. This idea defines Republican political ideology, usually in explicit contrast with the "Anglo-Saxon" model. In the schools, the state has the obligation to ensure that each pupil's freedom to learn, to cultivate her or his individuality, is protected. In this respect, the Republican approach can be given a philosophically liberal underpinning.[17]

Finally, these two vignettes point to the third common feature, the importance of the distinction between *culte* (organized religion) and religion (faith, belief, *croyance*). Organized religion has a cognitively salient template for most French in the institutions of the Catholic Church: a liturgy, performed inside a familiar sacred place once a week, with teachings intended to guide private life. Claims to do other things in the name of religion (sell tracts, ring doorbells, wear headscarves) are outside the template (and outside constitutional protection) and could be prosecuted if they contravened "public order."

Islam's public ritual practices, which include sacrifice, scarf-wearing, and prostrations in exotic buildings, are felt by some to threaten public order. The headscarf and the mosque are not objectively more visible than the nun's habit and the cathedral, but they are, or were, subjectively shocking because they were new, foreign—or perhaps, as reminders of a bloody, recent colonial past, not foreign enough, not foreign in an innocuous way as a Baha'i temple would be. Muslims' demands to live their religion publicly also made explicit the contradictions *already in place* between French ideas about religion's private character and the still-public role of France's Catholic heritage. The public ubiquity of crosses and churches could be ignored—had to be ignored—for reasons of civil peace, but ignoring crescents and mosques was more difficult.

LAÏCITÉ THROUGH HISTORY

Narratives about laïcité give to these elements both a temporal continuity and a historical *telos* or purpose. The history of relations between the state and religions in France is one of frequent conflicts and temporary resolutions, but to the extent that the historian can discern underlying continuities, he or she can claim to find a distinctive French approach to the issue that, because it is part of French history, should be maintained. One such continuity lies in the state's control of religions, the tradition of the "Gallican Church." Furthermore, to the extent that this history has a direction, progress can be claimed. In the dominant narratives of laïcité, history has moved toward the removal of religion from the public sphere, the Hegelian working out of a logic of laïcité. The law of 1905, celebrated as having proclaimed the separation of church and state, was but the outcome of a long prior struggle, with its Revolutionary thesis and Restoration antithesis. The law against religious signs in schools then can be seen as carrying still further that same struggle, along that same direction, toward a fully realized laïcité.

A handful of contemporary historians and sociologists function as the recognized experts on laïcité. Jean Baubérot and Émile Poulat draw on the prestige of their academic positions; Henri Pena-Ruiz insistently puts himself forward in print and on television as laïcité's high priest; Jacqueline Costa-Lascoux appears on nearly every government commission on pluralism, immigration, or laïcité. A number of other historians wrote new books in 2005 to commemorate the centennial of the law of 1905.[18] These laïcité experts are "public" intellectuals in the two closely intertwined French senses of that term: they speak to a general educated public as well as to academic audiences, and they work with or in the state as well as in universities or research settings. Their common element is that they see the past two hundred years of French history as "about" laïcité.

Jean Baubérot writes most of the short books on laïcité, those pocket books that are suitable for reading on the subway and that are intended for the busy French man or woman who is trained to feel guilty for not being up on current topics. Other writers cite Baubérot's analyses most frequently, so I take his version of the long-term history of French laïcité as a starting point for our ethnography of French thinking and as a guide through some historical markers.[19] Baubérot argues that modern French laïcité emerged out of a long history of experiments with state-church relations. When, notably, the rather bloody king nonetheless called Phillipe le Bel (1268–1314) asserted his political control over the Catholic Church, he inaugurated the tradition of maintaining an independent French ("Gallican") church vis-à-vis Rome, and of controlling this church from the palace. Despite the sharp changes that occurred thereafter—the Edict of Nantes (1598) allowing the practice of Protestantism, the Revolution of 1789, the succession of Empires and Republics—this model of state regulation of the church continued to dominate French politics until the late nineteenth century. It is this model that differentiates French forms of religious tolerance from their British counterparts in Baubérot's history. Whereas in France tolerance was a matter of royal regulation of a recognized religion, in Britain it was a generalized recognition of freedom of conscience. Both countries have uneven records of following these precepts—massacring dissenters, persecuting heretics— but the precepts have continued to shape the two countries' policies.

Republic versus Church

The Revolution is of course the main political watershed in French history-writing. Baubérot traces two modes of thinking about religion that developed after 1789. One emphasized the importance of maintaining a national, public religion, whether as the Catholic Church or as the brief-lived revolutionary cults of the goddesses Reason and Freedom. The second mode of thought emphasized the right of each individual to follow his or her own conscience. This right was affirmed by article 10 of the Declaration of Human and Citizens' Rights, which states, "No one may be persecuted for his opinions, even religious ones, provided that their manifestation does not disturb the public order established by the law."[20]

This dual orientation underlay a series of pendulum swings between state establishment of and withdrawal from religion. At first the Constituent Assembly considered the Catholic Church to be the national religion and part of the "public order" and non-Catholics to be both protected and warned by the new law. But the church was conceived according to the Gallican tradition, and in the 1790 Civil Constitution of the Clergy, the state required priests to take a new oath to uphold the constitution. The "refractory priests" who refused were persecuted for, precisely, "disturbing public order." Robespierre's rule was accompanied by persecutions of all religions, drawing the sharpest reactions (and brutal countermeasures) in rural areas. By 1795, after Robespierre's fall and in an effort to bring to an end the revolt, the government retreated from supporting any religion. It guaranteed liberty of conscience to all but forbade the exterior clothing or rituals of any religions, including funeral processions and bell-ringing. The pendulum had swung the other way, toward the intensely privatized notion of religion as faith and conscience.

Napoleon inaugurated a new version of Gallicanism, not in the form of a separate constitution of the clergy, but, through his 1801 Concordat with the Pope, as an agreement by which the state recognized and limited the Catholic Church as well as, through articles that Napoleon attached to the text of the Concordat, the Lutheran and Reformed (Calvinist) churches. Six years later, Napoleon added Judaism to this list of recognized religions when he created the Great Sanhedrin, a revival of a religious court once convened at the Temple of Jerusalem, as well as a separate council of Jewish notables. But at the same time that he recognized religions, he deprived them of the right to rule over family life. His Civil Code of 1804 required marriage to be performed by a civil authority, it permitted divorce—an innovation the Catholic Church was to reverse several years later—and it regulated inheritance. A subsequent law gave to the state the control of the university and the secondary schools—but by omission left the primary schools in the hands of the Church.

The Napoleonic solution to the church-state problem left unresolved the strong tension in French society between religious affiliation and antireligious sentiment. On the one hand, nearly all French citizens belonged to the Catholic Church, which continued to see itself as the guardian of morality and the molder of young French minds. On the other hand, the Revolution, especially under Robespierre, had nourished and legitimated a strain of thinking that was strongly antireligious. This tension produced a long-term conflict between the "two Frances," divided in ways often considered to oppose atheistic and socialist Paris to the Catholic and conservative provinces, but that in fact pitted people against one another within every region and social milieu.

The salience of the Catholic Church in the Revolutionary struggles meant that public debate about the Revolution would nourish strong, bitter memories. Religion could not be eased gradually into a private sphere of faith and prayer through gradual social processes of secularization because it was too much in the forefront of bloody struggles. Moreover, during the nineteenth century the state itself swung violently between Republican and monarchical (thus Catholic) regimes. During periods of pro-Catholic royal rule, the state would not only accede to some of the Church's social and political demands, but also recognize the truth of some of the Church's theological claims. (It passed laws that fixed the penalty of death for profaning a consecrated host on the grounds of the fact of transubstantiation, in effect declaring that to profane the host killed Christ.)

Laws on schools passed during the July Monarchy (1830–1848), the Second Republic (1848–1851), and the Second Empire (1851–1871) illustrate the ambivalence of a state caught in this tension. The Guizot law of 1833 required the creation of normal schools to train teachers, and required that all teachers, even those working for the Catholic Church, pass a state exam, but it gave to the Ministry of Religion the task of supervising primary schools. The Falloux law of 1850 required schools for girls as well as for boys, but it allowed the local priest to request that a teacher who displeased him be transferred. On other matters as well, the Church first advanced and then was forced back in its efforts to regain control over French society. Divorce was made possible during the Revolution, forbidden in 1816, and then reauthorized in 1884. In 1884 a law forbade religious signs in public cemeteries.

In geographically and linguistically peripheral areas, the first two-thirds of the nineteenth century was a time of growing Church control over schoolchildren. This trend was perhaps sharpest in Brittany, where the four districts (*départements*) created after 1789 were demarcated according to the existing four Catholic dioceses (which themselves had been established to fit with the four major Breton dialects). The clergy in Brittany had gained greater control over education and school administration after the Concordat. Moreover, teachers taught in Breton, further undermining the relationship of citizens to the French state.

The tension between Church and Republic exploded during the 1871 Commune, the uprising in Paris that followed France's defeat by Prussia. The killing of priests in Paris led to bloody reprisals by the conservative state. The Commune's pall lay over the debates about schooling for some time; the myth of the "Prussian schoolteacher" who won the war of 1870 through his superior teaching made it a matter of national self-defense to create a new, universal social morality in the minds of French pupils. Under the Third Republic, new curricula taught a secular form of morality that drew on diverse sources—Christian theology, Kant, and Confucius—and aimed to produce a generic French citizen. This citizen also would be freed from his or her regional traditions. This was the era of "peasants into Frenchmen," the teaming up of railroads and school-teachers to instill, sometimes severely, a sense of belonging to France rather than to Brittany or Bordeaux.[21]

In today's narratives of the struggle for the soul of schoolchildren, the Republican hero is Jules Ferry, who, as minister of public instruction, forged the school space into which, for the first time in the history of the nation, the Church could not go. A series of laws between 1882 and 1886 secularized the public classroom. All teachers had to be lay persons. Chaplains could give religious education after hours, and school would recess one day during the week to allow children to attend catechism, but inside the classroom only lay teachers and secular teachings would be allowed.[22]

These laws sharpened the conflict between advocates of continued Church control of schools and those who opposed the Church. Now *laïcité* became an object of struggle and emerged as a word: the Petit Robert dictionary gives 1871 as its first recorded use. The conflict reached its apogee in the Dreyfus affair (1898–1899), in which accusations of treason against a Jewish colonel brought to the fore the anti-Semitism that underlay some opposition to laïcité. The Catholic daily *La Croix* proclaimed itself the "most anti-Semitic newspaper in France," and accusations of plots by the Masonic Grand Lodge were amplified by the pro-Church forces. Those favoring a return to an era where the Church was in charge of morality grew increasingly vocal. They were met with equally intensified anticlerical positions, which shifted from admitting the value of religious morality, including that of the Catholic Church, to opposing religion in general.[23]

This legacy of combat against the Church in the name of Republic has been handed down through civic instruction, popular media, and teacher-training courses. The legacy helps to explain the degree to which many teachers and intellectuals see the contemporary presence of Islam in the schools as threatening to turn back the clock on at least two struggles: the fight to keep religion from controlling young minds, and the struggle to forge a common French identity—to which we will add in later chapters the struggle for gender equality in public and private life.

Creating the Legal Framework

It was a troubled social climate that saw the passage of two fundamental laws regulating social institutions: the 1901 law permitting citizens to form voluntary associations, and the 1905 law that took public status away from organized religions but allowed them to reorganize as private associations. These two laws created the two kinds of voluntary associations—generally distinguished as "law of 1901" versus "law of 1905"— available to citizens and, since 1981, foreign residents of France.

The 1901 law has provided the legal basis for a wide range of social and cultural activities, including teaching and outreach programs carried out by religious leaders.[24] However, the law also aimed to weaken Catholic institutions. It required that religious orders (*congrégations*) obtain authorization from Parliament. When the strongly anticlerical Emile Combes became prime minister, he used the law to close Catholic schools. By the fall of 1903, ten thousand schools had been closed on the grounds that they had been created by religious orders, even though their creation predated the 1901 law—a retroactive application of the law clearly not intended by the Parliament. A 1904 law went even further, forbidding people who belonged to religious orders from teaching, although the absence of sufficient public schools and teachers led the legislators to delay enforcement. (About the half the schools closed in 1903 reopened soon thereafter under the leadership of former teachers who had received permission to leave their orders and become lay teachers.)

The second major law from this period, the law of 1905, officially and explicitly ended the regime of recognized religions begun under Napoleon. Whereas the first article of this law guarantees "freedom of conscience and the free exercise of organized religions," the second article proclaims that the state "neither recognizes, nor pays the salaries of, nor subsidizes any religion." But, after spirited debate between those who favored denying religion any legal status and those who wished to guarantee worship, Parliament added provisions allowing citizens to reorganize religious bodies as private religious associations that would own and operate religious buildings and enjoy tax exemptions.

The 1905 law envisioned religions as part of civil society, and in this sense marks a moment in the history of French regulations of religions that was notably liberal, in the European sense. But the Church refused to accept the law, and in 1907–1908, France passed new laws turning over ownership of church buildings to town governments, except for the cathedrals, which remained the property of the state. This provision applied only to already existing buildings, which means that today, government subsidizes the Catholic religion far more than it does other religions. The vast majority of Catholic church buildings are subsidized by the state or by municipal governments, whereas such is the case for only about one-half the Protestant churches and 10 percent of the Jewish temples in France.[25]

After 1905, the intensity of conflict between anticlerical and proclerical factions diminished. The Church reorganized some formerly religious schools as "free schools," which were allowed under new laws regulating education. These schools formed nonreligious associations (under the law of 1901) for sports and other extracurricular activities. After the Great War, a number of new measures brought greater state support for religious institutions. New technical and commercial schools were created through a 1919 law allowing private religious-backed schools to apply for state financing. In 1923–1924 the French government and the Vatican reached a compromise that included Vatican acceptance of the 1905 law and continued French acceptance of "free schools."

State aid to private schools continued to churn debate on both sides during and after the Second World War, in towns and villages as well as on the national political scene, until the 1959 Debré law settled the matter. That law allowed private schools to retain their "particular characteristics," including religious ones, and to receive state funds on the condition that they taught the national curriculum and accepted students without regard to "origin, opinions, or beliefs." In other words, a Catholic school could be subsidized and include Catholic teachings, but those courses would have to be optional, in respect of the freedom of conscience of its students. In subsequent years, attempts to change the terms of the Debré law either to restrict or to expand the capacities of private religious schools have been met with massive demonstrations. The 1959 status quo thus appears to reflect a social and political balance of powers between Church and Republican interests regarding schools.

The current regime of laïcité thus came to include a great deal of governmental activity on behalf of certain religions. First, governments finance the upkeep of those religious buildings that already existed in

1905, even as it gives full use of those buildings to their religious groups. Second, it organizes and finances chaplains' offices for each of the major religions, to serve in public schools, hospitals, prisons, the military, and eventually in airports. By 2005, the state was making efforts to train Muslim chaplains as it had Catholic, Protestant, and Jewish ones. Third, it makes explicit provision for religious representation in a number of domains. It finances Sunday morning religious broadcasts on the France 2 television station, which feature programs on Buddhism as well as on Judaism, Catholicism, Protestantism, and Islam. It approves papal appointments of bishops. The president invites the representatives of major recognized religions to present their respects at the beginning of each year, and included a Muslim leader for the first time in January 2004. Finally, as we just saw, it pays the salaries of teachers in those private confessional schools that enter into contract with the state.

This current regime of laïcité is of quite recent date, having settled into place only in the late 1950s. Indeed, the historian Marcel Gauchet (1998) argues that it was not until the 1970s that laïcité became the general framework for French thinking about new social issues, such as the nature of family, divorce, homosexuality, and the acceptability of the Islamic headscarf. But then it was time to challenge that framework, or at least to ask if it did not better reflect an old combat with a now worn-out Catholic Church than the state of play in contemporary France.

LAÏCITÉ IN PUBLIC SPACE

Most historians of laïcité emphasize the continuity of Republican thought. The Revolution laid down the basic principles; the Third Republic extracted the church from the schools; the Assembly ratified laïcité in 1905.[26] Some philosophers and historians underscore the long process of secularization that made possible this evolution.

Other views are possible. Some writers underscore the sharp conceptual break that came with the privatization of the church in 1905 and the continuing struggle within Republican thought between a centralizing (or "Jacobin") political philosophy and one based on associations or civil society.[27] The political scientist Olivier Roy (2005) points out that, although a number of philosophers have created theories of laïcité, these theories conflict with one another, and it would be better to say that laïcité is the sum total of laws dealing with the relationship of the state to organized religions. Others, particularly Henri Pena-Ruiz (2005), have made laïcité into the equivalent of a religion, an atheistic philosophy, rather than a legally defined set of limits on proselytizing. Yet any attempt to see laïcité as a shared philosophy risks ignoring the bloody combats that pitted the French against one another over the proper place of religion in French public life.

Much as some would see laïcité as a guiding concept in French history, the word does not appear in the very law (of 1905) that is celebrated as its embodiment. Its legal status rests on its inclusion in a key phrase in the Constitution of 1946, repeated in that of 1958:

> Le France est une République indivisible, laïque, démocratique, et sociale.
> France is an indivisible, secular, democratic, and social Republic.[28]

Nowhere in these texts is *laïcité* defined. One view, a recent one, is that it designates not a specific set of rules regarding religious expression, but rather a protected, privileged, multifunctional social space within which Republican principles could survive and prosper. President Chirac expressed this idea in his December 17, 2003, address on religious signs in public schools. He noted that laïcité protects the freedom to believe or not to believe, to express and practice one's faith, but also that "it is the privileged site for meeting and exchange, where people find themselves and can best contribute to the national community. It is the neutrality of the public space that permits the peaceful coexistence of different religions."

Now, if laïcité defines the character of public space, then it can be cited as the justification for excluding any signs deemed dangerous to the free exchange of ideas. This notion of protected public space goes far beyond the law of 1905, which constrains the state, not pupils or other ordinary citizens. But what is meant by "public space"? Should the state forbid the wearing of headscarves in all public places, or at least those that are supposed to be "neutral"?

The word *public* is used in France in ways that often bring together three distinct meanings. In one meaning, that employed by Blandine Kriegel in the discussions cited earlier in this chapter, institutions and actors who are part of the state are thereby "public," as in "public (or civil) service" (*service public, fonction publique*). In a second sense, all that is out in shared social space is public, as in a "public thoroughfare." Finally, anything that is in the general interest can be said to be in the "public interest," as when a private corporation is deemed to be of "public utility." Some uses of the term *public*, perhaps even President Chirac's speech, leave unclear which meanings are involved.

Public service and public schools are both clearly "public" in the first sense. Civil servants, including teachers and principals, are supposed to speak and act in accord with state directives. They also embody the state; school personnel, in particular, are supposed to act in accord with a certain idea of French citizenship, and to form, through example as well as lesson plan, the future French man and woman.[29] The law of 1905 prevented public institutions (public in the first sense) from favoring one religion, and, arguably, it also prevented public servants from signifying their own religion.

But even this restricted sense of *public* contains ambiguities. Is a public bank different from a private bank in its relationship to citizens? How far can a private school that contracts with the state to provide "the same curriculum" deviate in the way teaching takes place from what is demanded of the public school? These institutions may or may not be "public" in the second sense of openness, visibility, and shared social space. A bus is "public space" no matter who owns it, as is the street and the public park. A public school is not really as public as a park, because there are strict limits on who can enter, and the same holds a fortiori for those temples of Republican public (first sense) deliberation, the Senate and the National Assembly. Both spaces are highly guarded and for the most part closed to the public. On the one hand, the citizenry owns the temples of the Republic; on the other hand, the state limits access to them, making them visible but distant, and thus, perhaps, all the more imposing.

Public can also take on the meaning of the general good, and legally does so in the phrases *public interest* and *public utility*. The latter phrase has served historically to give warrant to associations that otherwise might be denied the right to exist, and was given explicit legal status by the 1901 law on associations. As we saw earlier, this sense of the word *public* derives historically from the idea of the "common good," which became the responsibility of the state. Space thus may be private in the first two senses, in that it neither belongs to the state nor is open to the public, but it may serve public utility, usually as a result of a contract with the state. Here we find the justification for private schools. The state funds private schools and pays their employees if they are considered to serve public utility. (The Great Mosque of Paris similarly is controlled by a private association "of public utility" and is aided by the state.) Private schools perform a state-determined function in the same manner as do public schools. They then become subject to state inspections. A private enterprise, such as a television station, may also be required to perform certain actions if by its very nature it should serve the public interest.[30]

Islam's Challenge

It is in the relatively recent, expanded meaning of a secularized public space, Chirac's sense, that laïcité was deemed to be under threat from Islam. As late as 1999, however, the threat had not yet been identified quite so clearly. The major historians of laïcité agreed that laïcité had by and large won its struggle, and that the next challenge was the integration of society. Islam's presence was acknowledged but not given a special place in the discussions. The May 1999 issue of *Le Monde de l'Éducation*, the publication of record on school issues, was devoted to "laïcité, an ideal to reinvent." The contributors to the issue emphasized the challenge of fully implementing laïcité in Jewish and Catholic private schools. In two articles, Islamic headscarves were mentioned but placed in the broader context of struggle against the Catholic Church, seen as continuing to mix religion into the science curriculum of private confessional schools.

Only five years later, the consensus in the media was that laïcité was in peril and that Islam was the cause. In January 2004, as the proposed law against religious signs in public schools went to the National Assembly, *Le Monde de l'Éducation* decided to devote its main section to "laïcité contested." The editors began the section by posing the question: "How could laïcité, one of the founding principles that French society took as established, find itself so threatened?" Now the tone was one of regret over missed opportunities plus alarm at rising dangers.

In its title, the lead article complained of "the lost territories of laïcité," a reference to an influential 2002 book, *The Lost Territories of the Republic*, which blamed problems in schools on "Arabic-Muslim culture" (Brenner 2002). The article quoted three "local actors." An adjunct director of a teacher-training institute (Institut universitaire de formation des maîtres, IUFM) regretted that teachers had still been focused on fighting the Catholic Church rather than seeking a new dialogue with Muslims. An inspector at the Ministry of National Education blamed current problems on the acceptance of North American multiculturalist ideas under former president François Mitterrand, at a time when France should have been legislating against the headscarf. A teacher of history and geography at a high school in Aubervilliers (northeast of Paris), where the most recent "headscarf affair" had erupted, pointed out the irony that the school had been able to handle all problems through dialogue until this one incident, which had inspired the proposed law. Other articles focused on student refusals: to study a text illustrated with a nude from classical art, to listen to the teaching on the Holocaust, to participate in swimming classes. One teacher recited verses from the Qur'ân to justify her position. For example, she quoted the verse "You should eat what you are served" in support of the requirement that all students eat the same food and that no separate halal menus be provided. Now Islam was *the* threat to laïcité; the combat had to be waged once again.

Misplaced Concreteness

Laïcité remains one of those "essentially contested concepts" that is politically useful precisely because it has no agreed-on definition.[31] Or rather, it is useful for political debates because its use conveys the double illusion that everyone knows what *laïcité* means and that this meaning has long been central to French Republicanism. It is not that the historical accounts are "wrong"—nearly all the recent histories are serious studies of concepts, debates, and institutions, and they have that high quality for which French historical writing is famous. It is that they provide a narrative framework that permits public figures—politicians, journalists, or public intellectuals—to speak *as if* there is an historical object called "laïcité" that emerged from bitter struggles (the wars of religion, the Revolution, the Paris Commune), led to the forming of a social contract (under the Third Republic), and was enshrined in law (1905) and constitutions (1946, 1958). In this account, laïcité represents the General Will and indicates the Common Good. It is a Historical Actor. It must, therefore, have a philosophical base that then can be drawn on to derive new laws and regulations—such as regimenting the wearing of religious signs in public space.

The difficulty with this notion is that there is no "it." Not only has there never been agreement on the role religion should play in public life—some in France hold laïcité to guarantee freedom of public religious practice, while others think that it prevents such practice—there is no historical actor called "laïcité": only a series of debates, laws, and multiple efforts to assert claims over public space. As those debates came to concern Islam, many public figures had recourse to claims about a venerable "it" that could provide solutions to the new challenges. But no such firm ground existed; no easy deductions of new laws from old principles were possible. What ensued were tempestuous debates about what laïcité *should* be and how Muslims *ought* to act, not in light of a firm legal and cultural framework, but in light of a disappearing sense of certitude about what France was, is, and will be. Hence the desperation; hence the urgency.

THREE

Regulating Islam

IN CHAPTER 2, I argued that in the late nineteenth century the idea of laïcité, born of the struggle between the Republic and the Catholic Church, was grafted onto a much older model of state control of organized religion. As public figures began to grapple with the growing public presence of Islam, they had to work within the terms of this hybrid model, a model that had developed well beyond the dictates of the laws to become a set of norms about the proper role and presence of religion. According to its terms, the state must control religion but keep it out of the public arena. It must refrain from "recognizing" a religion in the sense of favoring it, but it must "recognize" it in another sense, that of regulating and protecting it.

Islam has added new complexities to this model because of France's colonial adventures and postcolonial entanglements. As it acquired colonies and protectorates, France found itself a "great Muslim power," aiming to encourage "moderate" forms of Islam overseas and, as part of that effort, at home. Long after decolonization, the French state continues to see its creation of a domesticated "French Islam" as a matter involving foreign governments as well as French institutions.

French intellectuals and politicians are trained to make their way through such landscapes of legal, political, and logical tensions. They must make Islam wholly French while working with its foreign supporters, and they must keep religion out of state affairs while recognizing official Muslim partners or "interlocutors." In the everyday politics of practical laïcité, their efforts sometimes take surprising turns. We turn to three cases that shed light on the complex ways in which the precepts of laïcité are interpreted and applied with respect to Islam: the state's role in financing mosques, the development of Muslim sections in cemeteries, and the creation of the French Council on the Muslim Religion. These cases all concern the difficulties of maintaining theoretically prescribed boundaries between the state and religions and between France and the rest of the world.

ISLAM IN PUBLIC SPACE

Colonial ventures started it all off. As the French found themselves pulled deeper and deeper into North African affairs in the course of the nineteenth century, they found themselves supporting Islam in order to rule Muslims. The ways they did so left their traces on contemporary policies and on the nature of immigration to France.

Although the Muslim populations subjected to French rule lived in West and North Africa, the islands of the Indian Ocean and elsewhere, it was the histories of French rule in three North African states—Tunisia, Morocco, and Algeria—that most sharply marked French Muslim policies and attitudes. Tunisia and Morocco both were protectorates of France: Tunisia from 1881 to 1956 and Morocco from 1912 to 1956. The protectorate was a form of indirect rule, with a French chief administrator (the *résident général*) and an indigenous ruler, the sultan of Morocco and the bey of Tunisia.

The politics of these two protectorates sharply diverged, however. The Moroccan ruling line retained its power through French rule and after independence. This continuity of rule was critical for political legitimacy, because the king's right to rule came from his claims to descend from the Prophet Muhammad. Although institutions of Islamic education were transformed by colonial rule, Moroccans continued to attend higher Islamic schools, and sent a disproportionate share of men to become imams in French mosques.[1]

Tunisia, by contrast, developed hostility toward the political expression of Islam. Today's Tunisian government grew out of a secular nationalism that often has been hostile to Islamic movements. Brutal repression of "Islamists" and suppression of free speech after 1991, in particular, led many politically active Tunisian intellectuals to seek refuge abroad.

Many of these intellectuals founded religious schools and associations in France, and today they dominate the world of French-language Islamic education.

Algeria's history with France has been radically different. Incorporated as a colony in 1830, Algeria was home to generations of people of French ancestry. From 1871 on, French policy was to make Algeria into part of France itself rather than a protectorate or a colony. This French Algeria would be bifurcated. The colonizers would be fully French citizens, with French political and social institutions at their disposal. The Muslim colonized would remain as a separate, "indigenous" population with a distinct personal status.[2] They were governed by the legal regime of what after 1881 was called the "*indigénat,*" in which their family affairs were judged according to a version of Islamic law—unless they renounced that status and applied for citizenship. (By contrast, Jews in Algeria were automatically given citizenship by the 1870 Crémieux decree.)

Until independence in 1962, Algeria was administered by the Ministry of the Interior, while Morocco and Tunisia were ruled from the Ministry of Foreign Affairs. Algeria's three *départements* had the same legal status as those of metropolitan France, except that a dual electoral college ensured that less electoral power would be held by français musulmans d'Algérie (Muslim French of Algeria) than by Christians and Jews. As late as 1961, by which time all Algerians had become legally full French citizens, the Paris police chief Maurice Papon could issue a directive to limit the freedom of movement of these French Muslims, reminding officers that Muslims could be detected by their facial features. Among the legacies of colonial rule was the memory among Algerians that, as the entrepreneur and advocate for "positive discrimination" Yazid Sabeg has put it, "France established in Algeria a social and interethnic organization based on communalism and discrimination, ignoring its own republican principles."[3]

The Great Mosque of Paris

Beyond the confines of French territories, the Third Republic sought to build a strong French presence in the Islamic world and to make France a "great Muslim power."[4] One way to achieve this goal was to construct an Islamic edifice, a great mosque.

The idea first surfaced in 1895, but it was only after the First World War that the project was developed, at a time when France sought to win the favor of Arab nationalists.[5] The government encouraged Muslims living in French-controlled territory to make the pilgrimage to Mecca. In order to create a French presence on that sacred land, France appointed an Algerian, Abdelkader ben Ghabrit, to direct the Society of Pious Trusts and Islamic Holy Places, based in Algiers.

The French government also gave to that association the task of creating a Muslim Institute in Paris. Because the 1905 law concerning laïcité prevented the state from directly financing religious activities, the government made sure that the Institute would be a cultural center, with conference rooms, a library, residences, a bath, and a restaurant as well as a mosque. In 1921, Abdelkader converted the Society into a French association and the government arranged for the land on which the mosque was to be built, in Paris's fifth arrondissement, to become the private domain of a public entity, Assistance Publique, so that the complex could legally include a mosque.[6]

This complex way of fashioning a legal status and finding funds for the Institute and its Great Mosque followed the old political pattern by which the state promoted and controlled religious institutions. But it also inaugurated a new *legal* pattern with respect to Islam. The state used the possibilities accorded by the 1901 law (which permits the state to finance nonreligious associations) in order to indirectly finance the Great Mosque. The state provided the land and gave funds to the Society, which was not a religious body even though it dealt with property to be used partially for religious purposes. The Society then sought additional money by taking up collections in French-dominated Muslim territory. By 1922, the Society was ready to start building.

If the Institute was to be technically a private, French institution for legal reasons, the Great Mosque had to have a very public, international presence for political ones. The entire process of creating the mosque was highly publicized as the symbol of a peaceful Islam, one that worked wholeheartedly with that great Muslim power, France. In 1922 a representative of the Moroccan sultan laid the building's cornerstone. Maréchal Lyautey, in his dual function of résident général of Morocco and the sultan's foreign minister, inaugurated the construction of the building itself. Moroccan artisans carried out the decorative work. The Institute was inaugurated in 1926 by the president of the French Republic and the sultan of Morocco. The ruler of Tunisia came one month later to officially open the conference hall and to show that the project was a common endeavor among French territories. The inauguration occurred just two months after France and Morocco had finished the bloody war of the Rif against an Islamic nationalist movement, and the prominent role played by these rulers affirmed an Islam of accommodation and collaboration against a dissident Islam—a role that the Paris Mosque has never ceased to play in France.[7] France also claimed the mosque as a monument of thanks to the thousands of Muslim soldiers who had fought and died for France.[8] In practice, however, it became a place for French to enjoy an exotic cup of tea and for respectable Muslim visitors to worship; shabbily dressed Muslims were turned away from its prayer hall.

Between 1954, when Abdelkader died, and 1992, when the current rector, Dalil Boubakeur, assumed office, the Great Mosque was fought over by competing interests in Algeria, Tunisia, and Morocco, with the French government working to prevent complete control from falling to Algeria—and ultimately failing, as it is currently effectively, if not legally, under Algerian control.

The mosque's history illustrates the two general problems of legitimacy confronting the French state and its Muslim "privileged interlocutors." First, the state wishes to appoint those who represent its subjects, at the risk of thereby weakening the legitimacy of these appointed "representatives." From its very origins the Great Mosque of Paris was supposed to be created and led by Muslims for Muslims, but only if at the same time those Muslims could be designated by the state—which made them appear as the state's instrument.

Second, the state wishes the mosque to be the symbol of "Islam of France," but its leader serves at the pleasure of the Algerian government. Of course, prior to 1962 Algeria was part of France, but independence did not mean the end of dual control of the Great Mosque. Old habits die hard, and both sides sought to retain their power over the shape of Islam in France, where the majority of worshippers were Algerians either in origin or in citizenship.

At times the interior minister, who now has jurisdiction over the mosque, still conducts what might appear to be foreign affairs. In 2002–

2003, the minister, Nicolas Sarkozy, obtained agreement from the relevant foreign consulates for his program of building a representative body of Muslims in France. In late December 2003, Sarkozy obtained from the imam of Cairo's prestigious Al-Azhar Mosque, M. Sayyid Tantawi (who claims to be Sunni Islam's highest authority), a nod of approval for a ban on headscarves on the grounds that, although Muslim women should wear headscarves, sovereign states had the right to make their own policy. Sarkozy claimed that the imam's blessing was in return for the creation of a council for France's Muslims. In matters of Islam, domestic and foreign policy continued to be intimately related.[9]

How Does the State Support Mosques?

Although the Great Mosque of Paris has a specific colonial history, the current logic of state-mosque relations is little different from that at work in the 1920s. To have a Gallican Islam means having visible sites for organized religion, such are enjoyed by Catholics, Protestants, and Jews. The state is interested in creating respectable places for Muslims to worship not only to place them on an equal footing with others, but also so that they can be made visible and accountable. As Interior Minister Nicolas Sarkozy said in 2003 to the Stasi Commission, "How can we expect them to obey the law if we don't invite them to the table?"[10]

Even though politically and constitutionally the state has an interest as well as a responsibility to support the capacity of Muslims to worship, the legal way to do so is not always clear. French legal scholars interpret the law of 1905 as preventing the state from simply building and financing a mosque for a community—with the exceptions of those parts of Alsace and Lorraine that were outside of France in 1905, and several overseas territories. Directly financing a mosque would contradict the statute's requirement that the state not finance or subsidize any organized religion. But two other ways are open. The state may directly fund a nonreligious association (formed according to the law of 1901) or it may take other measures to aid a religious association (formed according to the law of 1905) short of direct aid.

As an illustration of current strategies, let me turn to the story of a project under way to build a mosque in the city of Bobigny, northeast of Paris, where the government has worked with a group of Muslims. One of those Muslims is Hakim El Ghissassi, editor of magazines and

Web sites and promoter of public colloquia throughout France on topics relevant to Muslims. Hakim lives in Bobigny. On two occasions in 2004 I discussed the mosque project with him. In February, we talked in the office of his Muslim monthly magazine, *La Medina*, in Saint Denis. He began by contrasting the strategy his group had followed with the "electoral blackmail" strategy pursued by many other Muslim groups, in which people offer a block of electoral support in return for a promise to build a mosque. In several cities around Paris, local activists have spoken with pride to me about their use of their electoral power to achieve results—in their eyes, an example of their integration into France.[11]

Hakim, however, explained why in Bobigny they had created an explicitly Islamic association (following the 1905 law) to develop the mosque project rather than the more usual and much easier practice of creating a cultural association (following the 1901 law) to build a cultural center, next to which there would be a mosque. Bobigny Muslims have four places to pray on Friday (one of which is the cemetery mosque, discussed later in this chapter), but many end up praying on the sidewalk, and on feast days the city has let them use a municipal gym. The mayor (Bernard Birsinger) paid his regards to Muslims worshipping in the gym on the Id al-Fitr celebration in 2004.

"We did not blackmail the mayor as has happened elsewhere," explained Hakim. "Rather, he realized that there was a large community of Muslims and that they needed a place to pray. It did take us four years to convince him, but we did, and we now have a plot of 2400 square meters on which we are allowed to build a three-story structure. The mayor wanted us to form an association according to the 1905 law on religious groups because it was, after all, for a mosque. Doing it this way gives us tax exemptions. It also means that the association is limited to promoting religious activities, perhaps including a school if it is religious, but no cultural activities.

"The 1905 law otherwise regulates the Israelite and Protestant religions. The Church never accepted it. They had dioceses created in 1927, based on a 1908 law that regulates them now. Perhaps this is why the mayor preferred that Muslims use the law of 1905? [The mayor, a Communist, is notoriously anti-Catholic and his move could be seen as snubbing the Church.] Our association has rights to the land in the form of a long-term lease [*bail emphytéotique*] for eighty-seven years, paying a token rent of one euro a month. The municipality may do this even thought they may not pay for anything; the association has to pay all the utility bills, for example. [Eighty-seven years, I learned later, means that the Muslim's lease will run out the same year as the leases granted to other religious groups.] The city also guarantees the loan for the construction of the cultural center and the mosque."

I also wanted to hear what the Bobigny city government had to say about the case, so a few days later I took the tramway to Bobigny from another northern suburb, and spoke with José Pinto, the advisor charged by the mayor with handling matters regarding "intercultural relations," legal problems involving foreigners, and religious affairs. Pinto is an engaging and pleasant man in his late fifties. He came from Portugal more than twenty years ago, and for many years worked for the Social Action Fund, a public corporation that aids associations, before joining the Bobigny city government.

Pinto explained to me that there were Sikh and Hindu temples in Bobigny as well as Christian and Jewish places of worship, and also a number of religious groups that had not been recognized by the city government. The city publishes a directory of all the associations existing within its borders, and he referred to it frequently during our conversation. For him, if you did not appear in the directory, then you did not exist. He said that if the city had not officially recognized a group, then it could not appear in the directory and no one from the city government would visit its site. (I noted to myself that the municipal government does energetically "recognize religions.")

I asked him what it took to be recognized.

They have to form an association "law of 1905" if they are in Bobigny, unlike most other cities where they may exist as a 1901 law association. When the mayor was a deputy in the National Assembly he sat on the committee that produced the report on *Islam in the Republic*.[12] This experience led him to take the position that if you are a religion you should declare yourself as such. In the case of the mosque we gave them a long-term rent, for exactly the same period of time we gave the Israelites, so that no one would say, "but you did this or that for them and not for us." At the end of that period the property reverts to the municipality and we then take care of the building and all the costs. This means that we have to be kept informed of any changes or construction in the building, because we have an interest in it.

It turned out that the same people who created the 1905 association to develop the mosque also created a 1901 association to promote cultural activities. M. Pinto had not, however, recognized the latter association nor had he included it in the directory. "The address was incorrect, letters were returned, and the people involved in it have not yet understood that they have to separate the two associations." Subterfuge is fine—that was how the government had been assisting religious groups all along— but M. Pinto had his limits; bureaucracy has its rules. As an immigrant-bureaucrat, José Pinto has been particularly concerned to ensure that Muslims do what he did—become good French citizens by following the rules.

"It took four years to get all this accepted by the Muslims," he continued, "because of their way of thinking. It does not take much to create a 1901 association: finding three people to be officers is sufficient. But for a 1905 association you have to have twenty-five people, and follow a number of rules, including allowing inspection of your books, and in return you get tax exemptions. They have to have some rooms that the municipality can use as well as other people not members of the association. For them it means entering more definitively into the framework of the Republic, and many were not ready to do that. We proposed the legal framework and asked them to discuss it, we brought in Hakim El Ghissasi to talk with them and it took all this time to convince them to do it. What we say is: if you want to come out of the basements, come out into the light! Don't just say that we discriminate, that you are victims of racism. We propose these solutions; take them! It is like the young woman the other night [at an assembly in Bobigny, discussed in chapter 8]. She kept decrying the racism she faces. . . . They have to accept the Republic."

In early October 2004, I saw Hakim El Ghissasi again and learned that the Bobigny Muslims had firmed up the two associations' lists. He told me that a Moroccan heads the 1905 association and an Algerian the 1901 association, "as one would predict, though it just worked out that way." (In France, Moroccans serve more often than Algerians as religious officials, and Algerians control many cultural associations.) The next problem to resolve was to find an imam who would satisfy both groups: if the imam was an Algerian the Moroccans would be upset, and vice versa. "So, we found a young man from the Comoro Islands, so there is no problem with any one population."

The Bobigny pattern caught on. In 2004, after years of deadlock, the city of Aubervilliers, north of Paris, agreed to recognize two associations, one religious and one cultural, to build a mosque and a cultural center. This arrangement points to a greater willingness by local governments to contribute to the financing of religious associations, at the very same time that the headscarf affair has sharpened tensions over Islam. But this is not a contradiction, for it is by "guaranteeing" organized religion, the language of the 1905 law, that the state and municipalities can also regulate it. José Pinto and his counterparts in France see their task as "bringing Islam into the light," which means both aiding Muslims to create visible places for worship and education, and pushing them toward accepting the Republic, with its laïcité and its integration.[13]

Can There Be Public Muslim Cemeteries?

I also prevailed on José Pinto to take me on a tour of the Muslim Cemetery in Bobigny, a singular entity in France that challenges, from a different direction, the notion of the laïcité of public space. He took me in through the old entrance to the public cemetery, which is subtly but clearly Islamic, with small signs in Arabic (see figure 1). The gateway once included calligraphic mosaics, but they were painted over in an effort to make the Islamic character of the space less evident. The gate gives onto a courtyard with a mosque at the end, which is still used for Friday worship and for prayers for the dead. This entrance has no indication in French that the road leads to a cemetery. Most people use the main entrance, which is directly off the road through town and leads to a parking lot and then to the graves, bypassing the mosque entirely. Pinto explained that the construction of the new entrance was in response to complaints about the presence of the mosque in a public cemetery, and that even now he receives complaints about the mosque.

The cemetery owes its existence to the nearby Avicenna Hospital, originally called the "French Muslim hospital" but renamed in 1978 after the Muslim physician Ibn Sina. The hospital, inaugurated in 1935, was intended for Algerians living in the region, and indeed was limited by law to accepting Muslims who came from the French colonies. "Often they had very specific illnesses, particularly tuberculosis," explained Pinto, "and in any case the hospital administrators did not want to mix French people with North Africans." If someone died, usually his or her

FIGURE 1. Old entrance to the Muslim Cemetery in Bobigny, 1994 (photograph by author)

relatives would send the body back to Algeria or another country for burial, but if there were no family members or if they were very poor the body had to be buried nearby. Although the Society of Pious Trusts (the same society that governs the Great Mosque of Paris) urged that such a cemetery be created, it was the prefect of the Seine *département* who in 1931 authorized the creation of a hospital cemetery, to be paid

FIGURE 2. Graves in Muslim Cemetery, Bobigny, 2004 (photograph by author)

for by the hospital (rather than the city). The authorization was part of the centenary celebration of the colonization of Algeria. The cemetery was built in 1936 and inaugurated in 1937.[14]

Both the cemetery and the hospital were administered by the prefect of the former Seine district of Paris until 1962, when they became part of the network of Paris-region hospitals run by Assistance Publique, the hospital service for the needy. Although the hospital was opened to all patients in 1945, the cemetery remained limited to Muslims. As in the case of the Paris Mosque discussed earlier, a private holding of a public entity could retain its confessional character. In 1996, however, that part of the cemetery that contained the graves was taken over by a multimunicipality agency that included representatives from the contiguous cities of Bobigny, La Corneuve, Drancy, and Aubervilliers. At this point it became a municipal, public space, and could no longer legally be limited to Muslims.

Today there are about seven thousand tombs in the cemetery. It has a number of sections, some in disrepair and some recently rebuilt. Those graves that were built in the 1970s often had two people buried in them;

explained Pinto. "This was before the Wahhabis were here," he said, referring to the strict approach to Islam associated with Saudi Arabia; "They demanded that the practice cease." Many of the newer graves had been reconstructed for people who had died earlier. Older graves are very simple. There are many Turkish graves, probably reflecting the fact that people from Turkey would not be buried in Islamic fashion in Turkey and so chose to be buried in France. The graves are constructed so that the Muslims face toward Mecca.

José Pinto was part of the team that undertook to "regularize" the graveyard's administration in 1995. "First we compiled lists of the dead and where they were buried. We contacted relatives and gave them the opportunity to purchase concessions and build proper graves. The concessions can be for five, ten, or thirty years, and after that they can be renewed or passed on as inheritance. If they are not renewed, then the ground is plowed over. If someone dies with no money and no one to help, then he or she is given a five-year concession; we are not going to refuse burial to someone because of lack of finances."

I was intrigued as to how people could be assigned burial in a public space as a function of their religion. Until the communes took over the cemetery, the Paris Mosque had to certify that the deceased was a good Muslim before he or she could be buried there. Municipalities could not undertake such a role. Pinto explained: "Well, this is a public cemetery so we cannot refuse anyone burial because of his or her religion, but we can make decisions, you know." (Here he made the French expression with hands and mouth to indicate that "it can be taken care of.") Pinto then led me through the complexities of flexible uses of public and private property to allow religion and laïcité to publicly, visibly, mix. He explained to me that the area of the cemetery grounds that lay just inside the front gate, including the mosque and extending right up to the fence around the graves, was private, and belonged to the Paris hospital service and social welfare service (Assistance Publique)—and the mosque continues to be maintained by the service.

Pinto explained that

> because it is private, it is acceptable to have the mosque there, although people complain sometimes because they consider it to be public space. But once you pass into the area with the graves, then you are in public space belonging

to the municipalities, and on these grounds you may not have any religious signs. But each concession, the grave sitting on its own foundation, is private, belonging to each person, and so on it you may have religious signs, such as the Islamic ones on these graves or crosses on the grave for Christians—as long as there is no danger that they will fall over and touch the ground. I have noticed in other cemeteries that often there is a large cross in the center but when I look closer it is always on a grave, that of a priest usually, that they have arranged to be right in the center of the graveyard.

This complex articulation of religion and laïcité through nesting spaces has a legal basis. According to a law of 1881, no confessional cemeteries were to be tolerated in France; all were to be secular. But a directive from the Interior Ministry in 1975 authorized mayors to permit "de facto groupings of Muslims within communal cemeteries." This directive technically left it up to mayors or prefects to determine who was a Muslim, a task that none of them wanted to undertake. A 1991 directive responded to their complaints to this effect, reinforcing their right to allow de facto groupings (usually called "squares," *carrés*) but also emphasizing that the cemetery was a "neutral" and "public" place, and that it was not up to mayors to verify "the Islamic character of the deceased." Rather, it was left up to the families to decide how to bury the deceased and where to do so within the cemetery; the state rendered that determination purely private.

Here lies the ingenuity of the scheme: a private outer area that retains its Islamic signs and mosque, and then public cemetery grounds, free of religious signs, but dotted with little islands of private concessions, which may elaborately and ostentatiously signify their religious character. Not that it is a scheme acceptable to all. People frequently complain to the municipalities and write angry letters to the editor.

In a letter to *Le Monde* in the edition of September 30, 2004, for example, a "historian of cemeteries" complains that the "recent reintroduction of areas for specific religions in secular communal cemeteries, made possible by decrees that deform the law, is a dangerous practice, and we have yet to see the communalist [*communautariste*] consequences." She presents a history with two defining moments: in 1791, the transfer of cemeteries from parishes to towns, and in 1881, the law directing officials not to recognize the deceased's religious affiliation or lack thereof. In her eyes, the law had been flouted by authorities who were too eager to placate the religious communities in their midst. They had weakened laïcité and strengthened communalism.

THE SEARCH FOR A MUSLIM "PRIVILEGED INTERLOCUTOR"

Controversies surrounding the state's role in regulating and supporting Islam have been complicated by the diversity and discord characterizing French Muslim organizations. In France, the state wants a single, national body with which to negotiate and deliberate, and from which it may draw legitimacy for its decisions. Since the 1980s, successive governments of both the Left and the Right have tried to create a "representative body" (*instance représentative*) for the Muslim religion. The latest such effort led to the 2003 creation of the French Council for the Muslim Religion (Conseil Français du Culte Musulman, CFCM) and regional councils (Conseils Régionaux du Culte Musulman, CRCM), for which elections were held in April 2003 and again in June 2005. Despite some ambiguous official statements, this new structure was not designed to "represent Muslims" (mosques, not individual Muslims, did the choosing, and only some mosques took part) but rather to give the French state a Muslim counterpart for practical discussions of policy.

As Vianney Sevaistre (who was, as you will recall, the chief of the Central Bureau of Religions in the Interior Ministry in 2003) explained the objective of this and earlier efforts, "the dialogue between the faithful of a religion and the state requires that the former have an identified interlocutor."[15] As an example, Sevaistre points out that the Ministry of Justice appoints prison chaplains on the recommendation of the appropriate religious body. For Catholics that body is the Bishops' Conference of France; for Protestants it is the Protestant Federation of France; and for Jews it is the central Consistory. Muslims have no such body. It is the responsibility of the Interior Ministry, continues the bureau chief, to guarantee public freedoms, in particular the free exercise of one's religion, and therefore to create such a body.

In Sevaistre's example, the role of this body is to certify that a chaplain has the appropriate knowledge and skills to perform his duties. The other major tasks that the ministry identified early on for this body included resolving disputes about Muslim cemetery plots, organizing flights to Mecca for the pilgrimage, training imams for mosques, and, particularly thorny on a practical level, organizing the animal sacrifice on the Feast of Sacrifice.

The legitimacy of the Interior Ministry's actions would be contested from various positions, but it depended critically on the parallels drawn with bodies governing other religions' relationships with the state. For Catholics, the Bishops' Conference of France in effect brokers between the Vatican and the French state and has done so for centuries, beginning with the 1801 Concordat with Napoleon and including the agreements made in the 1920s concerning the state's responsibility to maintain Church buildings as elements of the French heritage (*patrimoine*). The Protestant Federation of France, created in 1905 in response to the official separation of church and state, controls Protestant television broadcasts on state television, furnishes chaplains for the army and prisons, and in general tries to "coordinate" relations with the state. Two bodies speak with the state regarding Jewish affairs. The Consistory, created by Napoleon in 1808, regulates the inspection of food and pronounces on religious matters, and the CRIF (Conseil Représentatif des Institutions Juives de France), created as an underground network in 1943, claims (with some difficulty) to represent the many distinct associations of Jews in politics and public life.[16]

There have been three major efforts to create a Muslim "representative body," beginning in 1989, 1995, and 1999.[17] The first two failed largely over the role given to the Paris Mosque. As we shall see in detail in chapter 4, 1989 was the watershed year for public attention to Islam in France, with the first "headscarf affair" following on the Ayatollah Khomeini's fatwa against Salmon Rushdie for his *Satanic Verses*. Suddenly, there was an Islamic threat posed from within and from without. Interior Minister Pierre Joxe responded by creating an advisory Council for Reflection on French Islam (Conseil de Réflexion sur l'Islam de France, CORIF), which first met in 1991. It collapsed the following year when the rector of the Paris Mosque, Tedjini Haddam, was named to the new governing council of Algeria. The French government considered that he could not continue as rector, and (in consultation with Algiers) named Dalil Boubakeur to replace him. The CORIF disagreed with the choice and saw its usefulness ended.

The next attempt was made by the notorious Charles Pasqua, who became interior minister in 1993. A strong law and order man not known for finesse, Pasqua threw his force behind the Paris Mosque. In 1994 he gave the mosque the monopoly to certify slaughterhouse workers as qualified to kill animals in a halal manner. This right can bring in considerable amounts of money, as slaughterhouses seek such certified sacrificers to attract butchers, who themselves compete for the Muslim trade. But the Paris Mosque failed to create a workable system for certification, leading the ministry to grant two other mosques (in Évry and Lyon) the same right. In 1995, Pasqua formed a new Representative Council of French Muslims around a Charter of the Muslim Religion, centered on the Paris Mosque. This new structure left out the two other major federations of Islamic associations, the UOIF and the FNMF (see the discussion later in this chapter) and never had any authority or influence.

The third effort began with Jean-Pierre Chevènement, the interior minister in the Jospin government from 1998 to 2000, who created what he called the "Consultation of French Muslims" in November 1999. To this group he invited five Muslim organizations, representatives of six independent mosques (meaning not affiliated with one of the major federations), and six "qualified persons," Muslims favored by the government as "moderate" and intended to provide an intellectual counterweight to the large organizations. (Subsequently, two additional organizations were added and one mosque withdrew.) In January 2000, Chevènement succeeded in having these participants sign a charter that set out the "principles and legal bases regulating the relations between public powers and the Muslim religion." The text caused a stir because the government agreed to drop a clause guaranteeing the right to change one's religion.[18] The structure created in early 2000 continued through two subsequent ministers and was the basis for the eventual CFCM central bureau.

Because the successive ministers tried to incorporate the various components of Islam in France into the Consultation and the Council, by looking at their composition we can gain an idea of the sociology of Islam in France.[19]

A Brief Political Sociology of French Islam

Although France keeps no statistics on the religious beliefs or practices of its inhabitants, estimates of the number of Muslims resident in France today range from four to five million people, nearly all of them immigrants and their children, and about one-half foreign nationals. These estimates immediately bring to the surface controversies about proper and improper ways of classifying people in France and about deciding what it means to be "of" a religion. The government's High Council on Integration followed earlier scholars in estimating the number of Muslims at slightly more than four million, but insists that the number of people "of Muslim religion" would be closer to one million, the rest being "of Muslim culture."[20] The Council based its estimate of religious Muslims on surveys concerning how often Muslims pray in mosques. (Because French census takers are not allowed to gather data on "faith," figures on religions in France draw from immigration histories and surveys on religious practice.) Basing this estimate of those of "Muslim religion" on mosque attendance was consistent with the government's subsequent decision to organize elections for the CFCM around the mosques and award electors by the size of the mosque.

About 60–70 percent of Muslim immigrants to France have come from three countries of North Africa. Algerians and Moroccans have contributed the largest numbers, followed by Tunisians. Turks and West Africans form the next largest groups. Certain generalizations about these populations are useful for understanding the interplay of ethnicity and religion. As we saw earlier, Moroccans play a particularly strong role as prayer-leaders in mosques, probably because of the relative continuity in religious training in Morocco. Most of the major heads of religious schools and institutes are Tunisians, and many of those had been forced to leave Tunisia by the Tunisian government. Algerians (many of whom are Berber-speakers from Algeria's Kabyle region) have the longest and deepest ties to France, are particularly visible in organizing political and cultural associations, and are strongly present in the civil service. Turks are sharply divided over the question of laïcité because of the strong divisions in Turkey on the same subject. These generalizations must be nuanced, particularly in light of differences in education and social class across generations of immigrants from any one country, but they do reflect a set of social and historical differences.

Differences among Muslim organizations both reinforce and cross-cut these ethnic differences. Seven organizations have been represented in the Consultation and the Council. Three are much more politically important than the others. One is the Great Mosque of Paris, discussed earlier, with its networks of affiliated mosques, Algerian governmental support, and favorable image with some in the government (including President Jacques Chirac) as the strongest force for "moderation." The mosque can claim some degree of allegiance from Algerians, who represent the largest number of Muslims in France, and from other Muslims who mistrust the more "religion-minded" Muslim organizations, but it has been less successful in creating a set of activist supporters.

The National Federation of French Muslims (Fédération Nationale des Musulmans de France, FNMF) today is associated with Morocco, but it began in 1985 when the World Islamic League wished to support an alternative to the Paris Mosque. French converts to Islam were among the early leaders. As of 2005 it was a network with only a Paris storefront as headquarters, but with a respectable number of affiliated mosques, most of which were led by Moroccan imams. Its leadership was contested as Mohamed Bechari was challenged as president; among potential successors was the longtime imam of the Strasbourg Mosque, Abdellah Boussouf.

The Union of French Islamic Organizations (Union des Organisations Islamiques de France, UOIF) is the most visible organization of Muslims in France. Founded in 1983, it became known widely in 1989 when it championed the cause of the girls expelled in the first publicized head-Scarf affair. As its name implies, the UOIF federates local associations throughout France. Most of these associations are cultural associations with associated mosques; the UOIF claimed over 200 of them in 2005. The UOIF has related organizations for young people and women, and forms part of a larger European network of scholars. Since its inception the UOIF has sponsored an annual "Muslim gathering," held these days at the former airport site Le Bourget. Its leaders, Lhaj Thami Breze and Fouad Alaoui, are Moroccans, trained in political science and neuropsychology, respectively, but the UOIF is not identified with any one Muslim-majority country.

The remaining Muslim organizations represented on the Consultation and Council are weaker. Decisions at times have been taken without their involvement. The Coordinating Committee of French Turkish Muslims (Comité de Coordination des Musulmans Turcs de France, CCMTF) is the arm of the Turkish government bureau charged with religious affairs and was represented on the Consultation. In France it exists alongside the Millî Görüs Islamic movement, which controls the large Eyyüp Sultan Mosque in Strasbourg. Because Turkish politics are so sharply divided over questions of the public representation of Islam, the Turkish French organizations have been strongly divided as well (although this division may soften as the result of political changes within Turkey). On the one hand, the CCMTF and individual Turkish public intellectuals associated with that organization take a hard line against scarves in schools and on other issues (and tend to ally with the Paris Mosque). On the other hand, Muslims affiliated with or sympathetic to Millî Görüs are among the strongest advocates, not only of the rights of girls to wear scarves but also of the requirement that they do so. They tend to ally with the UOIF.

One organization is truly residual, in that it claims to speak for Muslims not already spoken for. The French Federation of Islamic Associations of Africa, Comoro, and the Antilles (Fédération Française des Associations Islamiques d'Afrique, des Comores, et des Antilles, FFAIACA) has generally played the role of denouncing domination by the major organizations and speaking out for the role of "qualified persons," but does not play a major role in decision-making. Muslims from sub-Saharan Africa have little power in the CFCM, and on the local level sometimes organize separately from North Africans. Some find their strongest ties to be through Sufi brotherhoods with strong links to their countries of origin. Muslims from other current and former French dependencies, particularly the Comoro Islands, Mayotte, and Madagascar, sometimes play local mediating roles. In two cases I know of near Paris (in Bagneux and Bobigny, the case mentioned earlier), Muslims chose a Comoro man to be imam in order to avoid struggles among North African country groups.

The Tabligh Jama'ah is the final movement to have been represented in the Consultation. The Tabligh is a worldwide movement headquartered in India that engages in proselytizing, particularly among "lapsed" Muslims. In France, an internal political dispute caused it to split into two rival organizations. Both groups, Faith and Practice (Foi et Pratique) and Mission and Call (Tabligh et Dawa) were represented on the Consultation, each with half the votes of the other organizations; neither fielded lists for the CFCM elections (but in 2005 they formed electoral alliances with the FNMF).

Several of the major mosques in France also were invited to participate in the Consultation. The mosques of Mantes-la-Jolie, Évry, Lyon, al-Islah in Marseille, and Saint-Denis in La Réunion retain a degree of independence with respect to the major organizations. Each has its own particular affiliations, however. The mosque at Évry, south of Paris, for example, corresponds to images of what mosques should look like, with a dome and a minaret. It also has one of the strongest multiservice profiles, with an active business certifying animal sacrificers, a service of sending corpses back to home countries for burial, and courses in Arabic and the basics of Islam for children and adults. The mosque is avowedly Moroccan, built by craftsmen from Morocco and run by Moroccans, but does not prevent others from worshipping. Each of the other independent mosques has its own history and activities.

Not all mosques have chosen to join this process. While Marseille's al-Islah has fielded candidates, mosques in Lyon, Toulouse, and Strasbourg either have remained outside the government's activities or have changed their positions in a continual process of bargaining. Prominent among dissenter mosques is Larbi Kechat's Adda'wa Mosque in Paris's nineteenth arrondissement. Kechat has chosen to remain outside government circles, at least since the 1990s when he was arrested by Charles Pasqua on suspicion of links to Algerian rebel groups (of which charges he subsequently was cleared). The mosque is best known in wider circles for the series of panel discussions on topics ranging from the specifically Islamic (jurisprudence, spirituality) to the more broadly social (adoption, AIDS), which include non-Muslim speakers.

Finally, the state recruited some "qualified persons," chosen mostly for their "moderate" positions and their lack of ties to foreign governments. Some, however, were attached to the same organizations already present in the Council. By 2004, the list included a lawyer active in cases involving Muslim immigrants (Fethi Derkaoui of Lyon); Malika Dif, a retired jurist; two key figures in French Sufism, the professor Eric Geoffrey and the leader of the Alawiya Sufi order Sheikh Khaled Bentounes; and the so-called "Great Mufti of Marseille," Soheib Bencheikh (who has no following in Marseille but relentlessly attacks the UOIF). There were five men and five women in this group.[21]

Distinguished as this group is, it does not include the leading Muslim public intellectuals engaged in teaching the religion to French Muslims and rethinking the bases of jurisprudence. Those people are not university-based intellectuals but activists, involved in schools, institutes, local mosque-based associations, publishing, or political activities. They generally try to preserve their independence from the government and in many cases have strongly opposed particular government policies (including the procedures followed to set up the CFCM). France thus is caught in a dilemma faced by most efforts to construct legitimate representation from the top down: those willing to be "co-opted" are also those with the least legitimacy.[22]

Forming the CFCM

The Consultation formed into two types of structures during 2000, and this overall architecture has remained in place through 2005. As a structure formed to plan the elections for the CFCM the members were called the Organization Commission (Commission Organisation, COMOR). They also formed seven working groups, one on each of the major tasks to be performed by the CFCM (trainings imams, licensing halal sacrificers, etc.). These groups brought in dozens of additional Muslim experts and activists. This working method continued under Chevènement's Socialist successor, Daniel Vaillant, and under the subsequent ministers in the government of the Right, Nicolas Sarkozy and Dominique de Villepin (a continuity maintained largely through the work of the councilors working on the Islamic dossier.)

By October 2001, the COMOR had established the election procedures for the new Council. Electors would be named as a function of the size of participating mosques. Local officials made inquiries with mosque leaders as to the size of their mosques. (It was shortly after 9/11, and calls received at night about mosque size created considerable anxiety.) The COMOR was unable to come to agreement about most of the other aspects of the election, including the roles to be played by the organizations, the mosques, and the "qualified persons."

Sarkozy wanted to be the minister who finally resolved this long-standing "problem," and he was frustrated at the difficulties of arriving at a solution. At a meeting in June 2002, Sarkozy demanded that the ministry find a new way to work because the thirty-six meetings of the COMOR "had only arrived at a *meager* result."[23] At his second meeting with the COMOR, on October 21, he set out principles to guide the elections to the CFCM, notably that minority "schools of thought" within Islam (for example, from sub-Saharan Africa) ought to be represented on the CFCM, that no single "school of thought" ought to dominate the final Council, and that Dalil Boubakeur would be the first president of the Council. (The ministry seemed to believe that "schools of thought" mapped onto Muslim organizations and that once a political solution to the problem of representation was reached, then the problems of religious disagreement would be solved.)

Faced with a seemingly endless struggle for power among the various associations, ministry officials sought to accomplish two goals. First, they wished to bring the negotiations to a close by devising rules for selecting members to the Council that would be at least minimally acceptable to all. Second, they wished to ensure that the two associations with the strongest control over participating mosques, the UOIF and the FNMF, did not end up controlling the Council. They tried to accomplish both goals by counterbalancing electoral power with the slots set aside for the minority associations (West Africans, Turks), the powerful independent mosques, and the "moderate" Muslim public figures.

Insisting that Boubakeur be the first president gave a prominent role to one of the state's favorite "moderate" Muslims, continued the policy of working with the Algerian government to regulate Muslim affairs in France, and provided an additional institutional counterweight to the UOIF and FNMF. Ministry officials were ambivalent about Boubakeur (Sevaistre was reported to have become fed up with his constant attacks on the UOIF) but he continued to play a useful role.

This choice dissatisfied the other major organizations, in particular the UOIF. Sarkozy paid a personal visit to the UOIF headquarters north of Paris to answer their concerns that the Paris Mosque had been given supremacy. And he made sure that the foreign governments with large numbers of Muslim citizens living in France were consulted. Over the summer of 2002 he spoke with the ambassadors from Algeria, Morocco, and Tunisia, and representatives of the Turkish embassy, and on October 8, the Moroccan ambassador asked that Sarkozy meet with ambassadors from the three North African countries. (Tunisia sent a representative.) The ambassadors approved the selection of Boubakeur as Council president and said that they would work to keep "the extremists" out of the process.[24]

In December 2002, the three large federations reached an agreement among themselves about the composition of the CFCM. The other members of the commission protested that they had been left out of the process, but most appeared to realize that the agreement was required to continue the process. On December 19, Sevaistre met with the COMOR at the ministry's retreat at Nanville les Roches. Sarkozy made several appearances at the meeting. To obtain agreement on the elections and the composition of the future Council, he demanded that the three highest offices in the new Bureau of the Council be reserved for representatives of the three most influential associations. Boubakeur would be president, and there would be two vice-presidents, each representing the other two major federations: Mohamed Bechari of the FNMF and Fouad Alaoui of the UOIF.

The first elections to the CFCM and the regional councils were held on April 6 and 13, 2003, in the twenty-five electoral districts into which France had been divided (one for each region and three for the Paris region, Île-de-France). Each mosque that decided to participate designated a certain number of electors, based on the size of the area used for worship, and these electors then voted for one or another of the competing lists of delegates to their regional council (CRCM), some of whose members would then sit on the Administrative Council and the General Assembly of the CFCM. Of the 1,316 mosques invited to participate, 995 did so—about three-fourths. They named 4,032 electors, and about 86 percent of the electors showed up to vote.

The electoral lists were tied to their respective countries of origin: there were Moroccan, Algerian, and Turkish lists. When the FNMF, the Paris Mosque, and the Turkish CCMTF agreed to divide up the offices of regional council president among themselves, and thus to oppose as a united front the UOIF, "it was at the highest level, in Algiers as in Rabat, that the signal was given for this agreement."[25] Indeed, at this election as with that of 2005, the process may have strengthened the power of the "home countries" over the French Muslim organizations. The smaller organizations formed joint lists with one or the other of the Big Three. Remarkably, given the degree of hostility among Muslim organizations, there were few accusations of electoral fraud. The FNMF and the UOIF emerged from the elections as the clear winners. The loser was the Paris

Mosque. Dalil Boubakeur was quickly summoned back to Algiers to "explain himself."[26]

In early May, the Council and the Assembly of the CFCM met to ratify the rules and composition of the new structure. The Assembly included 200 members, 75 percent of whom had been elected and the remainder chosen by the COMOR and the ministry. The Council had sixty-three members, two-thirds of whom had been elected; the remainder were in effect an expanded version of the Consultation's membership, with representatives of organizations and mosques and "qualified persons." This new Council adopted (51 to 9) the composition of the new CFCM Bureau. The Bureau accentuated the dominance of the major organizations: the Paris Mosque, the UOIF, the FNMF, and the Turkish CCMTF each had two members on the bureau, while the Faith and Practice branch of the Tabligh and the residual FFAIACA each had one. The five major mosques still were represented, but now there were only two "qualified persons," Dounia Bouzar and Soheib Bencheikh.[27]

What or Whom Does the Council Represent?

The details on the formation of the CFCM are necessary for us to pose the questions: Precisely what kind of body is it? Whom does it represent? Those with opinions on these questions usually draw parallels to bodies designed to represent other religious communities. Jews, for example, have both the Consistory, a body of rabbis called on to resolve religious questions, and the CRIF, composed of intellectuals and activists who speak out on issues of importance to French Jews. Is the CFCM more like the one or the other? One way to understand the Consistory/CRIF distinction is to see it through the French lens of private religious life versus public civic engagement. From that perspective, the Muslim body, which is called on to take public positions on issues affecting Muslims, is more like the CRIF. This view is taken by some Muslim religious leaders, who point out that the CFCM leadership is composed of political activists, not theologians or jurists. They propose the creation of a parallel body to pronounce on theological matters and to take up the training of imams, and argue that such a body would be the equivalent of the Consistory.

Others think that the CFCM is more like the Consistory than the CRIF, because it is expected to make judgments on religious matters, including the requirements for burial, sacrifice, and pilgrimage, and on the religious qualifications of chaplains and imams. From this perspective it is already a religious body, and not a body intended to represent Muslims. The many self-styled "secular Muslims" in France who are concerned with political matters affecting Muslims, from discrimination to security, are then free to organize into associations that would, like the CRIF, engage in public lobbying for particular concerns of their constituency. Indeed, some advisors to Dominique de Villepin during his time as interior minister in 2005 proposed, without success, that a separate body be created to represent "secular Muslims" (*musulmans laïcs*).

My interviews with a range of Muslim public intellectuals during 2001–2005, including a number who did not take part in the CFCM, found little opposition to the idea that there should be a body that deals with the state on practical matters of concern to Muslims, from providing slaughterhouses to organizing flights to Mecca. These sorts of activities always had been supervised or organized by the state, and few, if any, Muslims object to the idea that Muslims should have a stronger say in what the state decides. That is how things work in France. The CFCM was seen by many as a reasonable way of creating a national body that could advise the government with some degree of legitimacy among ordinary Muslims, many of whom are not at all fond of either the UOIF or the FNMF.

But it was far from clear to many Muslims just what sort of body the Council was supposed to be. The CFCM did not "represent Muslims" nor was it intended to do so. Sarkozy declared that it "does not represent the Muslim community," and Prime Minister Jean-Pierre Raffarin took care to distinguish between the "Muslim component of French society" and the idea of a "community," which runs counter to French Republican principles.[28] Furthermore, as was pointed out by the several associations of "secular Muslims" that emerged around the time of the elections, many, perhaps most, Muslims in France spend little time in mosques and thus could hardly feel represented by a mosque-based council. But the Council did not constitute a body of religious experts either. The delegates are not necessarily learned in religious affairs, nor are the three officials appointed to leadership posts in 2003, Boubakeur, Bechari, and Alaoui.[29]

Furthermore, the Council echoed the ways of colonial rule, where the resident would appoint ministers and local "leaders" who were supposed to speak for the people. In the case of the CFCM, not only did Sarkozy designate the Council's leadership, but he did so in consultation with the governments of those countries from which the leaders had come. Sarkozy's statement that he had made the rounds of the relevant foreign governments before completing his program was greeted with derision by those Muslim leaders not included in the revealed triumvirate.

The Council structure immediately found itself confronted with practical issues to resolve, and had to devise a division of labor among its bodies. The CFCM was supposed to deal with principles and the twenty-five regional councils were to handle technical questions. Thus, the CFCM might be asked (as it quickly was) to pass judgment on the *voile* (headscarf) question or on how Muslims ought to understand the Feast of Sacrifice, but the CRCMs would have to deal with specific voile challenges or the knotty problem of how to put in place slaughterhouses for the sacrifice. As we shall see, the voile posed a particularly difficult challenge for the Council on the national and regional levels.

How Far Should the State Go?

Although some politicians complained that Sarkozy was consorting with radical Muslim elements, namely, the UOIF (see chapter 5), most commentators lauded Sarkozy for succeeding where a long line of interior ministers from different parties had failed, and for co-opting Muslim leaders into what was in effect a state-run body. This period of euphoria in early 2003 led some to believe that finally the state, by controlling and domesticating Islam, would be able to assimilate Islam into the Republic. The provocative question posed in the title of a 2000 journal—"Is Islam dissolvable into the Republic?"—would finally be answered: "Yes!"

The Gallican moment for Islam encouraged others to suggest that the state could do a bit more for them, too. For a short period in late 2002–early 2003, calls came for a "tweaking" (*toilettage*) of the 1905 law to allow for state financing of houses of worship. Protestants supported this change despite their generally strong stand for laïcité (against the Catholic Church), in part because only church buildings dating from before 1905 have their upkeep paid for by the state, a clause that favors Catholicism. A number of politicians called for state financing of mosques so that Muslims would not longer need to seek foreign funding. As a former mayor of Mantes-la-Jolie, home to one of the largest mosques in the Paris region—one of the few that was constructed to be a mosque and was therefore dependent on foreign funding—stated, "I find it healthier that mosques be financed by public money than by foreign states."[30]

However, it was soon pointed out that the state already could grant nominal, long-term leases of land to mosques or churches, as in the Bobigny case, and that at the end of the lease the state then would assume responsibility for the building's upkeep. This approach seemed less radical than the direct financing of mosques, and indeed, as we saw earlier, it is increasingly practiced by Paris-area municipalities. President Chirac also made it clear during the spring of 2003 that he was opposed to any change in the 1905 law.

A second set of calls came for the government to finance the training of imams, again with the idea that doing this would reduce foreign control over Islam in France. The French state does not train theologians or imams, but under the terms of a 1875 law it already finances a portion of the Catholic Institutes in Paris and Lille. Proposals had been made to construct a faculty of Islamic theology in Strasbourg, where the Concordat legal regime still applies.[31] Although training imams could not legally be a state project, it could be run by the CFCM. The Interior Ministry determined that there were nine hundred to one thousand imams in France, and that 90 percent of them came from other countries: 40 percent were Moroccan, 24 percent Algerian, 15 percent Turkish, 6 percent Tunisian, and 6 percent came from Africa or the Middle East. One proposal floated at the time was to allow the CFCM to receive money from halal certification and to use those funds to finance an imam-training institute.[32]

Sarkozy's successor, Dominique de Villepin, returned to these ideas in 2005 when he proposed that the state finance the training of imams in secular subjects: history, law, and the French language. A pilot program in French was carried out in Marseille in 2005. But the curriculum council of the university designated to oversee the courses, Paris IV, voted against the program for reasons of "laïcité."[33]

De Villepin also proposed the creation of a Foundation for Islamic Works. French foundations are created and supervised by the state. This one would channel money from foreign states, particularly Saudi Arabia, to Islamic organizations in France. (These steps are exactly as one would predict from the past history of state regulation of religion.) But, as happens so often with projects identified with a particular minister, when positions changed in mid-2005, with de Villepin becoming prime minister and Sarkozy returning to the Interior Ministry, the future of these proposals became less clear.

The combination of state control and religious autonomy that characterizes the CFCM remains unstable. Tensions flared in late April 2005, when the interior minister asked the CFCM to quickly name someone to the new post of national Muslim chaplain for prisons. The UOIF secretary-general and member of the CFCM Fouad Alaoui resented the "instruction" given by the interior minister, pointing out that the CFCM already had a commission on chaplains that was to deliver a report to the CFCM so that it, and not the ministry, could make a decision, and on May 6 he resigned (temporarily) from the CFCM.[34] But the CFCM members could not agree among themselves on any candidates for the chaplain post.[35]

One thing was clear, that the state intended the CFCM to be its instrument in promoting its sort of Islam and ridding France of all other sorts. In 2003, Prime Minister Raffarin had ordered the CFCM to serve as "the enlightened word of French Islam to fight against deviant tendencies which could threaten our social cohesion." Raffarin himself played the mufti, quoting the Qur'ân to make the point, as an example of deviant tendencies, that forced marriages were incompatible with France: "No constraint in religion," he recited from the scripture.[36] Laïcité was alive and well because the state had its own Islamic body.[37]

PART 2

PUBLICITY AND POLITICS, 1989–2005

FOUR

Scarves and Schools

NONE of what I have said so far explains why the appearance of Muslim schoolgirls wearing headscarves in public schools has caused such uproar. Consider how "public" (in all senses) Islam has become in France. The French state and municipal governments have endeavored to aid Muslims in building mosques, to provide graveyard space for Muslim burials, and to create a quasi-state Muslim council. When they do so, they give official recognition to Islamic bodies. The state will certainly recognize and subsidize Islamic private schools by the end of the first decade of the twenty-first century. It has promoted the teaching of "the religious" in public schools. Government ministers have tried to coordinate the training of imams and to channel foreign funds to mosques through a state-created foundation. Why, then, did scarves in public schools create a scandal?

Scarves, of course, are not in and of themselves the problem. Scarves in silk, wool, or other fabrics are staples of a French woman's wardrobe. When in the 1960s and 1970s women from North Africa settled in France, the fact that some wore headscarves caused no outcries. Theirs was a common Mediterranean costume, little different from that worn by Catholic women in the south of Italy, Spain, or France itself.

It is less surprising that the crisis, if one there was to be, would take place in and around a school. The public school, or rather the idea of the public school, has for at least a century been the privileged and most sensitive site for debates about religion and the Republic. But when scarves first appeared in schools, teachers and intellectuals might have reacted otherwise: they might have ignored the scarves, or used the occasion to teach about Islam and religious toleration. They were under no legal obligation to react negatively; no one contended that the law of 1905 constrained *pupils*.

Teachers and principals reacted as they did more because of events taking place in France and elsewhere in the world than because of the niceties of laws and rules about laïcité. By late 1989, many in France saw Islam as a new threat and Muslim students as its carriers. They saw Islam this way because of two simultaneous developments: the children of Muslim immigrants in France were proclaiming Islam as their identity, and political leaders in other countries were proclaiming Islam to be their guide. Since 1989, conjunctures of events at home and abroad—war in Algeria, the attack on the World Trade Center and the Pentagon, problems in the poor suburbs—have continued to shape the rhythm of the headscarf story as it has exploded into or drifted out of public awareness. It is never just about scarves.

A More Public Islam

Although the large Muslim presence in France is far older than in other countries of Europe, the ways in which Muslims chose to publicly affirm their identity underwent a noticeable shift in the 1980s. That shift—away from an identity as immigrants and toward an identity as Muslims—is a large part of what made scarves the source of scandal rather than fashion.

France was the first European country to develop a policy of active labor recruiting abroad. Beginning in the late nineteenth century, the state and private companies worked together to bring men from overseas, and overwhelmingly from French Algeria and the protectorates of Morocco and Tunisia. Through World War II these men worked for short periods and then returned home. Algerian colonists made sure that metropolitan France did not keep for itself the labor-power the colonists needed for agricultural production. But after the war, laborers (many of them now French citizens) increasingly settled in France, often with their families.[1]

But the French state continued to act as if the workers' stays were temporary. Families as well as single workers were housed in large projects built in poor suburbs or in industrial enclaves, where they remained isolated from the French cultural mainstream. The state offered the children instruction in "languages and cultures of origin" in order to facilitate their expected "return home."

Two things went wrong with this policy. First, the reception turned sour. The bloody Algerian War ended with independence in 1962. Millions of French colonists and soldiers returned to metropolitan France, bitter over the loss of Algeria. Recession in France (and elsewhere) followed just over a decade later. Algerian workers in France came to be viewed as former colonial subjects who now—especially after the recession of the mid-1970s—were taking jobs away from native French.[2] The far-right National Front was nourished on these colonial memories and economic fears—its leader Jean-Marie Le Pen had fought as a paratrooper in the Algerian War.

Second, Algerian independence accelerated the demographic transformation of the immigrant population from male temporary workers to resident family units. More families from North Africa came to France after 1962 than before, and when Algeria and France halted labor immigration in 1973–1974 it became difficult to immigrate unless one did so in order to "reunite a family."

The children of these new families began to demand their rights as citizens or residents of France. Starting in the early 1980s, they presented themselves as a new generation of Arabs in France, as the *Beurs*. The word *beur* is a reversal of *arabe*, a transformation that follows the rules of French slang (*verlan*). The word became recognized throughout France in late 1983, when Beur men and women marched across France for their equal rights. They hoped that their "March for equality and against racism" would end racist violence and bring them into the French social and labor mainstream, but soon thereafter conflicts between immigrants and nonimmigrants erupted and many of the new Beur associations disbanded. The legacy of the Algerian War, the long-term suspicion of Islam, the visible difference that "native French" thought they saw between themselves and these new strangers prevented the repetition of the standard immigration story.[3]

The years following the disappointment of 1983 were the low point for many children of North African immigrants. Many felt caught between parents who never convinced their children that there was much to long for in a "home country" of bloody revolution, and native French who would never accept them into the club. In 1984, the writer Tahar ben Jelloun (1999, English translation) described them as "a generation doomed to cultural orphanhood and ontological fragility."

At this point the Beur generation took two divergent paths. Some of the movement's leaders followed the route of previous immigrant groups and joined the Socialist party, where they campaigned for color-blind equality, notably in the organization SOS-Racisme founded in 1984 by Harlém Désir. Others, less hopeful that standard Socialism plus unions could close the identity gap with the French, looked for new sources of meaning. Some thought that Islam would offer an identity that would distinguish them both from their parents and from native French society, which did not seem to want them. They attended lectures sponsored by nascent French Islamic organizations and read books newly translated into French. They thought they had found a new way of living in France.

The growing sense that "true Islam" could provide a third possibility for constructing a subjective identity, beyond the undesirable "North African" and the unattainable "French," led some Muslims in the late 1980s to demand that they be allowed to practice their religion in a public way, by building mosques, carrying out collective rituals, and dressing in an Islamic way. Projects to construct "cathedral mosques" were put forward in Lyon and Marseille during the summer of 1989.[4] These demands were not always welcomed by other French residents, and the resentment over economic competition that had fueled the Far Right in the 1970s now was reinforced by resentment over visible cultural difference, an unalterable newness on putatively ancient French soil. This general problem of visible difference appeared with respect to specific issues of the use of space and of bodies. Many in France saw large mosques as incompatible with the French built landscape, and late in the summer of 1989, one mayor even bulldozed buildings used by Muslims for prayer.[5] Others were offended by the sight of Muslims praying in the street on feast days, when the available buildings did not suffice. But above all it was on the heads of three schoolgirls, in September 1989, that collective anxiety focused.

Hijâb, Foulard, Voile

Why did headscarves play a role in this search for identity? The terrain is confusing: Muslims and non-Muslims speak of *hijâb*, *jilbab*, *foulard*, *voile*, with little clarity as to the differences among these terms. The Qur'ân does not mention veils or headscarves at all, but speaks of the need to erect a "curtain" (*hijâb*) between women and men, which in specific contexts can mean keeping women separate from men in a house, or wearing concealing garments. But this second use is explicitly introduced only with respect to Muhammad's wives, in a passage where the Qur'ân mentions the long flowing garment known as a *jilbab*: "O Prophet, tell thy wives and thy daughters, and the women of the believers to draw their *jilbab* close round them . . . so that they may be recognized and not molested" (33: 59). The use of *jilbab* in this way was closely linked in the minds of believers to Muhammad, such that the phrase *she took the jilbab* was used to mean that someone became a wife of Muhammad. Veiling already was practiced in some parts of the Middle East by higher classes, perhaps to signify the possession of sufficient wealth that the veiled or secluded woman did not have to work in the fields. In any case, it is nowhere prescribed in the Qur'ân. Only one verse is directed to all women, and it enjoins women to cover their private parts and throw cloths over their bosoms.[6]

In France today, *foulard* can mean simply "scarf," although some people today would use *écharpe* for a "non-Islamic scarf," given the strong associations between *foulard* and Islam (and the luxury store Hermès sells scarves only as *carrés*, silk "squares"). Although the 1989 incident was the *affaire des foulards*, in the 2000s the singular *le voile*, "the veil," has been used more frequently in the media. Many Muslims also speak of the *voile*, often as a translation of *hijâb*. The difference between *foulard* and *voile* does not correspond systematically to a difference between two types of garments. A woman referred to as wearing *le voile* might be wearing a simple scarf, or a combination of two head coverings, one covering the forehead and the other the top of the head and the shoulders, or a more unified garment including head covering, blouse, and skirt.

The two terms do differ, however, in their connotations. A *foulard* is a scarf, after all, and the plural, as in *l'affaire des foulards* suggests different types and colors of scarves, as in French society more generally. A *voile* is a veil, and it is nearly always used in the singular, suggesting a uniformity of garment, and perhaps a uniformity of thinking. For some people the expression brings to mind the veils associated with an older, more demanding form of Catholicism, to which most would not wish to return. To "take the voile" once referred to a woman's decision to join a religious order and cover herself as a sign of her submission and modesty. Additionally, it conjures up images of Afghan women with their faces covered, "veiled" in the more usual sense of the term.

In this book, I often use the expression *the voile* either when translating from a French statement or to refer to a general French way of speaking. I leave the expression in French so as not to suggest, by use of *the veil*, either that I am talking about face-covering veils or that I accept the confusions in meaning produced by the broad contemporary French use of *le voile*. This strategy has the drawback of introducing one more French expression, alongside *laïcité*, but it has the advantage of emphasizing that I am referring to French ways of talking about a social phenomenon.

In most ways of speaking about Muslim women's dress in France, the many elements that make up markedly Islamic dress—head coverings, blouses and tunics, skirts and trousers, and perhaps gloves—tend to be reduced in conversation to the matter of how, and how much of, the head is covered. Did the particular scarf cover the ears, leave the roots of the hair exposed or not, come down over the forehead? As we shall see, these degrees of head covering became, for many non-Muslims in France, important signs of the degree of religiosity or difference being signaled by a Muslim woman.

Who Wears Scarves and Why?

What has all this meant for Muslim women and girls in France? Since the mid-1990s, French sociologists have studied the lives of Muslims, particularly Muslim women, paying special attention to the roles played by headscarves.[7] Drawing on interviews with women from a variety of backgrounds, they have traced the range and variation in motives and meanings attached to scarf-wearing. Either despite or because these studies showed these motives and meanings to be complex, to be quite different from one woman to the next, and to shift over a lifetime, they were completely ignored by the Stasi Commission and by politicians calling for a new law.

In one of the early studies, carried out in 1993–1994, two sociologists, Françoise Gaspard and Farhad Khosrokhavar, set out to interview girls and young women who wore headscarves.[8] They found two major kinds of motives among these women. Some wore a headscarf as a way to satisfy their parents and ease their transition across the line of puberty and into late adolescence. Many of these girls adopted it during middle school years but then abandoned it during high school. They were not necessarily regular practitioners of their religion. But other, usually older girls began to wear headscarves as part of a conscious effort to create a new identity as they entered or left high school. For them, wearing a scarf was part of two simultaneous processes: defining themselves in Islamic terms and entering the world of post-secondary education and work. These women tended to be educated and successful, and to regularly pray, fast, and observe dietary rules.

These two types, along with immigrant women who had begun wearing scarves in their lands of birth and were not the concern of the study, led the authors to speak of "three meanings of the voile." They note that they did not find women with allegiances to political Islamic groups; to the contrary, all the girls and women emphasized their right to make their own decisions. Not that Gaspard and Khosrokhavar ignored the possibility that some of these girls would, even as they saw themselves as making free choices, find themselves caught up in a "neopatriarchy" of obedience to their brothers, their fathers, and eventually their husbands. But they saw a dialogue and "cold tolerance" as a better response by France than that of pushing these women out of French society and into social isolation.

Subsequent studies, most carried out toward the end of the 1990s, confirmed Gaspard and Khosrokhavar's findings that young women chose to adopt Islamic dress, including the headscarf, as part of efforts to negotiate a sphere of social freedom and authority and to construct an identity as a Muslim, and that the relative weight of these two reasons depended on their age and social situation. Many of the women also drew explicit contrasts between, on the one hand, their own efforts to become better Muslims through study and regular prayer and, on the other, the ways in which their parents merely followed tradition, by, for example, fasting and sacrificing but rarely praying. Some distinguished between two ways of wearing a headscarf: "as in the old country" (letting some hair show), and wearing it in an Islamic manner (covering the hair).

Those who referred to themselves as "practicing Muslims" (*pratiquants*) always mentioned regular prayer, often in distinction to the practices of an older generation.[9] As one woman said, "For example, when I am about to eat, I recite a prayer, and when I am about to leave the house, I recite another; my parents don't know that. . . . It is a daily combat; I try to teach them the 'true Islam.' And because they have spent their lives in regrettable traditions they have a hard time accepting what I say!"[10]

These women who distinguished their parents' traditions from "true Islam" did not associate Islam with their "country of origin." One said: "I became a practicing Muslim thanks to France, because it provides structures so that we might learn Arabic and our religion. I am glad to have come to know my religion, true Islam, because 'back there' it is too traditional and troublesome."[11] These sentiments help explain why the idea of "country of origin," when applied to these young Muslims, born in France, would seem to them to be so unsuitable. "Origin," to these women, does not have to do with their language, or everyday lives, or religion: they speak French, not Arabic; they consider themselves French in culture and find that it is in France that they have learned "true Islam."

Because the later studies chose to interview Muslim women who did not wear headscarves as well as those who did, they expanded Gaspard and Khosrokhavar's typology to include a wider range of orientations toward Islam and French society. Jocelyne Cesari (1998) lists a number of types, from secularized Muslims through three types of actors within Islamic associations (children of the projects, social climbers, and transplanted intellectuals), but finds in several of these types a similar desire to replace the religious orientations of parents with a more self-consciously Islamic life, a desire that leads some of the women to adopt headscarves. Nancy Venel (2004) delineates four types of French Muslims born to North African parents, from those who adopt French Republicanism wholeheartedly to those who seek to create an Islamic "neocommunalism." She, too, finds that across these types young women achieve an Islamic legitimacy and familial authority by adopting the voile.[12]

Three Women, Three Trajectories

These studies show how variation in social histories (country of origin, age, education) shape differences in how younger Muslim women in France approach religious practice, family life, and the question of Islamic dress. They converge on the idea that women adopt scarves as part of an effort to become better Muslims and also as part of an attempt to negotiate their own authority with respect to their family, workplace, or society at large. By showing that distinct components of "Islamic practice" carry distinct meanings—daily prayer being much more closely associated with "true Islam" for these women than is fasting—they also provide an important counterpoint to the heavy public reliance on survey data, used to suggest a low level of religious observance among Muslims. These studies tend to sort people into socioreligious types, however, and by the very use of this approach play down the changes, ambivalences, and complexities that characterize many young Muslims' lives (and the lives of most of us).

I thought I might get a better sense of these complexities if I listened to younger Muslim women discuss their lives at length. In late February 2004, I met with three women above a small pizza restaurant near Paris's Institut Pasteur. All three agreed to have the interview filmed, and they reviewed this section of the book before publication. They were in their midtwenties and traced their roots to the Berber-speaking Kabyle region of Algeria. Fariba was born in France, grew up in Algeria, and returned to France in 2001 for advanced studies in American history. Maryam works in administration and lives in Paris. Her parents moved to France from Algeria in 1976 and she was born two years later. Fariba and Maryam are both single. Souad is married to a North African man and lives in the working-class suburb of Boulogne. She works for a communications firm. She was born in France, just weeks after her parents arrived from Algeria in 1976.

These three women are by no means a representative sample of young French Muslim women. They or their parents came from a largely Berber-speaking region of Algeria; they are completely fluent in French; they had been free to exercise a good deal of personal choice in their pathways; they were serious in their reflections on Islam; they are in a young age range. We would hear different stories and gain different impressions from older women, Turkish and Senegalese women, women who did not claim Muslim identities, or very young girls who wore the scarves at an early age on the orders of their parents.[13] My goal was not to adequately sample Muslim women in France, but rather to give these friends a chance to talk about their paths through home, school, and work, and their choices concerning religious practices and the public display of religious identity.

The three have followed different paths in religion. Fariba grew up in a "practicing" family, from whom she learned Arabic and the Qur'ân, how to pray, fast, and so forth. She began wearing a hijâb (the term she used) at fifteen, and whenever I have seen her, she has worn a single-piece, long garment that covers her head, neck, and shoulders. She received an excellent education in Algeria and now in France, and views her trajectory as in some ways ideal: "I was bathed in religion," she explained, "but also in philosophy, so I asked a lot of questions. Fortunately, I also had the materials to answer those questions." In the discussions she sometimes took on a pedagogical elder sister role toward the other two women, encouraging and explaining matters to them.

Souad's life in Paris has been a "zigzag," as she put it. "I was not brought up in Islam," she told us. "All my parents knew was about Ramadan, to not eat pork, not drink alcohol, and not have sexual relations . . . before marriage" [they all laugh]. In high school she began to learn about Islam through reading books suggested to her by friends and began to pray. Because wearing any head covering was forbidden at her school, only after graduating was she able to wear a hijâb, "to please our Creator." She wore a tight brown cap, over which a long light-colored scarf cascaded. In our discussions she emphasized the importance of acting on the basis of knowledge and not just from tradition or culture.

Maryam does not wear a headscarf. She observes Ramadan and avoids pork but no longer performs the prayer. "I am half-way between a practicing and a non-practicing Muslim," she explained. She did begin regular prayer in 2001, and it made her feel respected, but gradually let it slide and now only recites some of the prayer before going to sleep. She insists that it is a matter of personal choice: "it is personal, concerns only me, voilà."

The three women discussed their different experiences learning about social boundaries. Souad emphasized the role played by French schools. All through her middle school, teachers would ask students to write down their nationality, and she would always write "Algerian."

> Souad: Not before high school did a teacher ever say: "you were born in France, you have a French identity card, so you are French." So it was in high school that I discovered that I was French, and it changed my life! [Laughter]
> Fariba: How did it change your life?
> Souad: I don't know: that I could vote? It just felt strange.

I then asked Souad how she was viewed by others; she and Maryam described how pupils self-segregated in school.

Souad: At middle and high school people sort themselves by group, as Maghrebins or as French. I felt that I shared more with Maghrebins than I did with the French. Already in the *sixième* [eleven years old] we felt the difference between those whose parents had money and the others. They put me in the advanced section because I had received a 20 in math the previous year [an unusually high grade]; they thought they perhaps had an intellectual. It traumatized me that they put me with the others [French]. There was one girl who said: "you, you're Arab, don't get close to me." I was the "Arab of the classroom." It was really a shock. I was the only one, and I found it very hard to make friends; I made one. You find yourself with people; you do not know their culture; you feel very bad, feel still more that you are not well integrated: "we don't want anything to do with you, you are Arab, dirty." They were taught this from their parents, the racism.

So the following year (*cinquième*) I came down to the ordinary level and was with people like me, of Maghrebin origin, and it was easier to get along, without the racism. And I really feel that the school system contributes to that because it is they who make the difference from the beginning, with only with French people at one level and all Maghrebins and others in the other already in middle school, so it's normal that later on the racism will grow in people's minds. So the schools have a responsibility.

Maryam: We were in groups, we felt a sort of complicity among ourselves. We did tease among ourselves, "Oh, be careful, you're Tunisian." The Algerians did this even among themselves, Kabyles and people from Algiers did have a tension among them. But it was among us, friendly.

Fariba claimed to have had an entirely different experience because she grew up in Algeria.

I consider myself Kabyle, Algerian, French, European; I claim two continents. I attach myself to no single territory, but my culture is essentially Algerian. I have picked up things from French culture, American, because I study that, but I have not lived the same discriminations because I grew up with colleagues and professors who were Algerians, and I was in Kabylie, I was among Kabyles.

At one point she said she did not mind being called "Arab," and I reminded her that she was not Arab. "In a sense I do consider myself Arab," she replied. "I am Kabyle, thus Algerian and Algeria is an Arab country and so I am Arab. I love the language; perhaps ethnically I am not Arab but culturally I claim that culture, it is a matter of pride for me to be Arab. Well, perhaps I am the only Kabyle Arab [they all laugh]. It is not a problem of identity, because my identity is outside of all that. I have many attachments."

Fariba is unusual in her cosmopolitan ability to embrace different sources of identity. The relation of Algerians from the Berber-speaking Kabyle region and the Arab-speaking parts of Algeria often are not as harmonious. Rarely openly acknowledged, the identity of a particular actor as "Arab" or "Kabyle" is often mentioned in private as a way of explaining her or his actions. Frequently I heard from an Arabic speaker that someone's allegiance to the state and to the ideas of strict laïcité was due to her or his Kabyle origins, and that the person wished to "settle accounts with Arabs." I heard such "explanations" with respect to the mediations carried out in schools over headscarf incidents by Hanifa Chérifi (of Kabyle origins), or to the willingness of Socialist Party actor Malik Boutih to take strong stances against communalism and head-scarves. These tensions grew out of French colonial policies that favored Kabyle residents, the high rate of Kabyle enrollment in French schools and emigration from Algeria, and hostilities between Arabic and Berber speakers in Algeria over questions of language and national identity.[14]

Both Souad and Maryam described a gradual process of coming to learn about Islam and hesitating over how to present themselves to the French world. Their renewed commitment to living publicly as commit-ted Muslims came at the time that they were fashioning their own identi-ties vis-à-vis those of their parents and their countries of origin. Their relation to headscarves played an important role in these processes.

Souad observed that she and others who "came from immigration" knew very little about religion.

> Once I got to high school, friends told me about my religion, I discovered an aspect I did not know, I studied, I read books, I found that enriching.
>
> It was clear to me that the headscarf was an obligation, and I felt the need to please our Creator, it was in that spirit that I wanted to wear it, but the social conditions at high school presented problems. I had to prepare to be rejected by others. I studied for my bac [the all-important school finish-ing exam] and practiced my religion but the voile was another thing. I

always did my prayer, that's something very important for Muslims, and I am proud of myself there. But there was always that desire to go higher in faith, to go closer to the Creator, to please him. So I put on a small hair band so that people would get used to it, because before I wore mini skirts, long hair, but never drank alcohol. In effect I was a bit of a tomboy and hung out with guys, who considered me their little sister and made sure I did not veer toward drugs and night clubs.

One day I decided to become a woman, not a boy, and I changed my behavior, because I had been very aggressive in my gestures and words. I realized that it is hard to live in society as a woman, because there is a lot of sexism, in French society as well. So, to return to the zigzag, my behavior as a woman, the fact that God asked me to do certain things, so I decided to go in that direction while adapting myself to the society where I live, and I succeed at this, for, when I am at work I wear the scarf not like I have it now but on top, swirled around like the Africans [makes gesture around her head]. That seems to work. I began wearing it as an intern and it worked. This shows that there are still people who are very tolerant. They knew me before and after the foulard, and their attitude did not change. They saw that my work did not change, even got better, and one said, if anyone criticizes you let me know and I will take care of it. I found that touching.

Maryam has never worn a headscarf, "even though I grew up with it around me." Her mother "wore a foulard but not the hijâb; there is a difference." Fariba broke in to clarify for my benefit what wearing a headscarf "in the Kabyle manner" would mean, tying an imaginary scarf behind her head rather than knotting it under the chin, as she and Souad did. Souad did not agree with the distinction made by Maryam: "We have to clarify that; an Eskimo wears a hijâb. There is no uniform; it does not matter how you hide the parts you wish to hide. So the way your mother wore a scarf was the hijâb, but in the traditional way, as in the mountains." They all laugh at this last remark. Then Maryam continued:

When I would ask my mother why she did not remove her scarf, she said she would feel she was going out completely naked. It was natural for her, wearing it outside was like taking her purse.

I do not know what I will do in the future. I did start praying, one person helped me begin and at work there were two practicing Muslims and I became close to them and they said it was the good path. I had seen my mother pray when I was young, and as I had lost my father I needed to find my own guideposts. My parents had not made me fast, they said you do it when you are ready, and so I started fasting a bit later than others in my group, at about fifteen years.

"At work there were people who told me to buy a small book to help me learn about Islam. It taught me prayer phonetically, because I do not speak Arabic, and for three weeks I studied the prayer and then began to do it. And it lasted one year. During that period, I do not know why, many things came to me, and I had the impression that people respected me: "Oh, you pray" [she opens her eyes wide as an admirer might]. Gradually I stopped praying, but regretted it very much; I felt I had returned to the beginning. And I have not forgotten the prayer, I still know it by heart and before falling asleep I recite some. And now I said I should go to where people say the prayer, so I have, and I met Fariba."

Of the three women, Fariba had talked most frequently with non-Muslims about her own dress. People often asked her why she wore a voile.

Once I asked them: "why do you ask that question? Do I ask you why you wear that sweater or those jeans? Why is it I and not you who has to justify my choice?" They said, "well, but jeans are not a religious sign." I said: "the voile is not a religious sign either." I do not wear it to make evident my religious leanings. If I could wear the voile while hiding it I would do it. Because in religion it is clear that you should do things for God and not for people. It is not to show my affiliation with other people but my affiliation to God. Why does it bother others? That is their problem. They have ideas somewhere that are not the same as mine.

All three women objected to efforts by others to attach objective meanings to the voile.

Souad: The voile is in the heart; faith is in the heart.
Fariba: Yes, faith is in the heart, but I am against the idea that the voile is a religious sign, or a sign of religious excellence; it is not because I wear the voile that I am a better Muslim than Maryam or a worse Muslim. It is a

personal choice that I take on. And the connotations that it has—"submissive woman," "terrorist"—that is *their* problem.

Souad: You get the impression that only women with voiles are oppressed in this world. When there are women who die from conjugal violence every day they are not necessarily in veils, but no one talks about them, people only talk about veiled women in certain countries who are struck, burned, but not about others who experience discrimination. The voile is now the symbol of oppression in the world.

Maryam: On the television, it is as if there are only two Muslim countries in the world, Afghanistan and Iran.

I asked them about their experiences in looking for work. They said that they had fewer difficulties than did their male friends who also were of North African background. Souad noted that where she lived more women than men from North Africa were able to find steady jobs—but only if the women did not wear scarves. "People want the woman to be without the foulard, they want her to free herself; they have this idea of the oppressed woman (*la femme soumise*) and that in giving her work they are going to free her from that."

This comment reminded Fariba of the broader issue of how others judged her appearance.

Sometimes even when I have not been listening to the news, I know what has happened by watching how people regard me. On September 11th, [2001,] I returned home from work, turned on the television and saw the catastrophe. I was shocked like everyone else. The next morning, Wednesday, I had almost forgotten what had happened, I took the train to work, and the looks I got from others reminded me that it was the 12th, of what happened the day before. At first I did not understand, I looked myself over, to see if there was something wrong with my clothes, what did I do? And then I made the connection. . . .

The other time that happened to me, it was when there was a French ship blown up, I had not heard about it, and I saw a great deal of aggression in people's stares, and said to myself I had better read a newspaper right away, and I saw the explanation. I function as a barometer of the popularity of Muslims. When there were sympathetic looks it was between the two votes for the president [in April—May 2002], when Jean-Marie Le Pen had done well, they felt guilty, and so in the subway if I was jostled a bit, people would say "Oh, excuse me, ma'am," as if to say, "I did not vote for Le Pen." So in some sense, I have never been spit on or struck or yelled at but I see a lot in those looks. And with the polemic on the voile there has been a lot of electricity in the air.

The three women agreed that men were much less likely to harass a woman wearing a headscarf. Maryam, whose hair is loose, reported frequent unwelcome advances by younger North African men in the subway; Souad said it was the same for her before she began wearing her scarf, "but when I began to wear it they proposed marriage. And I know one or two women who put on the voile in order to get married. That is a trap you must not fall into." This remark reminded Fariba that "when I lived in Algeria, before wearing the voile I was Fariba and after I began to wear it I was 'L'Islam.' If I do something bad it is not Fariba who behaves badly or is impolite, it is Islam. Happily, I was well bought up and so do not say offensive things and so that did not happen, but I know that people wait for the least fault on your part to blame the religion. You must be perfect and that is a heavy load!"

I asked them if they encountered women wearing garments that completely covered their bodies and faces, the *niqab*. They had mixed feelings about such women. Souad thinks of them as "very pure and completely detached from the world. One day I heard a girl in niqab talking this way and that. [She moves her hands rapidly and speaks in slang.] That clashed!" Fariba had seen women dressed in that way only in France. When she did see some, "it shocked me; I consider them to have made a stricter interpretation than I have. . . . They are not necessarily more pious."

For Souad, the encounters gave her a chance to reflect on others' responses to her: "I find myself vis-à-vis someone wearing the niqab like someone who does not wear the foulard vis-à-vis those of us who do wear it." She added that she thought that "people who dress like that think they are dressing as did the Prophet in the desert." Maryam responded to this way of looking at things by making what Fariba thought was a rather offhand remark: "If the Prophet were here today he would travel on the Concorde and wear jeans!" Fariba tried to reword the sentiment in a more acceptable way: "He would not see the bad in everything, as do some religious movements. Religion ought to simplify and not create constraints; if you feel happy in jeans then you wear those, if in other clothes, then you wear those."

This conversation makes clear that these three women, at least, have fashioned their public behavior both by their personal religious trajectories and by their sensibilities as to how others do and will see them. Each describes a long history of reflecting on religion and on her ability to adequately carry out religious obligations. And each also makes decisions about dress and behavior that take into account others' reactions. They reject the idea that headscarves are "religious signs," because they see the decision to wear hijâb as the result of a personal commitment rather than an intention to signal something to others. But they also acknowledge that making that decision does and should take into account the responses of others and the importance of schooling, work, and family; they see the effects that such a decision has (on attractiveness as a potential spouse, for example) as part of the entire picture. Wearing a headscarf in France today involves negotiations, anticipations, and weighing of benefits and costs. It is not simply an "obligation" or a "choice," but a subtle dance among convictions and constraints.

SCARVES BECOME AN "AFFAIR"

From the standpoint of many others in France, however, the headscarves were primarily a political problem. The original "headscarf affair" of 1989 remains a touchstone for all accounts of the matter. In December 2003, just before the Stasi Commission appointed by President Jacques Chirac was to deliver its report on laïcité, the television station France 5 aired a documentary aptly called *Egalité, Laïcité, Anxiété.* The program opened with televised reporting on key events in the political history of the voile, shown on a filmed television set in order to frame the narrative as about "events that made the news." The first clip showed the three girls involved in the 1989 incident saying they would never take off their scarves. The next clips showed political responses and subsequent incidents, then turning to a series of political and social troubles, presented as resulting from these scarves: the rise of the National Front, the burning of a girl in a poor suburb, Sarkozy booed by Muslims, and finally an interview with Bernard Stasi, the chair of the Stasi Commission.

The program's narrative downplays the possibility that politics could have led to the production of the "affair" in the first place, and focuses the political lens on the Far Right rather than on the Left, where the headscarves had been most vociferously denounced. Indeed, in some respects political attention to Islam grew out of the Left's disillusionment during the 1980s. The rosy glow attending François Mitterrand's 1981 victory faded quickly when, that December, the government pronounced the declaration of martial law in Poland to be "an internal affair" (alienating the anti-Soviet Left), unemployment climbed throughout 1982 and 1983 (angering the working class), and the National Front attracted impressive vote totals (disconcerting nearly everyone else). The Socialist government's unpopularity was verified by the party's poor showing in the 1986 legislative elections, which gave a tremendous boost to the National Front and victory to the Center Right. Jacques Chirac became prime minister. Unemployment continued to rise and the Socialists soon returned to power but accompanied by widespread discontent and a growing tendency to blame immigrants for the economic problems.

By the late 1980s, many leftist intellectuals were looking for new sources of political direction. Many former Communists had become disillusioned with the Soviet paradise even before the fall of the Berlin wall. Some, such as the Che Guevara associate Régis Debray and the former Maoist André Glucksmann, turned to the ideals of the Republic as their new source of value in political life. Others, such as philosopher Alain Finkielkraut, attacked the misplaced multiculturalism of the early Mitterrand years and the ethical relativism that it supported at home and abroad. In the midst of this anxiety over France's political and cultural turn came the bicentennial celebration of the French Revolution in July 1989. The Revolution was and is the touchstone of those on the Left who defend the Republic, and its heritage had come under revisionist attack in the preceding years from historians on the Right and on the moderate Left, represented by the reviews *Esprit* and *Le Nouvel Observateur*, whose editors subscribed to the counterrevolutionary historiography of François Furet. Under these attacks, many on the Left took only the Declaration of Human Rights and the principle of liberty from the Revolution's legacy, leaving uncelebrated the role of the state and the principle of equality. For some who considered themselves to be Left Republicans, such as Régis Debray and Jean-Pierre Chevènement, this response to counterrevolutionary thinking was a capitulation, a word

Debray soon would use for those who would allow girls with headscarves into classrooms.[15]

1989 also was the year of the Ayatollah Khomeini's international swan song, his famous February fatwa against the novelist Salmon Rushdie in which he declared that Rushdie's blaspheming of the Prophet Muhammad in his *Satanic Verses* proved that he was an apostate and fit to be killed under Islamic law. The Rushdie incident brought together several related fears about Islam: that it was intolerant; that Muslims, once in power, would kill those who left the religion and would cut off the hands of thieves; and that the relative success of the Iranian mullahs meant that Islam was on a worldwide roll, certain to come to power elsewhere. One month later, the Islamic Salvation Front (Front Islamique du Salut, FIS) was born in Algiers. The FIS translated widespread dissatisfaction with the ruling party and strong grassroots Islamic organizations into a political movement. The civil war in Lebanon among religion-defined political blocs continued. Religion, but particularly Islam, seemed to have crossed into politics in places very close to France.

Then, that September, three girls showed up for the first day at their middle school wearing Islamic dress. At a different moment, the girls' appearance would likely have passed unnoticed. Girls had been showing up at this and other schools with scarves for years, and either attended the school with their scarves or agreed to remove them during class. Indeed, an earlier class photo at the same school showed a girl in headscarf as evidence of the middle school's openness to cultural diversity![16] But now international "political Islam" appeared on magazine covers in the form of Iranian women in Islamic dress, adding a new dimension to scarves in French schools. The conjuncture of domestic and foreign threats made scarf-wearing into a national "affair."

The girls in question were Samira Saidani, of Tunisian parents, and Leila and Fatima Achaboun, sisters whose parents came from Morocco. They attended the Gabriel-Havez middle school (*collège*) in the town of Creil near Paris, a school built to serve the children of immigrant workers and attended by a large number of Muslim pupils. The girls refused the principal's request to take off their scarves in class and were expelled, on the grounds that the scarves infringed on "the laïcité and neutrality of the public school." After several rounds of negotiations among the school administration, the parents, and local associations (in particular the Cultural Association of Tunisians), the girls agreed to wear the scarves on school grounds but remove them in class. They returned to school on October 9, but ten days later they started wearing the scarves in class, breaking the agreement and leading to a new series of negotiations, now involving national Muslim organizations.[17]

At this point, the local dispute became a national incident, on which everyone eventually had to take a position. Although a few institutions, notably the Paris Mosque, the Arab League spokesman, and the Vatican's representative Cardinal Lustiger, called for lowering the rhetorical level and continuing negotiations, most others put out "principled communiqués." Danielle Mitterrand called on the schools to accept scarves, as did a number of Muslim associations, the chief rabbi of France, and the national secretary of the Teaching League (Ligue de l'enseignement). Some Christian and Jewish groups saw the mounting attack on scarves as the beginning of a crackdown on other "violations" of laïcité—priests entering schools, Jewish pupils not doing so on Saturdays—and urged toleration. On the other side were several teachers' unions, who called on the government to stand firm against scarves and for laïcité.

The mass media jumped on the incident. During the preceding years there had been no mention made of scarves in France: a search through the archives of Le Monde for the two years prior to the 1989 affair shows close to one hundred articles on veils and Muslim headscarves, but every article concerned a Muslim-majority country and no mention was made of Muslims wearing headscarves in France. But now the national press played up the connections between these scarves and broader dangers. Le Nouvel Observateur's cover story for October 5 was titled "Fanaticism: The Religious Menace" and depicted a girl in a full, black chador. On October 26, the even more sensationalist weekly L'Express titled its feature story "The Secular School in Danger: The Strategy of Fundamentalists [intégristes]." Le Point added its own opinion at the same time with a cover called "Fundamentalists, the Limits of Tolerance," depicting a chador-clad woman. The incident plus the Rushdie affair allowed commentators to link Iran, the chador, and book-burning to the plight of the three girls at the middle school.

The Right was relatively silent on the issue, but the Left was sharply split. Antiracism groups associated with the Socialist Party emphasized the Revolution's legacy of equality and laïcité, and resisted allowing religion into the schools. France-Plus asked the Socialist education minister Lionel Jospin to keep scarves and Jewish caps out of the schools. SOS-Racisme tried to sidestep the question, saying that the real issue was integration, not scarves, leading one prominent member, the lawyer Gisèle Halimi, a strong opponent of the scarves, to leave the association. A number of public figures concerned with the condition of women, including the state secretary for the rights of women, argued that the headscarf stood for the suppression of women. The majority of French people opposed scarves in schools, and in a November poll one-half said they thought that most immigrants living in France could not be integrated because of their differences. Some commentators denounced the scarves as the sign of international Islamic oppression. Jacques Soustelle, ex-governor-general of Algeria, blamed Islamic fundamentalists for provoking the crisis.[18]

Two open letters published in November by public intellectuals on the Left offered sharply opposed positions amid inflated rhetoric. One, titled "Teachers, Don't Give In!" was signed by the intellectuals and writers Élisabeth Badinter, Régis Debray, Alain Finkielkraut, Élisabeth de Fontenay, and Catherne Kintzler and ran as a cover story in the mainstream, putatively Socialist review *Le Nouvel Observateur*. The authors warned that the two hundredth anniversary of the French Revolution could become "the Munich of the Republican school." A second open letter, "For an Open Laïcité," appeared in the more socially activist review *Politis*, signed by Joëlle Brunerie-Kauffmann (a woman gynecologist who had fought for the right to abortion), Harlem Désir (the head of SOS-Racisme), and the social scientists René Dumont, Gilles Perrault, and Alain Touraine. These intellectuals did not support scarves in schools but opposed exclusion, claiming that keeping the girls away from school fed the interests of fundamentalists and the National Front, and they denounced the "Vichy of the integration of immigrants."[19]

Jospin understandably tried to avoid taking either side. (Was it Vichy? or Munich?) In his first statement, in early October, he stated that pupils should not show their religious affiliation in school but also that the school was designed "to welcome and not to exclude children." Later in October he favored reintegrating the girls in the classroom if dialogue did not succeed. The following month, seeking to avoid making a decision himself, he sent the question to the State Council, the last resort for cases arising from the public school system. (The same day the National Front held protests against the "Islamization of France.") President François Mitterrand did not express himself until the end of the November, when he, too, tried to have it both ways: for respecting immigrants, but against Islamic fundamentalists. A few days later, fourteen of his ministers announced the creation of a new advisory group on integration of immigrants (which would become the High Council on Integration).

If Jospin hoped that the State Council would take the heat by standing up for laïcité, he must have been sorely disappointed, for in late November the Council cited the French Constitution and the European Convention on Human Rights and ruled that the girls had the right to wear the scarves as long as they did not disturb school life or (in a sentence that was long even for such rulings):

> That students wear signs in order to display their affiliation to a religion is not in itself incompatible with the principle of laïcité, insofar as it constitutes the exercise of freedom of expression and of demonstrating religious beliefs, but this freedom does not allow students to display signs that by their nature, by the ways they are worn individually or collectively, or by their character of ostentation or protest would constitute an act of proselytism or propaganda, would compromise a student's dignity or freedom or that of other members of the school community, would compromise their health or safety, disturb ongoing teaching activities, or would disturb order in the school or the normal functioning of the civil service.

None of this changed the reality for those three middle school girls, who remained sequestered in the school library. At other schools in France similar expulsions took place, sometimes after teachers had gone on strike to protest the presence of a pupil in a headscarf. Toward the end of November, the king of Morocco intervened to ask (on Moroccan state television) that the Moroccan parents of Leila and Fatima have their children remove their headscarves in school. Their children complied on December 2 and were readmitted. The parents of the third pupil, Samira, were from Tunisia, which refused to have anything to do with headscarf-wearing girls. Samira refused to remove her headscarf and was never readmitted to the school.

The day following Leila and Fatima's readmission, December 3, 1989, the National Front scored its most spectacular victory to date, winning

61 percent of the parliamentary votes in the community of Dreux, west of Paris.

Over the next few years, other girls at other schools were refused admission with headscarves; some appealed their expulsions up the ladder of the school hierarchy and to the administrative courts. Several cases reached the State Council. The Council held to its original decision that girls may wear scarves as long as they otherwise act as good students. Indeed, of forty-nine legal disputes over headscarves that reached the Council between 1992 and 1994, forty-one ended in favor of the school-girl. But on a number of occasions, the State Council backed the school administration in expelling a girl if it could be demonstrated that she was frequently absent from school, engaged in proselytism, or refused to remove the scarf for required sports activities or chemistry classes—certain teachers judged the scarves dangerous when worn next to a Bunsen burner. Neither the Council nor the Ministry of Education issued a general ruling on the matter, on the grounds that the issue of headscarves was not a matter of principle but a matter that depended on the specific characteristics of each case (*affaire d'espèce*).

1993–1994: Raising the Stakes

Apparently, things were stable. But in 1993 legislators turned their attention to the scarf issue when two disputes brought in new elements. One case was from Nantua, a town northeast of Lyon. The "affaire Akouili" there involved four girls from Turkish and Moroccan families who were allowed to keep their scarves in class but who had been asked, yet refused, to remove them during gym class. While their case was in a disciplinary hearing, a majority of the school's teachers went on strike. The teachers complained, not that laïcité was violated, but that *le voile* was a danger if worn during gym and science classes, and that "it is discriminatory in its treatment of girls and segregationist."[20] The girls' parents and brothers spoke for them in public and, in a particularly ill-advised move, two self-proclaimed Islamic authorities declared publicly that Islam *required* women to cover themselves. The absolute nature of the claims—the voile is in its nature discriminatory; girls must wear it—raised the stakes of the public debate.[21]

If in the Nantua case it was a rather rigid version of Islam that appeared to dictate the girls' actions, in the second case, from Grenoble, the scarf-wearing student was clearly in charge of her own fate. Schérazade, a student in her final year at high school, had discovered Islam the previous summer. As she told her story to *Le Nouvel Observateur*, she read the Qur'ân in French, the only language she knew, and once convinced of its truth, decided to follow its message, and succeeded in convincing her father to return to proper religious practice.[22] She was expelled from school for insisting on retaining her scarf during gym class. When she lost on appeal, she went on a twenty-two-day hunger strike while living in an RV parked in front of the school and attracting worldwide press attention.

These two cases illustrate one dimension of the debate on the scarves: the issue of freedom or agency. Schérazade's articulate account of her independent journey toward Islam supports those who argue that women choose to wear the scarves as part of their (re)discovery of their faith. During the debates of 2003–2004, a number of young women, born in France and wearing headscarves, made this argument force-fully. But the Nantua case supports those who argue the opposite: that parents, elder brothers, and self-styled religious experts of foreign birth and shadowy credentials dictate the norms of Islam to the girls, who merely follow suit.

The same facts could be called on to support both positions. In some cases, school girls cited word for word the 1989 State Council decision and referred to key court cases. In some cases, they had read the "hand-book" for Muslim schoolgirls written by Thomas Abdallah Milcent, known in his writings as Dr. Abdallah, a physician who converted to Islam and who regularly advises women in headscarf cases in the Stras-bourg area. Abdallah (1995) provided readers with the jurisprudence on the matter, advised the girls how to behave before administrative tribu-nals, and provided examples of the proper letters to write demanding an audience, an appeal, and so forth. For some, the existence of the book and the legal knowledge evidenced by some schoolgirls showed that they were being manipulated by Abdallah and other "Islamists." For others, it showed the ability of Muslims to operate within the strict terms of the law and therefore of the Republic.

The Nantua and Grenoble cases received a good deal of media atten-tion and led a deputy to the National Assembly to warn that laïcité was being compromised. Intriguingly, the deputy was none other than Ernest

Chénière, the middle school principal who had created the first "affair" in 1989 by expelling the three girls.[23] The education minister, François Bayrou, responded in September 1994 with a directive that required principals to ban all "ostentatious" signs from schools. He made it clear that the directive was aimed at excluding all headscarves from schools, on the grounds that "their meaning is precisely to take certain pupils outside the rules for living together [*vie commune*] in the school." The major teachers' unions applauded the directive.[24]

The directive led a number of schools to expel students. During 1994, the number of contentious cases, involving adjudication by the principal or by a school disciplinary council, rose sharply from its earlier levels in the low hundreds to about two thousand. To deal with the rising number of incidents, Bayrou created a new office of ministerial mediator for headscarf cases, and named to the position a woman from the Kabyle region of Algeria, Hanifa Chérifi.

In 2003, Chérifi described to me how she worked. She would intervene only if the two sides could not agree on a solution. She would try to convince the girl to give up the scarf for the sake of her future, and try to convince the school to look for a compromise, such as wearing a "discreet" scarf, one that would allow some of the hair and the earlobes to show (and was judged by teachers to be less "aggressive"). She explained to a journalist in 2002 that she looked with favor on a girl wearing a scarf at the behest of her family (a scarf of "traditional, familial Islam"), and with disfavor on a girl wearing it despite the wishes of her family (a "fundamentalist" scarf). The former was tied in back with a knot, the latter swept forward to cover the chin.[25]

As in 1989, external events had contributed to the new attention to headscarves. Between 1989 and 1994, Algeria had become the site of a full-blown war between the generals and new Islamic movements. When the generals had denied electoral victory to the FIS in 1992, they radicalized many of its supporters and lead to the creation of the Groupe Islamique Armé (GIA), which may have contained ex-mujahideen from Afghanistan and probably was infiltrated by state security police. The GIA and the army began a cycle of violence and counterviolence, killing thousands in Algeria.

In August 1994, the government raised the stakes in the combat against "Islamism." When five French citizens were killed in Algiers on August

3, France found itself directly involved in what commentators now called the "second Algerian War." The hard-line minister of the interior, Charles Pasqua, launched a security crackdown in "difficult neighborhoods" in France and arrested a number of French Muslim public actors of Algerian origin, including Larbi Kechat of the Adda'wa Mosque in Paris's nineteenth arrondissement.

Television programs in 1993–1994 often linked the foreign to the domestic, placing coverage of "headscarf affairs" in the same time slot as coverage of ongoing fighting in Algeria (which at that moment was constantly on the news), rather than with other social issues. "For the average viewer, the conclusion is obvious: headscarf = Islam = terrorism," complained one young "believing but non-practicing" Muslim businesswoman.[26] Other observers pointed out that the renewed attention to headscarves came at a moment when proposed stricter laws on immigration were under debate and shortly before new elections. News magazines also mixed the foreign terror with domestic headscarves. L'Express had a special issue on April 29, 1993, on "The Islamists," covering France, Algeria, and Egypt. On the cover of Le Nouvel Observateur for September 22, 1994, we see a woman completely covered, with only her eyes showing, and the title: "Islam and Women." L'Express of November 17, 1994, featured a woman in a black head covering and the title: "Foulard, the Plot: How the Islamists Infiltrate Us."

Many of the same intellectuals who had so vigorously opposed allowing scarves in schools in 1989 now found themselves vindicated. The ex-Maoist André Glucksmann called the voile a "terrorist emblem,"[27] and "a terrorist operation," adding, "We don't teach pupils in uniform except under Nazism."[28] The telegenic Bernard-Henri Lévy (the literary Salvador Dali of 1990s France) pointed to Islamic fundamentalism as the new greatest evil, comparable to the Nazis and the Stalinists, and called for support for the Algerian generals. Although others, such as François Burgat in Aix-en-Provence, saw the army as the major cause of the violence, such dissidents were (physically as well as ideologically) on the margins.

More than one hundred girls were expelled after Bayrou's 1994 directive. Two girls later recalled how their teachers said that they could not have what was occurring in Algeria repeated here.[29] In the Jean Rostand lycée in Strasbourg, nearly forty girls insisted on retaining their headscarves. They were placed in another room for about two months, until, after a disciplinary council meeting, they were expelled. One of them later recalled how she was called before the principal, who handed her a sheet of paper saying that she was expelled as of 10:30 on that day and then added: "It is 10:30; at 10:31 I want never to see you again." She was in her final year of school, the year of preparation for the all-important baccalaureate exam: "I felt a great solitude, because the lycée was my life, you would run into fellow students and talk about homework, classes, but now I had nothing to talk about with them. And I could not be in school, so how could I learn?"[30]

Many of these cases came from Lyon, and a group of Muslim women started the Union of Lyon Muslim Sisters in 1995 to organize courses outside of school for expelled students. Schoolteachers volunteered their time. The Union raised money for the students' transportation costs, for a stipend for teachers, and for the costs the students had to pay to enroll in distance learning courses provided by the Centre National d'Education à Distance. At no time did the Education Ministry provide guidance for the expelled girls: "integrating" them seemed to be less important than separating them from those girls who already appeared to be "integrated."[31]

Saïda Kada was one of the Union organizers. In a 2004 interview, she told me that the girls usually were expelled on grounds that they had been absent from school rather than what she saw as the real reason, that they persisted in wearing headscarves. "The Bayrou directive did not allow for expulsion simply on the grounds of wearing headscarves. If someone is younger than sixteen, then the state has the obligation to educate them, and may do so via distance learning only if the pupil is ill or is frequently traveling, and this recourse is supposed to be authorized by an inspector."

Some of the expelled schoolgirls took the schools to court. If they appealed to the State Council and showed that their scarf was the sole reason for the expulsion, they won, as had been the case before the directive.[32] In a 1997 case, for example, the Council specified that "the scarf cannot be considered as a sign that in itself has the character of display or making demands."[33] But the schools did win cases when they could demonstrate that they had expelled girls who had failed to comply with school rules. In a 1995 case from Lyon and in three cases from Lille decided during 1996–1997, the Council sided with the schools, finding in each case that the girls had been expelled not because they wore scarves but because they had violated codes of conduct: they refused to attend gym class, or protested against their own expulsion, or "engaged in proselytism." But if the Council suspected that such claims by school heads were merely covers for the real intention to expel them because of their scarves, then they supported the girls: such was their decision in a 1997 case from Strasbourg.

Thus by the end of the 1990s the Council had developed a clear and consistent jurisprudence on the issue: schools could expel girls if they failed to attend all their classes or if their case led to protests, but not merely for wearing scarves. The number of "incidents" had fallen dramatically after the 1994 peak, to about 150 each year through the late 1990s and early 2000s.[34] In the media, the "Islamist peril" became one of several stock stories that cycled regularly across the covers of *L'Express*, *Le Point*, or *Le Nouvel Observateur* in their efforts to alarm and attract buyers, joining the other regular topics such as the Freemasons' alleged control of the state, the dangers posed by religious sects, and the high price of apartments in Paris.

2002–2003: The Voile as Sign of Social Problems

Within several years, however, new concerns linked foreign to domestic unrest. The violence in Algeria reached France in the mid-1990s, when bombs exploded in Paris and Lyon. At the same time, many in France were beginning to speak of their nation's "ghettoization." A series of government reports described malfunctioning schools and a growing lack of contact between the ethnic France and the children of immigrants. After briefly triumphantly contrasting the integrated Republic of the black, brown, and white World Cup champion soccer team of 1998 with the segregated Anglo-Saxon societies of Britain and its more disastrous cousin, the United States, France now was threatened with eating cultural crow.

Islam's role in this general problem became more publicly denounced in 2000. The new High Council on Integration issued a report on "Islam in the Republic" in that year. The report rejected banning scarves outright lest young girls be driven into the dreaded communalism of the poor suburbs and the private Islamic schools that might be created to hold them. The report followed what had been the official state position on scarves since 1989. However, the High Council's deliberations also created a vocal minority that soon thereafter sought broad public and political support for a scarf ban.[35]

Public reporting on the voile began to heat up in 2002, less because of changes in the schools than because of heightened post-9/11 fears about Islam. These changes were indirect, however. France had already set in place antiterrorist machinery in the 1990s, and the police and the Renseignements Généraux, France's FBI, had compiled records on Muslims who traveled outside the country. Muslim leaders told me in October 2001 that they now found it easier to have their papers renewed, because they were known to be "safe," and those in control wished to divide the "good" Muslims from the "bad."

The attacks on the Word Trade Center did lead the mass media to train their lenses once again on possible internal threats attributable to Islam. Headscarves were even more likely than before to be seen in a negative light. When in March 2002 a new voile affair occurred at a high school north of Paris (at Tremblay-en-France in the Seine-Saint-Denis *département*), the Education Ministry mediator Hanifa Chérifi signaled a change in tone. She told journalists that although previously many claimed that the voile gave girls a space of freedom between the family and the society, "we have neglected the intrinsic significance of the voile: to remind women, starting at puberty, that Islamic morality forbids mixing of the sexes in all public spaces, including the school."[36]

Late in 2002, a series of new scarf affairs began to appear in the national media. They began in Lyon. Lyon has been an important center for new Islamic movements but also, unfortunately, for radical activists. The bombs that exploded in summer 1995 were set off in Paris and Lyon. The most notorious figure to emerge from the 1990s was Khaled Kelkal, brought to France from Algeria in infancy and living in the Lyon suburb of Vaulx-en-Velin.[37] In December 2002, a teacher at La Martinière high school in Lyon, Jean-Claude Santana, complained to the school administration that a sixteen-year-old student named Fatiha was wearing an Islamic headscarf in violation of school policy. The girl had begun to wear a scarf in early December after Ramadan, starting with it rolled up as a "bandana," a dress style that had been allowed, and then gradually unrolling it so that it covered her hair. On December 12, a teacher asked her to remove it. She refused and found herself in the principal's office, where she still refused to remove the scarf and was suspended. She was readmitted when the district superintendent made a phone call to the principal. Later that month one of her cousins joined her in wearing a foulard, leading the teachers at the school to hold a meeting: "they feared a contagion" and a wave of new foulard-wearing students.[38]

Shortly after Santana's complaint, the media descended on Lyon. Saïda Kada recalled how the television station France 3 tried to interview members of the Union of Muslim Sisters to get their reactions. "We knew that Santana had put them up to it, so that he could charge us with causing trouble and thereby justify her suspension. So we said nothing." In most such cases that year (and other years) teachers had succeeded in persuading students to remove their scarves. But at La Martinière, when the students and teachers returned from vacation in early January, the pupil in question continued to wear her scarf. She was sent out of class, and then was suspended from all school activities by the teachers (who had agreed among themselves on this course of action); however, two teachers continued to allow her into their classes. In February, Hanifa Chérifi was asked to intervene. She had the student readmitted to classes. The episode reached the *Wall Street Journal*, which quoted Santana as saying that "religion is something very private and intimate, like your sex life" (a quotation seemingly designed for American notions of how French people talk).[39]

The teachers asked for the school's disciplinary council to meet (necessary for definitive expulsion) but the superintendent refused, saying that he feared that if they expelled her and were overruled by the administrative court (which was likely, given that wearing the scarf was the only accusation made against her) she would be hailed as a victim. And, he continued, her scarves, which were colored and often in floral prints "are more discreet than the scarves worn by Islamists." The teachers met and issued a statement that "the student considers her scarf to be a sign of her belonging to her community and her religion, thus it is meant to attract attention (is *ostentatoire*), and our internal rules forbid that." Before the early (February) spring break, they voted to go on strike as soon as they returned from vacation. Upon their return, however, the superintendent urged them to meet with him and with the rector of the Lyon mosque,

Kamel Kabtane. They refused, saying that the involvement of the mosque leader was inappropriate. They asked for the disciplinary council hearing and for a clear rule on school dress. Then on March 13, 80 percent of the teachers went on strike.[40]

Hanifa Chérifi gave me her account of the Lyon case on May 1, 2003, as May Day processions passed before our café in the Place de la République. She had been called to Lyon in February, and found that the girl had been placed by herself in a separate classroom since December. "I said, 'you cannot have an Islamic classroom in a Republican high school,' and this phrase had an effect, because they put her into the regular class after that. There were three teachers who were vehemently against her, and in each of their cases there had been an earlier, negative relationship with Islam: they had been in Morocco, in one case there was a marriage that ended badly. The other teachers remained quiet, did not wish to oppose what the three were saying."

The girl had been wearing her bandana in class since the beginning of the school year in September, explained Chérifi, without anyone ever noticing, it was so minimal. She attended all her classes, so the teachers could not accuse her of missing class. When the girl was suspended, "she told the principal that she would not remove the bandana because she wore it for religious reasons, and once she said that, then the three professors started agitating for her to be removed from class." She had an older sister who had attended the same school and had not worn a scarf at that time but now did. She urged her younger sister to continue fighting and to find a lawyer. Chérifi added that "the family was from Morocco, and the elder sister spoke about her respect for her father, that this was continuing their tradition; I was impressed by that." If Chérifi respected the girl's attitude, she was less impressed when the district superintendent (the Recteur de l'Académie de Lyon) said he was going to ask the advice of the head of the Lyon Mosque: "Imagine, in a laïc Republic, the head of the schools asking a religious official what to do!" I asked her if she ever asked advice from religious experts. "Never, because I am there to carry out the laws of the republic, and if I asked religious experts I would get several different opinions." In the end, the education minister heard of the superintendent's plan and told him that he could not consult the religious official. The teachers ended their strike when the superintendent agreed to meet them.

Chérifi saw the voile debates as misleading: "Underneath all the talk about laïcité there is racism. The children of immigrants are not encouraged to continue their studies. I stopped mine at sixteen, and took them up only much later." She tried to arrange compromises, usually along the lines of the bandana that had worked in Lyon for awhile. "The professors all hate the voile," she explained, "but less so if the ears and the neck show, so when I talk to girls, first I explain that things will go easier if they do not wear the voile. 'Do you really want to continue fighting all the time, through your exams, so that you can be more Muslim than the others?' They may go into public service, which here in France includes everything from a postal carrier to the head of an office, and in all those jobs it is forbidden to wear the voile. If they decide to take it off it is better, because then that will take them out of that fundamentalism. But if they cannot do that, then pushing it back to make it smaller will help, and it does."

The Lyon case introduced to popular consciousness the possibility of the bandana, a form of head covering that would seem less Islamic to teachers and thus more acceptable but perhaps cover enough hair to satisfy some Muslim girls. The bandana became the great hope of those who wished the whole thing would go away.

But the case also showed that some groups of teachers were willing to disrupt the school for everyone in order to prevent the presence of a girl in a headscarf. They argued that laïcité, if properly understood, went beyond the rulings of the State Council. As Santana put it in an interview: "We defend la Laïcité. Not the idea expressed by the State Council, laïcité with multiple standards [à géométrie variable], strict for adults and 'tolerant' for pupils, considered as consumers of a pedagogical public service. The school is a place where we share universal values of freedom, equality, and fraternity. The school's mission has a liberating ambition: to give citizens-in-the-making the means to free themselves from social, cultural, ethnic, or gendered determinism. You do not attend school as you go to the post office or to another public service."[41]

Here was the basic challenge to the State Council: laïcité, claimed Santana, is about protecting pupils from pressures, and thus requires active intervention by the state against pupils and families who try to exert such pressure. We are now far beyond the idea of the state's neutrality, far beyond the requirements of the law of 1905, in the midst of an argument about the freedom of the pupil to choose: should she be free to dress according to her religion, or should she be free to explore her convictions without undue family pressure? The grounds had shifted; a confrontation seemed more likely.

FIVE

Moving toward a Law

BY SPRING 2003, many in France had the feeling that the social fabric was fraying at the edges. They read about violence done to young women, high-school pupils who had little love for the Republic, anti-Semitic taunts flung at Jewish children by Muslim ones, and they looked for solutions. Of course, most knew, or thought they knew, that if only everyone had jobs, and good housing, and a sense that the Republic belonged to them, then they would be less likely to insult and hurt and threaten. But those prospects seemed dim even for "native French." Were there other, more easily treatable causes of these problems—causes that passing a law might eliminate? Laws are relatively inexpensive, and in France sometimes provide a collective catharsis, with a hope for an eventual real change.

POLITICIANS TAKE OVER

The floating angst of the first few years of the millennium found a focus in 2003. I date the beginning of a bandwagon effect for passing a law against scarves in schools to a speech made in April of that year by Interior Minister Nicolas Sarkozy. Sarkozy, France's "chief cop," as he liked to call himself, and the icon of a new "tough love" approach to France's problems, singled out the unwillingness of Muslims to follow the law as the major obstacle to their becoming full citizens of France. The law in question was not about schools; it concerned removing head covering for identity photos, but it drew a link between the Muslim woman in a scarf and the failure of Muslims to embrace the Republic. The link clicked with many in France. Although defending laïcité remained the ostensible reason for the debates, commissions, studies, and proposals that followed, the enthusiasm and momentum pushing all those debates forward came from the diffuse sense that the scarves were the key to a whole host of problems. Ban the scarves and things will, somehow, get better: boys will stop harassing girls, "Islamists" will stop harassing "secular" Muslims, and teachers will get more respect. Much as in the now much-debated "broken windows" theory of crime's decline in New York City, the "veiled girls" theory of France's anomie and disaffection implicitly saw a cascade of good things coming from bared heads.

Not that such a theory of cascading social benefits was ever put forward in quite that way. Rational though the French like to think themselves to be, rational choice theory is hardly alive and well in France. But something like such a theory underpinned the claims and the associations made during 2003 and 2004. It motivated the juxtaposition of images, or the selection of guests for a talk show, or the telling of horror stories about bad things happening when veiled girls were present. The endless hearings before the president's Stasi Commission on laïcité built up the sense that, as one of the commissioners put it to me, "teachers can do no more, and something has to be done," and that banning the veil was the best candidate at hand.

In this chapter I take us through the political events of this key period, from Sarkozy's speech in April to President Jacques Chirac's declaration of support for a law in December 2003. Chapter 6 examines all that followed that speech—afterthoughts, debates at the National Assembly, and the first year of the law's application. This rather breathless run through the politics surrounding the law's passage is followed, in the final section of the book, by an analysis of the scarf malaise and its component fears. For these fears—about communalism, Islamism, and sexism—reflect deep-seated approaches to the world and ideas about how the world works. This analysis allows us to better understand how it was that journalists, politicians, and intellectuals could (and wished to) persuade people that the law was a necessary response to dangers facing France.

Sarkozy's "Answer to Le Pen"

As you may recall from chapter 3, by December 2002 Nicolas Sarkozy had managed to cobble together an agreement among the major Islamic organizations—the UOIF, the FNMF, and the Paris Mosque—on the structure for the new French Council for the Muslim Religion, the CFCM. He had been able to assume the cooperation of the Paris Mosque leadership because they had been the state's "house Muslims" for decades. The Moroccan FNMF operated less in the public sphere than as a network of mosques—it did not even have a headquarters. The UOIF was another story, however. Its claim to legitimacy derived from its oppositional stances (for example, on headscarf matters) and its clear ties to international Islamic movements. Co-opting the UOIF was Sarkozy's major challenge and his major success.

At the same time, mingling with the "veiled women and bearded men" of the UOIF was politically risky for a man who had set his sights on the presidential election of 2007 and who had made his name through a law and order campaign. He opposed passing a new law on laïcité, which helped him with the UOIF but set him up for attacks by his many rivals on the Right. By March 2003, the prime minister, Jean-Pierre Raffarin, and a growing number of politicians across the spectrum had come out for a prohibition on scarves in schools.[1] Sarkozy had to shore up his position as a champion of the Republic.

He did so by depicting himself as a latter-day Napoleon bringing light to Egypt—or in this case to the UOIF headquarters in the La Corneuve suburb of Paris. "I passed three hours with their executive board at their headquarters at La Corneuve on December 6, 2002. It was a gesture, not a concession. It was a way to bring to that place the voice of the Republic."[2] Now, the UOIF's corner of La Corneuve is a relatively safe industrial area near public transportation and cafes, and hardly isolated from the Republic. Sarkozy's neocolonial rhetoric was designed to let us understand that he had courageously bridged a gap between France and the foreign Muslims who needed to be integrated into the Republic, as he made clear in the same interview when he posed the rhetorical question of what the Republic had to gain "by continuing to admit imams who speak not a word of French and who defend an Islam incompatible with our values."

Sarkozy nonetheless was accused by many politicians of crossing the "yellow line" between the state and religion by working with the UOIF.[3] His response was consistent with the principles we examined in chapter 2. When asked if his activities in organizing the CFCM did not violate the principle of laïcité and the 1905 law, he retorted: "What does the law say? The Republic guarantees organized religious practices without favoring any single one. I devote equal energy to allow all our compatriots to live their faith. Islam is today the only religion without a national unifying organization."[4]

Yet the scandal sheets continued to warn of the dangers posed by the UOIF. Journalists paid increasingly close attention to headscarf incidents, although there were no more of them in early 2003 than in previous years. Sometimes those journalists overreached. In early April 2003, the irrepressible *L'Express* devoted its cover story to a supposed secret network of Islamists associated with the UOIF who were trying to seize power in France by manipulating elections. The magazine revealed that this radical network communicated by inserting secret information into the empty tracks of a recent CD released by the singer Carla Bruni. The police laughed off the story, but it added to a general sense among politicians and the public that someone needed to "do something" about political Islam.

Sarkozy's response to this unease came at the very moment when he was celebrating his new rapport with the UOIF. In April 2003, he made the first visit by a government minister to the annual gathering of Muslims sponsored by the UOIF. The Salon du Bourget, held in the hangars once used for Le Bourget airport, welcomes thousands of Muslims to three days of Islamic celebration. Stands sell books, CDs, and Islamic garb. Muslims from throughout the world give speeches with translations into French. People can feel free to wear Palestinian garb and cry out in Arabic. Boys and girls eye each other. Everyone drinks Mecca-Cola and Muslim-Up.

On Saturday night, April 19, Sarkozy made a grand entrance into the main hall, with cameras and security surrounding him. Fouad Alaoui, the UOIF secretary general, had just finished praising the UOIF for its strong showing in the just-completed elections for the CFCM. On this, the twentieth year of the Salon du Bourget, the mood was of high celebration. Alaoui embraced Sarkozy and called him "our brother." Sarkozy then read his speech (which, contrary to the usual procedure, had not been given to his hosts ahead of time). He celebrated the willingness of the audience "to be Muslims of France practicing an Islam of France," a phrase which elicited a few boos, and on which my neighbor in the audience commented, "We're not so sure about that." Sarkozy continued: Muslims must "present themselves in the light of day for who you are, citizens as are all the French." He congratulated Muslims on their participation in the Council elections, and remarked that they had taken place at the time of a war "that is not our own" (to which my neighbor in the audience added: "But it is ours," and then, pointing to me, "and it is his").[5]

Sarkozy continued: "For Islam to be completely integrated into the Republic, its major representatives should themselves be perfectly integrated into the Republic, and thus trained in France. We do not need to depend on other countries for finding imams who speak not a word of French." He received mild or strong applause for this and for his following remarks on the need for equal treatment of all religions and the important of the CFCM.

Suddenly, he changed his tone, and mentioned the rule that all residents must have their pictures taken for identity cards with their heads uncovered, adding: "nothing would justify women of the Muslim confession enjoying a different law." He also took to task the subterfuges by which cultural associations, which may benefit from government assistance, provide cover for religious associations, such as mosques, which may not receive such aid.[6] These remarks set the crowd on its feet, booing and whistling, and drowning out his subsequent remarks.

Sarkozy's speech caught the UOIF leadership completely unawares. The first of the leaders on stage to respond made a clearly ill-advised comparison between the "unjust law" requiring hair to show on identification cards and the Nazi-era laws requiring Jews to wear yellow stars.

The minister had timed his speech well. It fell two days before the anniversary of the "shock of April 21st," the first round of the 2002 presidential elections in which Jean-Marie Le Pen had defeated the prime minister, Lionel Jospin. (Jacques Chirac easily won the runoff.) Sarkozy himself later called his speech "my reply to April 21st." During earlier "headscarf affairs," Le Pen had seen his own influence soar and had managed to pull mainstream politicians toward anti-immigrant positions, first in 1989 and then in 1993–1994, when the nation's present and past presidents decried the influx of immigrants: François Mitterrand regretting that they had gone beyond France's "tolerance threshold," Jacques Chirac complaining of an "overdose of immigrants," and Valéry Giscard d'Estaing describing an "invasion."[7] Sarkozy was following what had become a standard electoral strategy, and it seemed to have worked: a poll published in the April 26 *Figaro* magazine indicated that among voters on the Right, Sarkozy had an edge over Chirac for the 2007 presidential elections.

Sarkozy's willingness to address the assembly, and the "hostile" response of the veiled-and-bearded crowd, made headlines in all major newspapers in the following days (even though in previous years the newspapers had virtually ignored the UOIF assembly). Sarkozy had launched "the new headscarf war" and had "put his foot in the veil." Some journalists (Catherine Coroller of *Libération* and Xavier Ternissien of *Le Monde*) wrote balanced stories about the divergence of opinion among teachers about scarves in schools, while others saw an opening for new exposés about radical Islam. *Figaro* on April 26, for example, headlined the danger of "Qur'ânic schools in your backyard," which were revealed in the article to be two schools run by the UOIF, neither of which was in anyone's backyard: one was in the rural Nièvre region and the other in a warehouse in Saint-Denis.

One should note that although the speech was interpreted as an attack on headscarves in schools, Sarkozy had not mentioned that issue. Instead, he attacked the practice of asking to wear one's scarf for an identity card photo. Identity cards are not as innocent as some may think. Jews in Nazi-occupied France were identified by their cards, before the yellow stars were required. In October 1961, the Paris prefect of police, Maurice Papon (later to be convicted of crimes against humanity during World War II), ordered young men whose identity cards indicated that they were Muslims to be brought to the police station if they were out after 8:30 in the evening or if they were driving. Stops were made on the basis of skin color (as, indeed, they are today in Paris), but the identity card sealed one's fate. Muslim men routinely were beaten and some killed— about two hundred were killed on one day by the police.

Although identity cards are supposed to show the face and head clearly, in 1983 the interior minister had stated in the National Assembly that his ministry had regularly allowed Muslim women to retain their headscarves for these photos.[8] Sikh men were not forced to remove their turbans for photos. But few knew the law on this matter, whereas many in France now knew that scarves were allowed in schools. Thus Sarkozy could better apply his "no one is above the law" rhetoric to the issue of identity cards than to the schools.

But in fact no one cared about identity cards, and for the politicians the issue clearly *was* scarves in schools. Two weeks later, Raffarin and Sarkozy together appeared at the opening ceremony of the CFCM. Raffarin praised religion—"the true energy is found today in the spiritual and religious"—but said that the veil issue "must be dealt with, asking what it is that leads certain pupils to take refuge in communalism." He also mentioned cases of pupils refusing to take oral exams administered by someone of the opposite sex, or challenging the content of the curriculum, and added that "the voile is a symbol for those who wear it, but also for those men and women who oppose it."[9]

What did French women and men think of the matter after Sarkozy's speech? A professional telephone poll taken by the firm BVA April 25–26, 2003, found people evenly divided about a ban on headscarves in schools, 49 percent to 45 percent for such a ban, a bit stronger for a ban on scarves on identity cards (53 percent to 39 percent)—the subject of Sarkozy's April speech—and one-third even supported banning headscarves "in the street"![10] (The percentages were remarkably stable over social and economic strata.) However, only 22 percent were for expelling girls who refused to remove their scarves in school. About half of those surveyed said that the headscarf was a way of lowering the status of women; this sentiment seems to have been stronger than a concern about the public presence of religion.

Sorting Out Positions

From Sarkozy's speech in April until the passage of the antiheadscarf law by the National Assembly the following February, scarves and Muslims were almost constantly in the public eye, with time out for the devastating heat wave that struck France that July and August. Looking back over the year that November, an editorial writer for *Le Monde* argued that it was the booing of Sarkozy in April that led the political leaders of the country to raise the stakes regarding the voile and led the media to highlight the debate on television and in print.[11]

Major politicians took one of three stands: for a law to ban scarves in schools, for something short of a law (a code, or clearer court rulings), or against any change. Government ministers began to stake out their own positions and spar with each other over this issue; the voile became one of several weapons in the fight for political advantage. Gradually, however, politicians who initially had adopted the second or third position climbed on the prolaw bandwagon.

François Fillon, the social affairs minister, was the earliest advocate of a new law, on the grounds that it would state clearly the Republic's position on laïcité. Sarkozy, although he opposed wearing scarves in schools, opposed a new law on the grounds that it would humiliate Muslims. Through their differences on a number of issues, those two ministers, although political allies, defined the space open to members of the majority party, the Union for a Popular Movement (Union pour un mouvement populaire, UMP). Fillon stood for the hard-line defense of Republican individualism. Indeed, when he succeeded Luc Ferry as education minister, he spent the summer before the law's implementation delivering what school officials described to me as the "hard line" they were to take regarding girls in scarves. Fillon also brought social affairs policy back to a defense of assimilation rather than just integration, urging, for example, that immigrants who did not sign up for government-sponsored language classes have that failure count against them when they applied for naturalization.

Sarkozy, by contrast, was the only minister to advocate a French version of affirmative action. On May 2, 2003, he told *Le Monde* that although "republican conformity is the rule in the public sphere," handicaps must be taken into account, and "positive discrimination is necessary to reestablish equal opportunity." His major example was Corsica, which he thought deserved a limited degree of political autonomy, but his active (what the French call *volontariste*) policy toward aiding Muslims in building mosques can best be understood as another dimension of his "positive discrimination" thinking.[12] The difference between the two ministers' positions on the scarf issue was just one instance of a broad disagreement over the extent to which the state should enforce a particular view of laïcité and neutrality.

During the spring of 2003, Prime Minister Raffarin occupied a middle position, urging new measures against the voile but stopping short of advocating a new law. In late April he declared that "the school is the premier space of the Republic and we must remain vigilant that we ensure that the supreme value that is the Republic is protected in the school, and that there are no ostentatious signs of communalism."[13] The minister most directly concerned by scarves in schools, Education Minister Luc Ferry, vacillated (as he did frequently during his tenure). Toward the end of April he came out against a new law, saying it would be unconstitutional, but in May he argued that a new law would clarify the rules for the schools.[14] And yet even then he argued that expelling girls would send them into Islamic private schools and would contravene article 9 of the European convention on human rights, which protects "freedom of conscience and of religion." In October he stated before the Stasi Commission that a law was unnecessary, given the small number of cases. (Ferry's lack of clarity marked him for removal from the cabinet at the next opportunity.)

Some deputies in the majority UMP were unwilling to propose a law forbidding the scarves because they feared it would be unconstitutional, but instead proposed a new "code" to interpret the law.[15] By late May, however, the tide had begun to turn on the Right. Some say that Chirac and Raffarin already favored a new law; others think that Chirac continued for several more months to hope that he might avoid this step.[16]

Within the UMP were some who saw the law as a way to neutralize Le Pen, blame the Left for having promoted multiculturalism or "differentialism," and take Sarkozy down a peg for his support for Muslims and resistance to a law. In February, Raffarin had asked the young and eager François Baroin (an Assembly vice-president) to deliver an unofficial report on the voile to a discussion club founded by Raffarin. Baroin's report, delivered in May, urged the Right to adopt the issue of defending laïcité against "a Left that has mainly converted to multiculturalism" and "certain immigrant populations" that do not understand laïcité. He recommended a "laïcité code" that would ban headscarves from schools. He also recommended the creation of a state-sponsored faculty of Islamic theology and the teaching about religion in public schools—thus combining, as did many politicians, a hard-line position on scarves with a willingness to control Islam by aiding it.[17] Laïcité meant that the state had to keep Islam in its place, not keep out of its way.

The National Assembly created its own committee. On June 4, Assembly Speaker Jean-Louis Debré named deputies to a Parliamentary Information Mission on Religious Signs, with himself as both president and reporter—an unusual step, but one consistent with his personal penchant for control. The Mission was bipartisan, and indeed responded to a call by the Socialist Party leadership for such a group.

Socialist deputies tended to be for a new law but also for massive efforts to deal with discrimination and unemployment (not that they had implemented such measures during their own turn at governing). An early convert was former education minister Jack Lang, who in the Mitterrand years had been a proponent of the "right to a difference," including the right to wear scarves, but now supported a law. The April 30 edition of the strongly antiveil *L'Express* smugly congratulated Lang for joining them in the fight against the veil, ironically referring to themselves as "those Cassandras who since 1989 have opposed, in vain, the judicial consecration of this negation of the equality of the sexes in the very place where that principle ought to be taught."[18] Former prime minister Laurent Fabius, in an address to the Socialist Party Congress that May, argued that "in the public space—thus first of all in the public school—demonstrative religious signs have no place." He proposed a new law that would "express this rule that would be the strict application, according to the law, of the principle of laïcité."[19] Fabius was joined by longtime ardent Muslim advocates of a strict laïcité, such as Malek Boutih, and by new, self-styled "secular Muslims" (*Musulmans laïcs*) such as the businessman Yazid Sabeg and the sole Muslim in Raffarin's government, Tokia Saïfi.

One had to travel farther to the left than the Socialist leadership to find opposition to a new law. The most prominent early statement of that position was in a letter published in *Libération* on May 20 written by a number of public figures, including the philosophers Etienne Balibar and Pierre Tévanian, and the sociologists Saïd Bouamama, Catherine Lévy, and Françoise Gaspard. They took no position on the desirability of the voile, but supported the school as an instrument of "emancipation and not expulsion." Regardless of whether it is the girl or someone else who thinks up the scarf, "it is by welcoming her at the secular school that we can help her to free herself and give her the means to her autonomy; it is in sending her away that we condemn her to oppression." The letter objects to blaming the girls for social problems: "To justify expelling them, people invoke, in random fashion, things in which the girls are not necessarily implicated: lack of discipline, massive absenteeism, racist and sexist (and often anti-Semitic) insults."[20] (*Libération*'s editor, Serge

July, supported a law; *Le Monde* cited the letter in a news story of its own in implicit support of its own editorial position against the law.) The letter was the germ of what became the "One School for All" collective against the law.

The UOIF's position that women should wear a covering (a hijâb), its relationship with Sarkozy, and the sense that it was allied with international "Islamists" meant that the group's every act and statement added to the sentiment for a law. Chirac confidants within the UMP played on the open Chirac-Sarkozy rivalry to argue that the voile in school was just one element of a broader plan by the UOIF to challenge the Republic. It did not help that the UOIF president, Lhaj Thami Breze, was reported to have said in an unguarded moment that "the Qur'ân is our constitution."

The taint of the UOIF was exploited by the Left. Jean-Marc Ayrault, president of the Socialist group of deputies to the Assembly, attacked the government for its reliance on the CFCM and pointed out that the Council had stated (in a session at the April assembly held after Sarkozy's speech) that the voile was a "religious recommendation." Ayrault attacked this "retrograde message" and Sarkozy for "this new 'Concordat' and its danger of communalism."[21] By September it had become clear that a law would be proposed and that Sarkozy eventually would have to support it. (Polls taken in October showed him to be preferred as a candidate for the presidency in 2007 by 50 percent to Chirac's 40 percent.)[22]

By and large, spokespersons for non-Muslim religious groups opposed a new law for fear that any effort to tighten up on laïcité could adversely affect them. In practice, laïcité is not always strictly observed. Some Jewish pupils absent themselves from school on Saturdays. Catholic priests sometimes appear inside schools to meet with pupils. After the divisive debates of the 1950s and 1960s, Christian and Jewish religious leaders preferred to work out issues discreetly. In May, the chief rabbi of France, Joseph Sitruk, came out against a law, recognizing that the skullcap would be banned along with the voile.[23] (He later retreated from the debate.) The same month, the president of the Reformed Church of France came out against a new antivoile law in his opening address to the national synod.[24] Cardinal Lustiger, who had opposed efforts by priests to work closely with Muslim leaders, nonetheless warned Chirac against changing the 1905 law lest he open "Pandora's box."[25] In September, the president of the Bishops' Conference of France, Monsignor Ricard, did question the capacity of Muslims to "distinguish between religious and civil law." But two months later he took a stand against a new law, saying that "if the state is secular, civil society is not" and that religious liberty must be safeguarded.[26] In December, the leaders of Catholic, Protestant, and Orthodox churches would send President Jacques Chirac a joint letter opposing a new law, for fear that it would threaten the presence of religion in public space.[27]

Summer Distractions

New issues arising over the summer of 2003 heightened the general sense that Islam had invaded the public sphere. When on June 14 the Senate held a debate that was open to the public on Islam and laïcité, a Muslim woman wearing a headscarf was refused entry. The Senate president learned of the fuss, and came to explain to the woman that the hemicycle was a secular space and that religious signs were forbidden. On July 3, a UMP deputy in the Assembly spotted a woman in a headscarf seated in the visitor's gallery and sent a note to the president of the Assembly on behalf of several troubled deputies asking that she be thrown out. "I defend the Republic and do not allow this sort of behavior," he said.[28]

Swimming pools came into the debate in June, as the summer grew hotter (it became the hottest on record). In some cities, mayors had allowed municipal pools to reserve hours for women. In southern Lille, one of the four municipal pools had offered such hours for two years when reporters finally stumbled on the practice in June 2003. The mayor, Martine Aubry (who had been a government minister under Jospin) had authorized the special hours upon request from city women. The same arrangement turned out to have been in effect in a Lille suburb. In other parts of France, Jewish associations had successfully petitioned to have sex-segregated hours at municipal pools, with no media attention. But in 2003, the existence of the "Arab" women-only hours shocked certain commentators. The president of the association Europe and Laïcité, Étienne Pion, considered the arguments for women-only hours—modesty, ease with babies—to be but "alibis to force the acceptance of communalist principles." The ante was raised on the Muslim side as well. The Islamic association in Trappes, south of Paris, put on a demonstration to force the mayor to grant separate women's hours. The mayor refused.[29] (He had, however, worked with the association to build a new mosque, as I discuss in chapter 7.)

When the story about Lille broke in June, Martine Aubry was quickly asked to explain herself during a municipal council meeting. The head of the opposition party in Lille (in this case, the UMP) publicly denounced sex-segregated hours for swimming pools as conflicting with "Republican practices of equality and gender-mixing" (*mixité*) and promoting a "closing-off of communities from each other" (*un repli identitaire et communautariste*). In her reply, Aubry suggested that by making "a small detour" from Republican principles "women can liberate themselves." One suburban Lille pool admitted only Muslim women, but Aubry assured the public that in 2002 users of the women-only time slot were 70 percent Muslim and 30 percent non-Muslim.[30] (No one appears to have found it remarkable that in a country where officially recording religion or ethnicity is forbidden, Aubry's office would have such figures.) By December, the minister of sports strongly condemned the pool hours for women as "a deep challenge to the value of our country and of sports."[31]

A New Affair: The Lévy Sisters

Almost anything about Islam that surfaced in 2003 made the newspapers, so when a standoff over scarves occurred at the return to school in September, journalists were waiting. At the Henri-Wallon high school in Aubervilliers, a northeast suburb of Paris, the Lévy sisters, Alma, sixteen years old, and Lila, eighteen, showed up wearing what were described as "veils that cover the ears, the neck, and half the forehead," in contrast to the acceptable "light scarf tied behind the head." A teacher asked one of the sisters to leave the class. She did so but returned accompanied by the principal, who argued that the girls needed to be allowed to "find themselves." Several of the teachers were irritated that their authority had been undermined.[32]

The teachers were further disquieted when they learned that the girls had a Jewish last name, leading some to think that their father was a "Jew converted to Islam." It turned out that the father, Laurent Lévy, was a lawyer working for the antiracism movement MRAP (Mouvement contre le Racisme et pour l'Amitié entre les Peuples, Movement against Racism and for Friendship among Peoples). Lévy called himself "Jewish and atheist." Their mother was from the Kabyle region of Algeria and had never worn a voile. They had separated. The girls had lived with their mother until shortly before the beginning of school in 2003, when they moved to live with their father. "It is their choice" to wear scarves, he told reporters. He hoped that they would give it up. "They began three years ago by not eating pork; two years ago they observed the fast and learned a bit of Arabic. They have worn the foulard for six months." He had been the first to be irritated by their decision to wear it, he said, and had tried to convince them that the voile represented a terrible burden for women in Muslim countries. They retorted that "they would never wear it in a country where it is required."[33]

As in earlier cases, officials sought compromise. An inspector from the school district tried to convince them to wear a scarf that would leave at least the neck, earlobes, and roots of the hair visible, what he called a "light foulard," versus a "foulard islamique." The girls refused, and they retained the voile during gym class. They were expelled on the 24th. Their official notice of expulsion cited their wearing of "ostentatious" clothing, clothing that was incompatible with gym class, and "disturbing public order" because of the demonstration that followed their provisional exclusion. These charges were worded so as to justify the expulsion in terms allowed by the State Council.[34]

After the expulsion, five of the teachers involved in the dispute wrote an open letter to *Libération*, in which they said that that they found the expulsion regrettable but necessary. They added that they opposed a law banning scarves and that such a law would "reinforce discrimination and therefore communalism." Thirty-four of the thirty-six students in Lila's class voted to strike. One of them complained that the school admitted students who wore "gothic" cloths, "even a T-shirt saying Vote for Satan: is that not religious? At least Lila and Alma don't scare anyone with their voile."[35]

But of course they did scare people. The fact that their parents had not approved of their decision led people to look for the radicals who must have put them up to it. The sisters swore that they only rarely went to the mosque, and never visited "Islamist associations," and their father confirmed this.[36] Their father accused teachers affiliated with the far-left party Lutte Ouvrière of having called in the media, and claimed that the decision to take them before a school disciplinary council had been made by the prime minister's advisors.[37]

As with previous highly publicized affaires—Creil in 1989, Nantua in 1993–1994, Lyon the previous year—the Aubervilliers incident provided an occasion for public figures to sound their slogans. MRAP's general secretary, Mouloud Aounit, used the expulsion to denounce *Islamophobie* in France. MRAP became an active partner in the negotiations with the school and the family. Malek Boutih, the general secretary of the Socialist Party but formerly a leader of SOS-Racisme, the group that had become a major force in the movement to ban the voile on the grounds that it oppressed women, applauded the expulsion of the girls because "it protects the destiny of all other girls."[38] The Communist Party, which joins with the Socialists on laïcité but which is divided on the question of a law, called the expulsion "a failure" because "the girls will continue to wear the voile and they are excluded from school." Sarkozy used the occasion to repeat his position that, on the one hand, "the rules of laïcité are required of everyone," but on the other hand, they must be respected "in such a way as to not humiliate anyone." The CFCM echoed the Communists (!) in calling the outcome "a failure," while its president, Dalil Boubakeur, tried to be both ultrasecular and Muslim, as usual, by saying that "the priority for the girls is instruction in the public, secular, obligatory, and free school," repeating the phrase associated by all readers with Jules Ferry and "high laïcité."[39]

Immediately after the girls' expulsion in mid-October, the CFCM declared that the existing jurisprudence ought to be applied (which arguably would compel the school to keep the girls) and that the voile was a "religious prescription."[40] In October, the UOIF (the major component of the CFCM) let it be known that it would welcome a law against the foulard in schools, because it would allow the organization to tell girls that the "condition of necessity" (the Arabic term *darurat* was used) required that Muslims obey civil laws even when they contradict religious principles.[41]

The Stasi Commission Deliberates

All these matters and conflicts were to be resolved by a commission appointed by President Chirac in July 2003. In creating a commission to report on issues associated with laïcité (but understood as focusing on headscarves), he may have assumed, and wished, that the result would be something short of a new law. After all, his party's political strategy had included targeting voters of North African origin and appealing to those who thought religion had a place in France. The Independent Commission of Reflection on the Application of the Principle of Laïcité in the Republic—known subsequently either as the Commission on Laïcité or, most commonly, the Stasi Commission, after its president, Bernard Stasi—began work without knowing what the outcome would be.[42] Most commissioners did not favor a new law. One of them estimated that only three of the nineteen members had made up their minds that scarves must be banned by statute from schools—and one of those three was caught on camera saying that she had begun her service unsure of the advisability of a law. Yet eighteen members voted for the law, with one abstention.[43] Why?

Some of the commissioners spoke to this question after they had submitted their report. Both in their public comments and in discussions with me, they tended to converge on one major reason: that those who testified had agreed that things had gotten terribly out of hand in some of France's schools, and that something had to be done. Even Alain Touraine, a sociologist generally opposed to the monolithic republican way of thinking that was very strongly represented on the Commission, initially abstained but ended by voting for the law. And yet no one was sure that a law against scarves would help matters much. Nor did the nation's deputies exhibit much certainty on that score when they debated the draft law several months later.

The report of the Stasi Commission made a large number of recommendations, only one of which had to do with clothing. The recommendations ranged from improving the condition of the poor, to fighting labor discrimination, to recognizing one state holiday each for Jews and Muslims. Many of the commissioners reported their frustration that only the scarf issue was taken seriously as an item for immediate legislation. But of course the debates and the anger that preceded the Commission's creation and that rose in intensity during their deliberations were all about the scarves—or rather, about the violations of France's social principles that the scarves summed up, represented, and perhaps encouraged. The issues were the place of Muslims in the Republic, and more particularly of Muslims who showed themselves in public as distinct from other people. The furor was not about discrimination, poverty, or the quality of schools, much as these issues were and are debated. They were not about Jews and Christians, or about the place of religion in the Republic, try as people might to diffuse and disguise the Islamic question in these more general concerns. The anger and the discussions and all the news articles and television programs were about whether and how Muslims could fit in within France.

Even in its official film biography, the fifty-two-minute *Behind the Veil* produced by the government cable and Internet station PublicSénat (modeled after C-SPAN and presided over by a proponent of the law), the Commission represents itself as responding to matters of veiling (as if the film's title did not already give this away). After a few introductory remarks, the film shows Bernard Stasi confronting the question of whether or not the Commission would hear a *femme voilée*. He recalls that a recent book was titled *One Veiled, the Other Not*, and that they could interview "the one who is." So little attention had been given to asking women in scarves what they thought that neither he nor the Commission's *rapporteur*, Rémy Schwartz, recalled her name. (It turned out to be Saïda Kada from Lyon, quoted in the previous chapter.) All the other clips shown on the film are about headscarves, even a clip of the commissioner Mohammed Arkoun complaining to the camera that the voile is such a "small matter" in Islam. Like it or not, the voile was the subject matter of the Commission's work.[44]

The nineteen commissioners were a diverse group, chosen to have a range of talents and to include intellectuals, administrators, politicians, and a few provincials. Bernard Stasi had begun his civil service in French Algeria, and had been mayor, deputy, minister, regional president, and European deputy. Two members of the Commission had practical experience with scarves in schools: Hanifa Chérifi was the mediator in these affairs from the Education Ministry and Ghislaine Hudson is a lycée principal. Maurice Quenet is the superintendent of the Paris Academy. Most were recognized for their scholarly records: Gilles Kepel is one of France's foremost experts on Islam; Mohammed Arkoun, the only Muslim member of the Commission, is recognized for the level of his philosophical writings on Islam; Jean Baubérot and René Rémond are recognized scholars of laïcité; Henri Pena-Ruiz is one of its firmest advocates. Jacqueline Costa-Lascoux has served on many government commissions dealing with immigration, and integration and Alain Touraine is a major figure in French sociology. Régis Debray moved from his prominent role as a member of Che Guevara's guerilla group to being a defender of the Republic against headscarves in 1989, a critic of media domination later on, and most recently an advocate of teaching the history, philosophy and sociology of religion in the schools. Patrick Weil is one of the foremost experts on the history of immigration and policies concerning integration. A few high civil servants and two mayors rounded out the list: Marceau Long, who was vice-president of the Conseil d'Etat when it issued its 1989 decision and the first president of the High Council on Integration; two mayors, Michel Delebarre and Nelly Olin; and three figures from "associative life": Nicole Guedj, who had to leave the Commission midway through its work to take up a ministerial position in the government; Gaye Petek, an activist for the integration of Turkish immigrants; and the businessman Raymond Soubie.

What the Hearings Were Really About

The Commission was supposed to hear from the diverse opinions of French people about laïcité. How was that topic to be defined? Of course, the agenda was the voile in public schools, but the commissioners by and large wanted to address a larger array of issues. What was the larger array of issues? Was it laïcité, or was it a set of social problems somehow linked to Islam? Had it been the former, then one would have expected the commissioners to focus on the place of religion in public life (the schools, politics), on whether changes in the 1905 law were required to adequately fund the building of mosques, churches, and temples, the ways in which laïcité is taught in schools and to future teachers, the curricula followed in private religious schools that receive state subsidies and are supposed to follow the national curriculum, the appropriateness of the high degree of state involvement in regulating religion, most recently regarding the CFCM, and other, related questions about laïcité.

These issues were not, however, those on which the commissioners focused. Yes, representatives of several religions were asked for their opinions about the 1905 law, and an intriguing suggestion was made to give Jews and Muslims each a state holiday, but most of the testimony turned on problems of the poor suburbs: violence against women, challenges to authority in the schools, poverty, and, central to most of the testimony, the voile. In each case, topics were deemed relevant only insofar as they involved the public actions of Muslims and the question of the headscarves. So, when unemployment was introduced as a problem afflicting many residents in the poor suburbs, the hearings did not then pursue the causes of and best solutions for unemployment, but stopped at a general plea for doing something about the problem. For problems of discrimination, the Commission stated that it was regrettable and something ought to be done, as it contributed to tensions, but that was not the focus of the report either and little new light was shed. The major specialists on those questions did not testify; the topics were thrown into the mix, one might speculate, to "cover the bases."[45]

In its very choice of persons to hear and questions to pose, the commissioners suggested—in the manner of television hosts assembling topics and people for a talk show—a set of causal links among the voile, Islam, violence against women, and a breakdown of order in schools. Other causal links were alluded to but not pursued, suggesting peripheral status. The real topic of the investigation, then, was approximately "problems in and around poor schools that are linked to the rise of Islam," and the working hypothesis was something like "wearing headscarves threatens central values of the Republic." Let me be clear: I do not think that the majority of the commissioners began their work assuming the hypothesis to be true: some thought the headscarf to be a relatively unimportant piece of the entire social puzzle. But the organization of the Commission's work, the choice of people to hear and places to visit (determined by the *rapporteur* Remy Schwartz, who collected lists of suggested witnesses from commissioners and who had previously argued that girls were pressured to wear headscarves in schools), all focused everyone's attention on this topic and on this hypothesis, rather than on the topic of laïcité, or on the topic of why it is that things are in such bad shape in these neighborhoods.[46]

Furthermore, the commissioners did not include anyone likely to present the views, experiences, and interests of the girls concerned. As one member later told me: "It was unfortunate that there was no one with sensitivity about Islam. René Rémond had that for Catholicism and Patrick Weil for Judaism; Muhammed Arkoun has no real ties with the Muslim community, things have moved well beyond him."

The Stasi Commission did listen to a wide range of people: heads of major religions and associations, ministers and mayors, police (regular and secret), and teachers and principals of public middle and high schools. The commissioners responded in quite distinct ways to different kinds of witnesses. They listened attentively to teachers and school principals. They were suspicious of or antagonistic toward those few Muslim witnesses who opposed a law. At one point, Jean Baubérot chided his colleagues for suspecting a priori everything stated by Fouad Alaoui, the secretary-general of the UOIF. They did not hear from young women who had been expelled, nor from the many sociologists who had studied their choice of dress. (The sociologist Françoise Gaspard had conducted such a study, but she was called to testify before the Commission in her role as a prominent feminist politician.)

Even witnesses who targeted other causes of social problems ended up strengthening the case for a law against headscarves. Arguments that the causes of current social problems lay in the failure to seriously address problems of poverty, segregation, and racism did not lead the discussion away from the voile, but paradoxically tended to keep the debate centered on the voile as the most visible and public sign of a social problem. For example, the minister who most forcefully emphasized the need to attack economic and social problems was Urban Affairs Minister Jean-Louis Borloo, who was building his career on urban redevelopment. Yet he, too, began by selecting as the major problems the equality of men and women, girls in headscarves, and attitudes toward those girls who do not wear the voile. He then focused on the problem of insufficient funding for social and economic problems in the poor suburbs, but returned to the issue of the voile.

"Everyone agrees that there are three ways to wear le voile: a defensive way in the face of violence by boys, who attack girls because the girls advance faster in school; as a way of leaving the Republic in which they do not see themselves as having a place; and because of *intégrisme*, 'green fascism.' " He then turned to only the first two and outlined what his ministry has done and could do with more resources.

Borloo's intervention exemplifies the way in which politicians and others at one and the same time could say that the root causes of social problems lie elsewhere and yet support, intentionally or otherwise, the cause of passing a law against scarves in schools. In arguing that we need a massive investment in poor neighborhoods, for example, he said that making such an investment would "place the religious in the domain of the religious, and you will see the question of the voile in school retreat, because it no longer will be the arm of combat, the place where everything mixes—the colonial, justice, the adolescence, all." In this claim, Borloo asserts once again that the voile is the site for this illegitimate mixing of things that ought to be separated.

The commissioners posed questions in such a way to suggest that they had decided that veils, and Muslims, were the problem. Saïda Kada was the token "veiled Muslim woman," as she was introduced to the public by the PublicSénat spokesperson.[47] In the only moment of agreement between her and anyone on the Commission, she complained that everyone seemed to talk as if banning the foulard would resolve the problems of the poor neighborhoods and schools. Bernard Stasi immediately agreed, saying that "we too have been annoyed that the debate seems to be limited to the question of a law on the foulard."

And yet immediately thereafter, the commissioners launched into a series of questions that all concerned the voile. With two exceptions—interesting questions by Alain Touraine and Jean Baubérot that went unanswered—all the questions were of two sorts. The commissioners either demanded that Kada explain why Muslims do this or that (outfit little girls in voiles, fail to denounce the stoning of women), or they attacked her and people like her for encouraging girls to leave school, or for forcing society to adapt to her rather than the other way around. It was as if the appearance of the only invited public witness in a scarf (in fact she brought another with her without telling the Commission and angering some of its members) so mesmerized or enraged the commissioners that they could not ask about the problems they claimed to think were also important: the role of religious education in schools, the social and economic problems of the ghettos. Nor was there any manifest interest in learning more about the activities of Kada's network in Lyon, which arranges home schooling for girls, or interest in learning how girls and women might respond to a law. Very much unlike the responses to ministers, teachers, or unveiled social actors, no questions asked of her were informational.

The testimony by Nicolas Sarkozy is worth considering because of his own central, if contested, role in publicly articulating a new place for

Islam in France. He spent much of his time defending his active (*volonta-riste*) approach to Islam. He summed up the 1905 law with the motto "The Republic accepts all religions and favors none," which he said required acknowledging the spiritual importance of organized religion. His reading of laïcité was as follows: "laïcité is the recognition of the human need to hope and therefore to believe" (meaning "to have a religious belief"). The main role of the state is to actively guarantee equal footing to all religions: "The state has to watch to ensure that each religion has exactly the same rights as all the others." Islam, he continued, does not have the same rights as the others: too few mosques, no chaplains, no French institute to train imams. The best way to combat communalism is to grant Islam those rights, in a kind of "positive discrimination" for Muslims: "The first Republican value is not equality but fairness" (*équité*). Sarkozy emphasized both the "neutrality" of the state and the active role this required on the part of the religions minister: "As Ministre des Cultes, it would be wrong for me not to participate in the great moments of religions. It is in this way that one must understand the requirement of neutrality."

Although Sarkozy also repeated his opposition to the voile in school, separate hours for women at the swimming pool, and, in general, the notion that religions could negotiate laïcité, the overall thrust of his testimony was to argue for a greater public recognition of the role religion has played in history and plays in every person's personal life, and for including Islam in those acts of recognition. In an eloquent set of closing, somewhat impromptu remarks, he urged a France that gave women the right to vote only in 1945 to show some humility when preaching gender equality to Muslims, and he attacked those who, decades after France encouraged the massive migration of Muslim workers to its shores, would even pose the question of whether Islam is compatible with the Republic. He reiterated his opposition to a new law, warning that it would humiliate Muslims and radicalize people on both sides of the debate.

The law and order minister Nicolas Sarkozy, booed by the crowd at Le Bourget, and the "veiled woman" Saïda Kada, an activist on behalf of Muslim schoolgirls, strikingly converged in their opposition to a new law. Both Sarkozy and Kada urged the government to continue to allow case by case handling of school disputes. Sarkozy approvingly mentioned a recent case in Orléans where a girl agreed to replace her voile with a bandana: "both won, no one was humiliated." Both warned that a law would lead to a hardening of positions: indeed, Kada reported that the school districts, the academies, no longer allowed girls under the age of sixteen to pursue distance learning. Of course, they disagreed on much as well. Sarkozy disclosed his own images and emotions about the voile when he recounted how, after stepping off the podium at Le Bourget and heading toward the exit, he was greeted by young women in scarves who wished to talk, and then commented: "I was struck by the fact that many of them were at university, were born in France, and why then the need to caricature their identity?" He then answered his own question: "It is because they see their identity caricatured in the eyes of others."

These comments, made at a relatively informal moment in the hearings, reminded me of the strange phrase *cold tolerance* proposed by Gaspard and Khosrokhavar, and since then by others, as the best attitude toward Islam. Sarkozy cannot see the voile as a positive element of the religion whose rights he champions; it too strongly violates his sense of how women ought to present themselves. He cannot personally or emotionally embrace the public face of Islam even though he can offer it a spirited political and legal defense—indeed, he offered what was potentially the most effective argument against an antivoile law, that it would humiliate Muslims. He is surprised that educated women "born in France" could so disfigure themselves as to wear an Islamic headscarf. Islam is certainly compatible with the Republic, he argues, as one of many avenues toward hope by way of faith. But its public manifestations must be strictly limited by laïcité, although this limiting must be handled deftly, and (here is where he would be most guarded) ought to, in time, be brought closer to French norms of behavior.

(Some) Educators Speak Out

Finally, let us consider the overall effect conveyed by teachers and other personnel from the Education Ministry, the people most directly concerned by a possible law—other than Muslim schoolgirls themselves. Educational personnel were divided on a new law. Many teachers doubted its effectiveness. In December, three of the four major confederations of teachers' unions were to ask President Chirac not to propose a new law.[48] Some feared that focusing on the scarves would harden positions and make their work more difficult. In the classroom, they look for compromises.

But it was mainly school principals and educational administrators who were heard by the Commission. They encounter scarf issues as legal or potentially legal battles, and they considered a new law likely to make their task of resolving disputes easier because it would not require them to either find nonscarf grounds for expulsion or negotiate a compromise. Administrators look for definitive solutions.

This analysis is supported by a comment made in early September, when both the Debré and Stasi commissions were beginning their work. Eric Raoult, deputy from Seine-Saint-Denis, one of the Assembly's vice-presidents, and far from a favorite among Muslims, reported that the deputies on the Debré Commission had begun divided on the issue and all had modified their initial stands. "Those who pleaded for the freedom to wear a voile in the classroom have heard the principals demand a legislative framework. Those who were for a law heard teachers explain to them how sometimes, for adolescents, the voile is at one and the same time a family obligation, a sign of identity, and protection against what they feel as aggression by boys."[49]

Furthermore, few believe that the teachers and principals who were selected to testify before the Stasi Commission represented the range of positions held by their colleagues in France. Those teachers asked to testify usually had encountered a girl in a headscarf, and had stories to tell about problems involving Muslim pupils.[50] But their experiences were hardly representative. Indeed, 91 percent of all teachers in France had never even *encountered* a student in a headscarf at their current school.[51] Nonetheless, the teachers who testified tended to generalize their sense of crisis to other teachers and other schools. A high school teacher from Lyon referred to the many problems told to her by others in the Lyon area; a middle school principal in Paris said that all her colleagues reported incidents similar to those she described; teachers claimed that all the other teachers at their school agreed with them. The testimonies thus gave the impression of a unified sentiment among teachers and principals throughout France.[52]

The commissioners heard stories about pressure placed on girls to wear the voile. Several teachers and principals claimed or implied that families pressure the girls, usually by inferring this pressure from the girls' ages or from changes in their behavior. One teacher recalled how a girl's knowledge of the State Council's ruling led him to wonder whether she had been coerced or trained, leading some on the Commission to shrug their shoulders and give each other knowing looks. A command of the legal framework could have been celebrated as empowerment, but when girls in scarves knew the law, it was assumed to be evidence of coercion.

In most cases, the teachers and principals presented a series of incidents of turmoil and challenge. For example, Thérèse Duplaix was in her sixth year as principal at the Turgot high school in Paris after having taught in other schools in the Paris region. She recounted incidents of students praying in the school, girls coming to school in headscarves, conflicts between mothers and daughters, trouble-making boys, voodoo ceremonies, proselytism, students bringing Islamic books to school, anti-Semitic insults, fighting, students claiming that lessons conflicted with Islam, students of different religions debating their positions, Jewish students missing Friday late-afternoon or Saturday classes. Her assistant added that "there is an aggressive presence of religious signs . . . and we cannot teach in such a climate." She recalled a conversation with a young woman in a voile the previous evening, who was very aggressive, "so we need a strong reminder of the law."[53] (Duplaix's strong bias, and the problem with the Commission's selection of witnesses, were more clearly revealed the following March, when she was denounced by many of her teachers and students for helping to create a television documentary that depicted her school as in a virtual state of war between Jews and Muslims; see chapter 7.)

This set of incidents was repeated by other teachers and principals. How did it lead them to advocate a law against headscarves? Arvaud argued that France needed to reaffirm a common understanding of laïcité, that this reaffirmation had to banish proselytism and "revealed truths" from the sphere of laïcité, and that because France's schools and their teachers are now very diverse, they can no longer agree on their own on how to translate laïcité into concrete, daily policies. Headscarves were for her the visible sign of "intangible laïcité." But some teachers will accept scarves, others not; therefore, "if we wish to preserve the national character of our values on which our personnel act, we cannot let local law prevail." When asked why France needed a law rather than a ministerial directive (*circulaire*), she replied: "I am not a legal scholar, but I have a certain idea of the Republic. I consider that the law is what the Republic does, and the laïcité is one of the founding values of the Republic. . . . A directive is like the notes I make in my office."

Although some teachers were not themselves convinced that a law was necessary, they, too, listed problems they encountered at their schools, thereby leading to the overall sense on the part of the commissioners that, in the words of one of them, "teachers cannot continue; something must be done."

The Final Push

On December 11, the Commission issued its report, in which the commissioners urged the government to fight discrimination, train imams, provide Muslim chaplains, and teach laïcité. Overall the report took strict or strong positions on issues of laïcité and on issues of social inclusion. Although for months thereafter commissioners complained that people focused only on a few of its many recommendations, in fact most of those recommendations were too general to be worthy of note: break up the ghettos, teach about laïcité, respect burial practices, and the like. These and other recommendations, such as that regarding the training of imams, had been recommended by many previous commissions. On only a small number of issues regarding Muslims and laïcité were there substantive (and thus controversial) recommendations in the report. The Commission stated that hospital patients do not have the right to refuse to be treated by a doctor of the opposite sex. They proposed a new law ensuring that people using government services would "conform to the requirements for public service to function," a vague statement that could be interpreted to ban citizens from entering the post office wearing a headscarf. And finally the body recommended that: "In schools, middle schools, and high schools, appearances and signs displaying a religious or political affiliation be forbidden, conditional on respecting the freedom of conscience and the specific nature of private schools under contract with the state. All sanctions are to be proportional and taken only after the pupil has been asked to meet his/her obligations." This proposition was followed by an explanation explicitly stated to be "inseparable" from it: "The forbidden appearance and signs are *signes ostensibles*, such as large crosses, voiles, or kippas. Discreet signs such as medallions, small crosses,

Stars of David, hands of Fatima, or small Qur'âns are not regarded as signs displaying a religious affiliation."

The second part of the conclusion was titled "Respect for Spiritual Diversity," but in fact, aside from the general suggestion that the state create a national institute of Islamic studies, it was limited to the proposal that Aïd al-Kebir and Yom Kippur become national holidays. The idea was a new one, but immediately quashed by Chirac.

The report was unanimous except that one commissioner, Jean Baubérot, abstained on the proposal for a law against religious signs. But two of the nineteen commissioners were absent the day of the vote: Régis Debray, who was writing his own book on the subject at the same time, and Maurice Quenet. Two others, René Rémond and Alain Touraine, held out before finally voting with the majority; Rémond later publicly termed the law "useless."[54] Alain Touraine, interviewed shortly after the report was presented to Chirac, seemed to say that he voted for it because had the Commission been divided no one would have paid any attention to the report. As did many deputies in the subsequent debates, Touraine salvaged from the report the idea that with it, France sent a message to communalists that "we do not want communalism, that rational thinking exists, that equality between men and women exists, that citizenship exists."[55] At least one other member wanted to vote against the proposed law but found the pressure unbearable.

Between October and December, politicians on the Left and the Right had closed ranks behind a new law. Some doubted its advisability but knew they could not oppose laïcité. One member of the national Socialist leadership reported that at the meeting that led to the declaration in support of the law, "everyone rallied to it but considered it stupid" (une connerie), and many who would later speak passionately for it were reluctant converts.[56]

By the time the Commission issued its report, public opinion had swung firmly behind a new law. A new poll conducted by BVA on December 3 found that 72 percent of those interviewed favored a ban on all "visible signs of religious or political affiliation in public schools"; the number rose to 83 percent for those who leaned toward the majority Right, the UMP.[57] This figure contrasted sharply with the mere 49 percent in favor of a law in BVA's April poll, and represented an increase over the 57 percent and 65 percent approval rates found in two polls taken in November.[58] Other indications pointed in the same direction. In an email forum set up by the National Assembly, 75 percent of messages supported a law.

It is hardly surprising that increasing number of people favored a law against religious signs in public schools. They heard politicians calling for it. Between September 2003 and February 2004, they would have read an average of two articles each day on the voile in each of the three major news dailies, including stories about a series of Islam-related threats to the Republic: covered women at swimming pools threatening mixité, patients refusing to be treated by male doctors, jurors wearing scarves while in court, and Muslims approving the stoning of adulterous women and booing the interior minister.[59] Some of the media reports concerned serious problems, such as anti-Semitism or attacks on women in the poor suburbs, albeit linked to scarf-wearing only vaguely at best. Other reports were highly fanciful, such as the Carla Bruni CD hoax. But the overall effect of all these reports was to move the public—and some on the Stasi Commission—toward the general sentiment that "something had to be done." The commissioners began to feel that they had no choice. "If we propose another ministerial directive, people will laugh," exclaimed one of them during their discussions.

Media prolaw coverage intensified just as the Stasi Commission was due to deliver its report on December 11. On December 5, Chirac attacked the veil as "aggressive." The next day, Saïda Kada testified before the Commission in its final public session, the first woman in a headscarf to do so, to extensive coverage. On the 7th, Le Monde published a report about challenges to laïcité in the hospitals (see chapter 7). On the 8th, Elle published an open letter denouncing the voile, which "returns us all, Muslim and non-Muslim women, to intolerable discrimination against women," which was signed by a long list of notable women, from the actresses Isabelle Adjani and Isabelle Huppert to the intellectuals Julie Kristeva and Françoise Héritier. Elle reported the results of a poll of Muslim women living in France taken in late November: 49 percent supported a law and 43 percent opposed it. Élisabeth Badinter, asked to comment, said that the 43 percent only said they opposed the law because of pressure by fundamentalists (les intégristes).

FIGURE 3. Editorial cartoon after President Chirac's speech proposing a new law, *Le Monde,* December 18, 2003 (by permission of *Le Monde*)

The juxtaposing of certain news items also sent a message. *Libération*'s issue of December 10, the day before the report, pulled out all the stops. The cover story concerned girls in poor neighborhoods who denounce pressures placed on them by Muslim boys under the headline: "Their voile, I want to rip it off: nonveiled girls testify to the pressures that they undergo daily in their neighborhood in Paris, Lille, Mulhouse, or Avignon." Next to it was a story on the 1966 assassination of seven monks in Algeria, and three news boxes: on Tunisia, where the voile is banned in the schools, on Turkey, same story, and on Algeria and Morocco, where although there are no such laws, "women suffer increasingly strong pressures to wear the voile." *Libération*'s editorial position was clear: Islamist terrorism, resistance against voile-pressure in Muslim countries, and the tensions in France were all of a piece.

On December 17th, Chirac spoke to the French public to propose a law against signs that "clearly show" (*manifestent ostensiblement*) a religious affiliation. He had already publicly showed his hand during a visit to Tunisia twelve days earlier, when he declared that wearing the voile is "a kind of aggression that is difficult for the French to accept" (implying that one could not be "French" and wear an Islamic headscarf).[60] Despite potential opposition from some Muslims who were being courted by Chirac's party, it was clear why the president wanted to see such a law pass. The French public increasingly wanted something to be done about "all the problems," and the French tend to look for a law to solve things. Since early in 2003, several key figures in the party, including François Baroin, François Fillon, and Jean-Louis Debré, had been urging Chirac to support it. He could steal some thunder from his most visible political rival of the moment, Nicolas Sarkozy, and also force the interior minister to back away from his initial opposition. He would reduce the capacity of the National Front to make electoral hay out of the issue in the spring 2004 regional elections.[61] Why not?

SIX

Repercussions

ONCE President Chirac delivered his December speech proposing a new law against religious signs in schools, it became clear that the National Assembly and the Senate, France's two legislative bodies, would vote for the law in some form. Majorities on both the Left and the Right already had declared their support. A poll taken the day of the speech showed 69 percent of the population behind the president.[1]

But many continued to oppose the law, and indeed the first few months after the speech saw the greatest amount of protest. Some disliked headscarves but did not think that schools should expel girls who wore them. Others were concerned that the law violated religious freedom. Many who worked in the schools preferred the flexibility of the status quo. Some pupils prepared to defy the law at the start of the new school year.

DEMONSTRATIONS AND DEBATES

Opposition to a law was not only on the fringes. After a debate within its editorial committee, *Le Monde* took a strong position against the law the day after Chirac's speech, charging that such a law would "stigmatize, marginalize, and exclude a part of the population when the country has more than ever a need for integration." The overwhelming support for the law, the editorial argued, was because "the irrational is at work here," and it warned that some Muslim women soon would no longer be allowed to wear their scarves in the streets.[2] Two days later, another editorial charged that the government had played up the foulard to hide the real "social debates" over unemployment and the bankruptcy of Social Security, and that it pushed forward without consulting "the major interested parties: practicing French Muslim women, including those in the voile."[3]

But after Chirac's speech the center of attention passed from the Stasi Commission to the streets, where those opposed to the law could give voice to their complaints, and to the Parliament, where legislators could compete to see who was the strongest defender of laïcité.

Opponents of the law turned out for three major demonstrations, on December 21, January 17, and February 14. The January march was notable for the appearance of a new target for those who saw great dangers from Islamism in France. Few had heard of Mohamed Latrèche prior to the march. President of the small Parti des musulmans de France (Party of French Muslims) based in Strasbourg, he mobilized thousands of men and women in Paris and thousands more in other cities to march chanting "there is no deity but God" (*la ilaha ilallah*) and "God is great" (*Allahu Akhbar*). These phrases are the normal ones for Muslims to chant in public in Muslim-majority countries, but they are unusual in the French context, where everyone translates their particular concerns into Republican phrases, and where some associate the phrases used in the January march with *jihad*, or at least *islamisme*. Latrèche himself exacerbated these reactions by speaking with reporters about the "Zionist media" with whom he would "settle accounts" later. Even *Le Monde*, generally sympathetic to the protests, emphasized Latrèche's threats, choosing for its headline a quotation attributed to him: "He who insults us we must terrorize politically."[4] The UOIF, to its later regret, participated in the march.

The Anatomy of a March

Organizers of the February march tried to undo the damage by emphasizing the ecumenical character of the opposition to the law. The collective One School for All placed themselves in the front of the marchers and were accompanied by North African (but not specifically Islamic) groups such as the Fédération de Tunisiens citoyens des deux rives as well as Islamic organizations such as the independent Collectif des musulmans de France, centered in Saint-Denis, and the Jeunes musulmans de France, associated with the UOIF.[5]

Figure 4. Demonstration against the law on religious signs in schools, Paris, February 14, 2004 (photograph by author)

People come to demonstrations in Paris with a set of expectations: The marchers will move slowly from the Place de la République to the Place de la Nation. They will be organized into distinct cortèges, and the people on the front line will be selected to send a particular message to the journalists who take their photos before the marchers begin to move. Many of the groups will have nothing in common except a general agreement with the cause and desire to march. Chants will follow familiar rhythms and melodies.

On February 14, I arrived at the Place de la République about two in the afternoon, as marchers were assembling. As I emerged from the subway station I first saw two long tables containing the works of Marx and Lenin and other tables with Maoist and Trotskyite pamphlets. I wondered if I had wandered into the wrong place until I saw a few signs protesting the law over to the side. Some of the far-left organizations did oppose the law, despite their Marxist suspicion of religion. The latest

Figure 5. Demonstrators, Paris, February 14, 2004 (photograph by author)

bulletin of the Revolutionary Young Communists, called *Red* (in English), urged unity behind the antilaw group in the name of class solidarity and antiracism.

The front line of marchers gradually assembled. They clearly had been chosen to project a certain image of the group: ethnically mixed, all female, few headscarves. The message was: women are speaking for themselves, and they are secular, not *intégristes*. Women in scarves and men with short beards mixed with far-left groups toward the rear. Two girls were in wheelchairs to signal their hunger strike. A group of Strasbourg Muslims marched on their own.

The front line stood still for a long time, singing songs, to let all the television cameras get good shots. Then the march got under way, a truck with loudspeakers moving slowly along just ahead of the front line. Several men and women sat on the speakers and called out chants. The chant leader for most of the way was Radia Louhichi, a young Tunisian woman with long, curly hair, who was active in One School for All (and who appears again in chapter 8). She vigorously kept the crowd going, interspersing chants with the hopeful cry "We are not tired." Among their chants were:

Première, deuxième, troisième génération, on s'en fout, on est chez nous!
(First, second, third generation, we don't care, our home is here!)
Police partout, école nulle part!
(Police everywhere, school nowhere!) [They often inverted the order of clauses in these two slogans.]
Français musulmans, fière de l'être!
(French Muslims, proud to be!)
L'École laïque choisit pas son public.
(The secular school does not choose its public [students].)

About half-way along the route the leaders paused to deliver a speech emphasizing that they were all united in the fight for the homeless, against expelling students, for minorities, and so on, before continuing to the Place de la Nation.

Some observations I noted along the way:

A reporter from an Arabic-language television station interviewed (in French) a man who explained that they had made overtures to non-Muslims and the march included all citizens to fight exclusion.

Posters read: "Stasi killed me"; "1 veil = 1 vote."

I walked ahead of the slow-moving march for five blocks. I saw a petite, middle-aged lady walking toward the group with a single sheet of paper on which she had written *Vive la laïcité*. As she neared the marchers she hesitated, turned her sheet over, and took a different path. I bought the afternoon paper and sat in a café, by the window. Two elderly ladies sat next to me watching the marchers. "When you are in a country you should show respect," said one. The other agreed: "We had to work very hard after the War. . . . We cannot really say anything. . . . This gets on my nerves."

One group of five young men, dressed in Palestinian outfits with red checkered scarves and long flowing pants, hung out alongside the march, but never joined it. At one point they took pictures of themselves. A group of girls in scarves and long gowns kept up with the march on roller blades (see figure 5).

Radia at one point announced that Tunisia was leading Morocco 2–1 in a soccer match, and most of the people in front cheered, a few men jumping up and down, and she cried out "vive la Tunisie."

At the end of the march, all gathered around the truck in the Place de la Nation to hear a succession of speeches by men and women, Muslims and non-Muslims, including one Sikh—the dilemma of the turban-wearing Sikhs was very much in the news and he was applauded loudly. One woman asked for donations. "We are not SOS-Racisme; we are not Ni Putes Ni Soumises; we do not have money."[6]

Applause lines from other speakers:

"The law divides people as did colonialism; this law is colonial."

"We built our feminism on our tenderness, on our solidarity."

"I rejoice that these are not 'Muslims' in the street, but men and women. . . .
    We are the people of France . . . in the tradition of France, demonstrating
    our concerns."

"Jules Ferry, Condorcet, Victor Hugo would turn in their graves if they knew
    that today, the schools exclude young people in the name of laïcité."

"All of you, stay in school, because we have had it up to here about people
    in the projects just going on to flip burgers at Macdo" [spoken by a young
    woman in a headscarf].

The march embodied the position of those opposing the law on the Left: there were no slogans, speeches, or banners that approved of wearing headscarves, and certainly no one said women should wear them. Few speakers wore head coverings, and they were in large majority women. The message was a secular and universalistic one: all in the Republic have the right to attend school. This message was linked to others dear to the Left: equal rights for all, an end to job discrimination, an inclusive form of feminism.

The National Assembly Produces a Text

Now we turn to a completely different setting, no less exotic: the semicircular amphitheatre (*l'Hémicycle*) in the Palais Bourbon where the deputies to the National Assembly meet. During four days in the first week of February, the deputies debated and voted for the proposed law on religious signs. (The Senate followed suit the following month.) There, too, the message was about the Republic and its universalistic principles, but the conclusion drawn was that the voile must be banned in the name of those principles.

As Marc Abélès (2000) has noted, one could easily stroll through the Palais Bourbon and imagine oneself in royalist days if one regarded only the imposing building and the paintings from the *ancien régime* that line its walls. It is "public" in that it is part of the state apparatus, but it is hardly freely open to the public.[7] To attend many of the open sessions you need an invitation from a deputy, which I had obtained before leaving the United States. Feeling myself the owner of a prize possession, I used my ticket to follow the hearings through to the end. Each day I was ushered up into the spectators' gallery only after leaving all objects other than a small notebook at the cloakroom. Once in the gallery you must remain silent and respectful—at one rather warm moment I made to take off my suit jacket, and was sternly frowned at by the guard sitting next to me.

Deputies make a great show of partisanship on the floor but clearly maintain collegial relationships. Nearly every time a Socialist deputy mentioned the name of their founding figure, Jean Jaurès, those on the right would jeer or call out their objections. One or two of the Socialist and Communist deputies (particularly the noisy mayor of Montreuil, Jean-Pierre Brard) made a regular point of objecting to any attempt by the president's party to justify government policies. But sometimes one would give a hearty "well said" to a colleague across the aisle, and Socialists and conservatives walked in and out of the *hémicycle* together. The owlish-looking president, Jean-Louis Debré—whom most agree was a terrible minister but became an excellent Assembly president—kept the speeches moving with good humor and the occasional remonstrance (often directed at Brard).

Equally important to the Assembly's functioning is the chair of the Commission on Laws, a post occupied in 2004 by Pascal Clément, a deputy from the UMP. This commission chair discusses any proposed law and amendments with his committee ahead of debate, and then works with deputies from the opposition to develop a best-case scenario. At any critical juncture, the Assembly president calls on him for a recommendation.

The spatial set-up emphasizes hierarchy and ideology. The president sits at the highest point in the room, at a desk on the third level of the elaborate presidium. Behind him staff members deliver messages to and from deputies. At a desk below him sit from three to five people taking notes on the proceedings. Two take down the words of the speakers, while two others record all the other interjections: "applause," "smiles from the Socialist benches," "gesture of disagreement from the minister," and any other interruptions. Their operation are so efficient—one scribe replacing another with a tap on the shoulder, the exhausted writer hurrying out with his or her text—that an initial version of the speeches is available on the Assembly's Web site three hours after every speech, to be issued in print form, free for the taking, at 10:00 the next morning at the Assembly bookstore.

The deputies sit, as they always have, arrayed from the speaker's left to right, with coalitions thoughtfully situated between opposing parties. Most of the time, most of the desks are vacant. A lot of the business takes place in the halls. A lot of people are elsewhere.

The debate on the law on religious signs in schools was unusual in that a clear majority of deputies had agreed beforehand to pass some form of a law against religious signs in public schools. The sole note of disharmony was caused by—the government's own education minister, Luc Ferry! Everyone suspected that he was unhappy with the law—how else to explain his maladroit performance before and during the debates? He had pointed out that under the proposed law, anything worn by a student that was not "discreet" and that had religious meaning could be banned, even beards. Coming after the revelation that Sikh males would find it difficult to attend school with their turbans—we have Sikhs?— Ferry's speculations risked making the entire project appear ridiculous. So little confidence did the prime minister have in him that he took the unusual step of presenting the opening case for the law himself, rather than, as is usually done, asking the minister most directly concerned to make the case. Ferry had to sit, silent, in the minister's seat during this embarrassing proceeding. (Indeed, either Ferry or an assistant had to be present at all times during the debate to represent the government.) When Ferry did speak, in response to objections made to the law, he was interrupted by unusually loud catcalls. Most of the Socialist Party deputies walked out, in an unusual show of disrespect. One yelled out: "Great, you respond before we have presented all our objections!"

The Assembly president had taken the unusual step of allowing any deputy who wished to do so to address the assembly, rather than asking each faction to put forth a limited number of spokespersons. The decision meant that the debates went on for an unusually long time, more than twenty-four hours in all. Deputies clearly wanted to go on record in support of the Republic and against *islamisme*. As many deputies admitted during their speeches, this law was intended to be "symbolic": to send a message to Islamists and to French citizens alike that France stood for principles of laïcité and gender equality.

I attended the sessions with a colleague, Claire de Galembert, and as we took a taxi back from dinner after a break, our driver, learning our destination, railed against the politicians: "It is what the French always do: if there is a problem they pass laws, even if no one respects it. They did that to ban pit bulls, but no one cares! What idiocy! If they come to school with their voile let them leave and take correspondence courses: that's all, what idiocy!" Perhaps the negative vote on Europe a year later reflected some of this sense of how valuable political debates were for ordinary Frenchmen.

The text of the law as it was debated read as follows:

> *Dans les écoles, les collèges et les lycées publics, le port de signes ou tenues par lesquels les élèves manifestent ostensiblement une appartenance religieuse est interdit.*
> (In public primary and secondary schools, wearing signs or clothes by which pupils clearly display a religious affiliation is forbidden.)

In its final form, as ratified and proclaimed by the president, the text added clauses that prescribed dialogue with the student before any disciplinary actions be taken, specified that it would go into effect at the start of the following school year, where it would apply among France's territories, and that it would be evaluated after one year. That the main body of the text did not change during the debate is due to Pascal Clément's success at reaching agreement among the major parties prior to the debate.

Prime Minister Raffarin opened the session with the government's case. He framed the issue as follows: "The question is our capacity to preserve our values and to transmit them to immigrants," he said. He explained that these values included freedom of conscience, equality between men and women, the "humanistic value" of fraternity, and laïcité, "which we built in dialogue with the Church." (Some Socialists later said, "It was war, not dialogue.") The new law will "respond to those who would place their communalist affiliation above the Republic's laws." The veil and other religious signs "take on ipso facto a political meaning and can no longer be considered as personal signs of religious affiliation." The law is needed to support school principals and teachers, who have, since the nineteenth century, "integrated immigrants with the children of France."

The leader of the Socialist faction, Jean-Marc Ayrault, claimed to be even more deeply concerned with laïcité than Raffarin. He repeated many of the prime minister's points on the voile but attacked the majority for doing little to combat discrimination and also for promoting "positive discrimination," which weakens laïcité.[8] He received applause from his side of the semicircle for the following points:

"You Muslims are fully citizens . . . with the same rights and obligations as everyone else."

"Yes, France is alone with regard to this law, but it has been for 100 years because we are the only country to have secular constitutions."

"France is a beacon for women who are prisoners of obscurantism and for oppressed minorities."

"No other nation has such a cultural mixing."

"We must preserve mixité in all public spaces." [Here he cited approvingly the work of Ni Putes Ni Soumises; see chapter 9.]

By my count, the people or events most frequently cited by deputies during the first night of speeches were, in descending order, Jean Jaurès (always by Socialists); the 2001 France-Algeria match where some spectators booed the *Marseillaise* (as evidence of communalism); Fadela Amara, the leader of Ni Putes Ni Soumises; and Jules Ferry (the last two cited approvingly by the Left and the Right).

Why a Law?

Pascal Clément, the chair of the Commission on Laws, followed the prime minister by taking the logic in a more legal direction, as was his role. "Why a law?" he asked. Because relying on courts created "legal insecurity, local law" when basic liberties are at stake.[9] We need a law, he added, because the European Court of Human Rights has stipulated that "only the legislator is authorized to restrict the exercise of basic liberties." But more fundamentally, "the law, because it is the expression of the general will, will have a broader educational value."

Similar arguments had guided the Stasi Commission's work. To simply affirm the courts' rulings, or to direct the education minister to produce a ruling, would not send as clear a message as would a statute. There is a tendency in France to assume that a statute is much better than jurisprudence because it clearly states what is permitted and what is prohibited. (In this respect French jurists are closer to Islamic "fundamentalists" than they are to the traditional Muslim legal scholars or to Muslim reformers.) French people have more respect for, or place more emphasis on, a statute than a court decision. Because there is no single equivalent to a Supreme Court in France, no judicial decision has as much moral and political value as do, say, decisions of the U.S. Supreme Court.

Many deputies and public officials also argued that statutes are clearer and thus easier to administer than are court rulings or ministerial directives. This argument seems weak. All legal norms that apply to education, whether they come in the form of statutes or court rulings, are translated into administrative directives, *circulaires*, by the Education Ministry. It is these orders that school administrators apply. So it makes no difference to ease of application whether the directive draws from a statute, a court ruling, or some other source.

But Clément also argued in his speech that only a statute could restrict basic liberties without being overruled by the European Court of Human Rights. He based this claim on conversations with Jean-Paul Costa, the vice-president of the European Court (and a member of France's State Council).[10] Costa played a critical role. France had come in for considerable criticism from the Court on various grounds, and to be slapped down for violating human rights is especially humiliating for a country that loudly proclaims its own pioneering role in declaring human rights. A statement by the European Court that France's "symbolic" law violated human rights would be devastating.

In his testimony to the Stasi Commission in October 2003, Costa had predicted that a law prohibiting signs that were *ostensible*, that were intended to draw attention to one's religious identity, would be acceptable to the Court. Although the Court had been vigilant in protecting rights to religious expression, it also had recognized the right of each member state to define its own conception of the relationship between religion and state. France could make a plausible case that its conception, based on laïcité, required that public school students refrain from imposing their religious ideas and identities on others. But, he added, the law must serve a legitimate end, be clearly stated, and be "proportional" to the problem, meaning not excessive relative to the problem it was intended to solve.[11]

Ironically, given the opposition by many of France's political leaders to Turkey's admission to the European Union, that country's experience provided the strongest evidence for the government's position. In a series of cases, the Court had supported actions taken by the Turkish state that had been challenged in the name of religious freedom, including, most famously, Turkey's shutting down of the Refah (Welfare) political party. Costa testified that the Court had upheld the ban because the party advocated Islamic law and Islamic law was contrary to the Council of Europe's principle of equality for women. Turkey therefore did not violate religious freedom by banning the party. Costa inferred from this part of the decision that the Court would welcome a law that, in the name of gender equality, sought to protect girls from pressure to wear the voile. Furthermore, the Refah party had campaigned against laïcité, and laïcité is a constitutional principle in Turkey, and thus would be upheld by the Court. Costa went further and declared that "if you wish to forbid religious signs at the schools, you *need* a law," on the grounds that only a law gave the specific acts of excluding girls a strong enough legal base to avoid being overturned. It was this opinion that Clément relayed to the Assembly and that effectively countered the objections of some deputies.[12]

Costa's views also were decisive for the National Assembly in deciding between two alternative wordings of the law. Jean-Louis Debré's Parliamentary Mission to study laïcité had recommended a sweeping prohibition on all "visible" signs. Leaders of the Socialist Party held the same view, and during the debate they repeated why they had preferred that language. The Stasi Commission had simply said that pupils should not be allowed to wear articles that "displayed their religious affiliations," before clarifying that Islamic veils, kippas, and large crosses alone were banned.

During the Assembly debates, Clément reported that he had learned from Costa that, whereas the European Court would probably support a French law that was "proportional" to the problem, it would likely view as excessive the prohibition of all signs of religious faith, such as the small crosses that many French Christian children wear in school. A law that banned all "visible" signs would cross the line from justifiable protection of France's system of laïcité to unnecessarily limiting freedom of religious expression. The law needed to be worded in such a way as to allow "discreet" religious signs, such as small crosses. And of course this distinction would have the effect that was desired in terms of French domestic politics. The Commission had heard the wishes of representatives of the Catholic Church that small crosses not be banned. (The Jewish skullcap—the kippa in French, the yarmulke in the United States—would be banned, but because most Jewish pupils wearing the caps already attended Jewish private schools, subsidized by the state, the law would not affect many Jewish people.) The commissioners decided that banning all "visible" signs of religious affiliation thus would be legally and politically difficult, and settled on the final wording of the law, which prohibited wearing articles that "clearly display" or "draw attention to" (*manifestent ostensiblement*) the religious affiliation of the pupil.

TRANSLATING AND IMPLEMENTING

After the Assembly and Senate passed the law, the Education Ministry issued an administrative order on May 18, 2004, that restated the law and then made it clear that "the signs and clothing that are forbidden are those where the wearing can be immediately recognized for a religious affiliation, such as the Islamic voile, by whatever name, the kippa, or a cross of excessively large size." The criterion then is a kind of semantic transparency of the object.

But "immediately recognized" is a subjective notion, and since 1989 people have had difficult agreeing on how precisely to characterize various items of clothing. The State Council had spoken disapprovingly of "ostentatious signs" (*signes ostensibles*) but said that to force a student to remove the offending headgear it either would have to be *so* "ostentatious" as to constitute proselytism or provocation in and of itself, or be accompanied by acts of proselytism or provocation. This sort of language had led some teachers and principals to complain to the Stasi Commission and reporters that they could not be asked to determine on a daily basis which head coverings were "ostentatious" and which were not. It was these complaints that had prompted the Socialists to opt for "visible."

How to Recognize an "Ostentatious" Sign

Many school officials had shown a highly nuanced sense of how context shapes meaning. As the principal of a lycée in the town of Trappes, south of Paris, testified before the Stasi Commission, "What precisely is an ostentatious religious sign? A short beard? A foulard tied behind the head?" She continued with her own interpretation of the word *ostentatious* as having "the notion of something that is perhaps a bit aggressive." But "everything depends on the context. At Trappes we agreed to allow the 'little voile,' a discreet chignon tied behind the head. In another context than ours this could be judged ostentatious, but here it is not so, because other young women dress similarly but not with the same meaning, not for religious reasons. So it blends into the background and is no longer ostentatious." But, she added, the situation is different for the keffieh, the red and white checked shawl that has become a part of Palestinian male dress and by extension a sign of allegiance to the Palestinian cause. "That strikes me as ostentatious."[13]

This principal's subtle distinctions were based on her sense of whether the overall effect of someone wearing something is to be a bit aggressive or pushy (the French verb *agresser* locates the offense in the act rather than in a character trait). She took careful note of context, of the styles of clothing to which people are accustomed, and the fact that people may or may not make close associations between specific items of clothing and specific meanings. She focused on the effect of wearing clothing in a particular way rather than on the object itself, "the voile."

And yet, although the law was aimed at the "Islamic veil," it was written to be general, so as not to target only one religion. One consequence of its general wording is that male Sikhs were unintentionally affected. But many other potential signs of religious affiliation could eventually become banned. With few exceptions, none of the deputies speaking at the Assembly or the many public figures testifying before the Stasi Commission speculated as to which kinds of clothing could fall under the ban, or whether the semantically broader term *tenue* used in the law could extend to other aspects of one's appearance. Luc Ferry had been ridiculed when he suggested that because some young Muslim men wore short beards as part of their religious behavior, they could be targeted. Cartoonists had great fun with cartoons of the other Ferry, Jules

Ferry, considered the father of laïcité, wearing his full, black beard. But Luc Ferry's point was quite reasonable. (That he was more of a philosopher than a politician became particularly clear during this venture.) Could a shirt in the Prophet Muhammad's favorite color, green, be considered to be a manifestation of Islamic affiliation? What about a purple shirt during Easter?

Even in the case of headscarves, the testimony of the Trappes school principal shows how a scarf signifies religion only if there is local agreement among people that it carries that signification. A scarf in one context, or accompanied by certain behavior, means one thing, but in another context it may mean something else. But even this degree of sophistication leaves it unclear whether it is the intent of the wearer or the perception of others that decides when wearing an article amounts to "clearly displaying" religious affiliation.

If it is the wearer's intent that is decisive, then at least in theory you could ask him or her whether the item does indeed have that meaning. The school principal Ghislaine Hudson, a member of the Stasi Commission, relied on this subjective idea of meaning when enforcing the law at her lycée. She allowed pupils to wear head coverings, and some girls did wear bandanas in the fall of 2004. "We have to decide whether or not a scarf has religious meaning. First we see if the girl wears it every day or just sometimes. If she always wears it and it might be religious, then I might talk with her; teachers are instructed not do so lest they differ in what they say. I ask the pupil whether the scarf is a religious sign or not. Some say it does have religious meaning and then they have to remove it, but we allow her to substitute a bandana."[14]

This approach has a lot to say for it. As many students of the problem have pointed out, headscarves are worn by many women in North African and other countries as a matter of "tradition," which means something like: "this is simply what one does to behave properly, and there is little more to say about it." It would be incorrect to say that these women are displaying their religious affiliations every time they put on a scarf.

Thinking about intentions can become quite complex. What about the women who, according to some proponents of a law, put on a headscarf to protect themselves from harassment from ghetto youth? Depending on how an observer interprets the women's reactions, covering their hair may be intended to deceive callow youth into thinking that they are displaying their religious affiliations, or to neutralize the same youths' objections to their choice of clothing, or, perhaps, to display religious affiliation as well.

And what precisely is "religious affiliation"? Is it the answer to the question "of what confession are you?" When girls and women are asked why they choose to wear a headscarf, their response usually has to do with a greater consciousness of religious obligation, or to show their piety, or as part of declaring their independence from their parents. Their intention was to manifest their piety or maturity, not their Muslim identity.

The complexities of the subjective theory of religious display were well captured by a parody that circulated on the Internet of the Education Ministry's administrative order. In the parody directive, "A scarf worn by a Christian girl will be accepted, as long as she is not a nun, and the same for a turban worn by a Jewish pupil and a Sikh's large cross. . . . A registry will be kept of each pupil's religion to make clear which signs each may not wear." The parody was logical: because a turban cannot indicate Judaism, the Jewish pupil in turban would not be breaking the law, and so forth.[15] But the implications ran completely counter to Republican hopes for effacing religious differences within the school.

But alongside the subjective interpretation of clothing there is a second possibility. Perhaps "religion is in the eye of the beholder." Then you would be displaying your Muslim or Catholic identity to me by wearing a scarf or a cross if and only if I perceived you to be doing so. Indeed, this interpretation seems consistent with the ministerial directive, which specifies that it is articles that "are immediately recognizable" as having religious meaning that are banned. It also allows teachers or principals to simply declare an item of clothing as falling under the ban because *they* see it as indicating a religious affiliation, a way of proceeding that is clearly easier for them.

Enforcement, 2004–2005

None of these issues were explored before the ban was to go into effect, in September 2004. Indeed, quite a lot was left undetermined in May 2004. Despite claims that the law clarified the situation, school principals would still have to decide whether a sign conveyed religious affiliation and, if so, if it was discreet or obvious. Schools could pass internal regulations making the law more specific, but they risked sanction from the State Council (or, eventually, Europe) if they went beyond the law. No one knew what stance various Islamic associations and anti-expulsion coalitions would take.

By late spring there was a new education minister, the former social affairs minister François Fillon. He set out to eradicate Islamic signs from the schools. He directed principals to "look for the religious meaning that could be attached to certain items of clothing."[16] Some within the Education Ministry saw a newly aggressive climate toward Muslims in general. School principals had by and large supported the law, and their largest union (the SNPDEN, Syndicat national des personnels de direction de l'éducation nationale) also took a hard line, instructing principals to ensure that no one entered a classroom wearing religious dress even during the required "dialogue phase," and to exclude from that dialogue anyone but students and education officials (a directive aimed at keeping Muslim advocates for the girls away from the schools). They also left it up to individual schools to pass their own internal regulations, which legally could only be stricter than the law itself.[17] Some schools did pass internal rules that banned all head covering, obviating the need to choose among headscarves.

Prepared to defy the ban were several smaller Islamic groups, and most notably Dr. Abdallah Milcent, a convert to Islam and a self-appointed advocate for schoolgirls in veils in Alsace. Abdallah was close to the Turkish community, which tended to produce people taking the hardest lines for and against allowing scarves in schools, mirroring the tensions within Turkey itself. During the previous scarf crisis in 1994, Abdallah had published a "manual" that set out the jurisprudence in favor of the right to wear the scarves. Ten years later, in late June, he circulated its successor, "A Manual for the 2004 Return to School."[18] Abdallah set up a hotline and suggested that parents go on a week's strike if any schoolgirl was expelled for her headwear.

The UOIF, too, urged girls to test the law. On June 29, 2004, they issued a statement that urged Muslim pupils to show up for school "in the clothes they have decided to wear" and offered its own interpretation of the law, namely that it "explicitly permitted discreet religious signs." It urged that Muslims remain vigilant lest in their internal regulations schools prohibited all head covering, which, claimed the UOIF, would violate the law. (Few outside the UOIF picked up this legal claim, and the UOIF eventually dropped it.) Several days later, a gathering of imams in Lyon stated that they had opted to obey "religious principles" rather than the law. In contrast, the Paris Mosque and its allies, notably the associations allied with the Turkish government and representing Muslims from sub-Saharan Africa, the Comoro Islands, and the Antilles, tried to be ultra-Republican and directed Muslims to follow the new law.[19]

On July 5, the CFCM issued a statement saying very little (as its members agreed on very little), and promising only that it would play a role during the dialogue phase and would inform schoolgirls of lawyers who could help them. The CFCM also warned anyone working for them to avoid making their own statements, a clear slap on the wrist of Abdallah, a member of the Alsace CRCM, the regional council.[20]

Just before the September return to school, peace (of a sort) came from an unlikely source. Two French reporters were taken hostage in Iraq by a group demanding that France repeal the law or they would execute the hostages. The action immediately brought unanimity in France against the terrorists. The CFCM leaders offered their services to negotiate for the hostages' release, and soon departed for Baghdad. Editorial writers trumpeted the victory of "*Islam de France*," the proving of the CFCM's loyalty. One major Muslim publicist called on Muslims to cancel the demonstration they had planned in protest of the law. Dr. Abdallah's "Committee on March 15th and Freedoms" (March 15th being the date in 2004 when the law received its final approval by the Senate), stated that they would make no statement on the return to school, given the hostage crisis, "but we will take care of these internal French issues (*nos affaires franco-françaises*) when our countrymen have returned home."[21]

The UOIF skillfully managed its part in the affair. On September 3, it turned the regular Friday prayer at UOIF headquarters into a "national prayer" for the release of the hostages. In his sermon (which he must have known would be reported), the *khotib* explained (in French) that Muslims placed the hostages' right to life above the right to religious expression, but this did not mean that they had forgotten the second problem. "The Muslims who wear the foulard ask themselves why their fellow citizens feel so ill at ease with them, and they receive no response."[22]

The hostage situation made it much more difficult to protest the scarf law, and many girls said they would no longer push their cases at their schools—the UOIF indeed recommended that girls back off, a proposal that some Muslims considered to be a disappointing indication of what the UOIF's cooperation with the government would mean. Many girls had thought long and hard during the summer about what they would do on the first day of school. "It spoiled my vacation," said one girl in her final year, who decided against wearing it. The mainstream national media concurred with *Le Monde* that the first day of school, September 2, "occurred calmly." *Le Monde* pointed to Henri Wallon lycée in Auber-villiers, where the Lévy sisters had been expelled in 2003 but where in 2004 no cases presented themselves. One girl was allowed into the school with a scarf that covered just half her hair. "It has nothing to do with religion," she told a reporter, adding, somewhat inconsistently, that "if they make me remove it I will pray to God."[23] Although one girl said that she felt a bit like a hostage herself, because to wear the scarf could seem to support the terrorists, she admitted that the hostage-taking made her decision easier.[24]

Even after this calming of tensions, François Fillon continued to take a hard line on the issue, calling the law "the symbol of a halt to the process of rising communalism."[25] There were tensions in some schools. Schools differed in three respects: whether or not they allowed "discreet" head coverings, how they engaged in the required "dialogue" with the student, and what scope they gave to the law—did it apply to the class-room, the school grounds, or all activities connected with the school?

The famous "bandana" now acquired considerable importance as a way out for schoolgirls and principals. A school principal could allow cloths that partially covered the head either on the grounds that they were not religious (because the religious injunction requires total cov-ering) or on the grounds that they were discreet. Some principals also decided that a bandana worn every day was more likely to carry a reli-gious meaning than one worn irregularly. Alternatively, a principal could forbid all such scarves, either by interpreting the bandana as de facto religious if worn by a Muslim girl, or by way of an internal rule passed by the school's governing council that would prohibit any head covering. The Education Ministry took a position on bandanas, saying that they could be accepted if (1) they were worn sporadically, thus not for reli-gious reasons (if they were worn for religious reasons, they would presumably be worn all the time), and (2) they were not unrolled to cover more and more of the hair during the school day.[26]

In some cases, girls in scarves were allowed into class and the dialogue begun between school authorities and parents. In a lycée in Trappes, known for its large Muslim population, a fifteen-year-old girl entered school determined to keep her scarf. "I have worn it for four years and I will not disobey God." She said that she would attend an Islamic school if told to take it off. But her teacher said that she would be allowed into class and they would allow two weeks for dialogue, which usually worked out well. After school, the girl said that she had rethought the matter and might take it off; she would have to discuss it with her parents.[27]

The Strasbourg area, with its large population of Turkish origin, produced the most difficult cases and in particular a focus on the hair itself. In the first few days, some girls wore wigs to class to hide their hair, a practice otherwise found among ultra-orthodox Jews.[28] One fifteen-year-old girl of Turkish origin, who had worn the voile in school for several years, showed up with a knit cap and was refused entry. She was brought to see the principal, who told her to take it off. When she refused, she was kept in a windowless room all day. Distraught, that night she cut off her hair and shaved her head. The next day she showed up again, with the cap, and again was shown to a separate room. The school did not have an internal rule against head covering, and many other students had caps or bandanas. One teacher resigned her post over the law. Calling herself a "North African atheist," she was opposed to "this coercive aspect consisting of wanting to liberate people despite themselves. What kind of society are we creating?"[29]

A number of Muslim observers of the scene indicated that they were less worried about the law itself than about the general trend it had produced toward limiting public religious behavior. Some of the satisfied commentaries by those favoring the law indeed suggested some "next steps." L'Express, for example, went to see what would happen at a middle school in Vaulx-en-Velin, a "notorious" suburb of Lyon. All was calm concerning scarves, but the law did not "vaccinate the school against all the problems of the religion." A growing number of girls avoid swimming lessons by finding a doctor to attest that they are allergic to chorine, reported the magazine. And some students take out sandwiches at the moment of the end of the fasting period. Here, "the teachers need guidelines."[30] The images of illness and vaccine to characterize Islam continued even after the law.

Finally, teachers and politicians confronted the question of how broadly the law should extend. Should it apply just to the classroom or also to the school grounds? Ghislaine Hudson, the principal in Melun, prohibited the voile in the classroom and responded case by case to other events. She told me that when a pupil collected donations for earthquake victims in Morocco (an activity permitted by Hudson) on the school grounds wearing a headscarf, Hudson told her to remove it lest the school's action of charity be misinterpreted as having a religious dimension.

What about mothers who volunteer to accompany the classes on school outings? The law does not appear to apply to them, but what if they were seen as school personnel, who must avoid indicating religious preference? The school inspectors in Seine-Saint-Denis district drew the line down the middle, saying that parents who regularly took care of students must avoid all such signs, but that those who did so only occasionally were exempted. Other school districts took a stricter line, and of course schools were also free to do so. To further complicate matters, because mayors assist schools with transportation and in other ways, they can assert their claims, as did the mayor of Montreuil, east of Paris. The Communist mayor (and outspoken deputy), Jean-Pierre Brard, said that no parent going along on an outing would be allowed to display religious signs.[31]

The issue soon spread far beyond schools. In some cities, mayors refused entry to city hall to women in headscarves. On September 11, 2004, a woman was not allowed to act as witness to marriage in a Lyon suburb because she refused to remove her scarf "to allow for her identity to be verified." The mayor of the city said he was simply applying a directive that required him to ascertain the identity of all witnesses, but then he betrayed his broader concerns beyond the letter of the law. "For several years now we have been pressured by communalist requests. Sometimes couples ask that the presiding officer be a women, not a man, or arrange things so that it works out that way." He explained that every couple is told that witnesses must have their foreheads visible up to the roots of the hair at the moment when they sign the register. "We must be firm, because marriage is an *acte civil*, and we risk being caught up in an endless spiral. Tomorrow, in polling places, women will demand to wear the burka."[32]

A second case suggests that the idea of "public space" may serve as the vehicle for further prohibitions. On September 22, 2004, a university student canteen in Paris refused to serve a student because she wore a headscarf. Although the new law does not apply to universities, in this case it was misunderstood as doing so: the food service director explained that "the law that was passed forbids the voile in public establishments. I don't see a problem here."[33] In March 2004, the mayor of a small town ordered a man working at the municipal pool to shave off his beard: the mayor judged the beard to be a "religious sign" that could not be tolerated in a place open to the public.[34]

"The Poor Sikhs"

Not anticipated in the original discussions was the problem of the Sikhs. After a certain age, Sikh males are required by their religion to cover their uncut hair, usually with a turban. Few in France knew what a Sikh was—some Sikhs said that they often were mistaken for "radical Muslims" because of their beards and turbans. Many of them live in Bobigny, Drancy, and other eastern suburbs of Paris. Officials consider them model citizens; the mayor of Drancy, Jean-Christophe Lagarde, said they were "infinitely respectful of the laws of the Republic"—except, now, for the law against religious signs in schools. (The deputy mayor of Drancy, who is also in the National Assembly, had voted against the law because of its impact on the Sikhs.)

The question of Sikh turbans had arisen before. One Sikh contacted by *Libération* had worked for years to be allowed to have his turban on when his photo was taken for identity purposes, and in 1995 he succeeded in getting the Interior Ministry to issue a statement saying that people whose religion required them to wear head coverings could keep them on in their photos. But once Sarkozy launched his campaign against foulards in photos in 2003, this arrangement collapsed.[35]

As one city official in Bobigny put it to me, "if they had just kept quiet no one would have worried about them." But the law said otherwise, and at the start of school in 2004, something had to be done about them. In some schools, a compromise (promoted by Dominique de Villepin, the new interior minister) allowed Sikh boys to substitute a "discreet turban" consisting of a cloth worn over the hair. No one believed that these boys would not be instantly recognized as

"Sikhs in discreet turbans," but they had compromised, and that was enough. But state officials were divided on the issue. In Seine-Saint-Denis, the inspectorate of the academy approved the "discreet turban" compromise. But some of the schools in his district had already passed internal rules prohibiting any head covering, and some professors refused to treat Muslims and Sikhs differently. Fillon, the hard-liner, overrode de Villepin's compromise and said that no turbans of any material could be allowed.[36]

Lycée Louise-Michel in Bobigny had the most Sikhs of any school in the Paris region. In 2003, the school had accepted nine Sikhs with turbans on the grounds that for Sikhs the turban "has an ethnic as well as religious value," which confused the issue nicely and kept them in school.[37] But after the third week in 2004, three Sikh students at the lycée had been kept isolated since the start of school in a room near the principal's office, not allowed to go outside, and required to arrive and leave at a different time than the others. They had showed up the first day with the compromise black cotton cloth on their heads, but in the meantime the lycée had adopted an internal rule prohibiting any head covering and this rule (along with Fillon's directive) nullified the compromise. One of the three pupils was in his final year of school. Teachers gave him homework and he completed it, but the principal's office held onto it.[38] The *Canard Enchaîné*, a satirical weekly that often scoops the major dailies, reported that the Education Ministry had proposed privately to give scholarships to the Sikhs who chose Catholic private schools and to subsidize several new teaching positions for those schools—a measure that, once it had circulated in the Sikh community, led eight students to say that they, too, would hang onto their turbans and attend private school![39]

The three Sikh boys were unable to find schools to take them and appealed their expulsions, losing their case at each level of the administrative hierarchy, and they remained out of school the entire year. Ironically, Sikh turbans, never the target of the law, were the clearest case of an infringement of its text.[40]

In October 2005, the Education Ministry reported that during 2004–2005, only forty-seven pupils had been expelled from school because of their refusal to remove religious signs, 550 incidents had been resolved through dialogue, and ninety-six pupils had left public school for private schools, distance learning, or to enroll in another country. (The last category usually involved residents of the eastern regions moving to Belgium or Germany.) Almost all of these incidents involved girls with headscarves.[41] The office of national mediator was eliminated. But one group claimed that in fact several hundred girls had never showed up at school, and thus were not included in the official statistics.[42]

The role of the school head was critical. At some schools, confrontation was avoided because the principal was able to convince pupils to remove their scarves at the school door, or because the school passed an internal rule prohibiting all head coverings. Other school heads saw the law as the opportunity to "take a stand" and in the process offended families and created confrontations, which led to school disciplinary councils and often expulsions. In greater Melun, south of Paris, for example, two neighboring lycées, with similar populations, had opposite experiences because of their principals' attitudes: at both, several girls showed up initially with scarves, but one principal was able to convince them to remove the scarves, while her counterpart at a nearby high school denounced the girls and produced a public confrontation.

The state had taken a stand against the voile, without any major, immediate repercussions, and the Education Ministry congratulated itself on the outcome. If one looked at the individual cases, one might experience some ambivalence. *Le Monde* reported on girls in Mulhouse and Strasbourg, in the Alsace and Lorraine regions where the highest rates of incidents were reported. One pupil was the class representative at her middle school and an excellent student, but now was following distance learning because of the law; others were finding it difficult to continue their studies without the support provided by the school environment. From their perspectives, the law seemed to have only negative effects.[43] Other Muslims with whom I spoke in 2005 worried that the main effects of the law would concern not the schools but rather the broader society, as more and more non-Muslim French felt it to be legitimate to demand that Muslims remove their headscarves in public.

What this decision would bring in the longer term was less clear. At the UOIF annual gathering in March 2005, many more stands than before were seeking funds to start private Muslim schools. But the existing experiments, at Aubervilliers and Lille, had difficulties making ends meet. Would the law of March 15, 2004, come to be seen as marking the beginning of a flourishing Islamic private school sector in France? Would it look like a push toward "integration," however that might be understood? Or would it be judged as one step in a hardening of tensions over laïcité and religion?

PART 3

PHILOSOPHY, MEDIA, ANXIETY

SEVEN

Communalism

PERHAPS it is now clear why a law against the voile, pretending to deal evenhandedly with "religious signs," would have proved so appealing to politicians: a thorn in the Republican side of teachers and, increasingly, public opinion, the voile was an easy target for deputies feeling a need to "do something" about France's problems. The voile could be construed as violating at least the spirit of laïcité, and the new law would appeal to the French penchant for legislation and it would survive eventual legal challenges.

But this account rests at the surface of things. *Why* was it that so many people became so concerned about "a bit of cloth"? We need to see how the voile touched several raw nerves at once, that these were nerves of some philosophical depth, and that the French news media did their best to inflame the resulting anxieties.

By early 2002, many French journalists, intellectuals, and officials increasingly linked the problem of scarves in schools with three other problems of society: communalism, Islamism, and sexism. Many in France became deeply worried and frightened about these problems, and therefore about the social effects of the voile. We can understand the degree of popular and intellectual support for the law—including support among Muslims—only if we appreciate the ways in which television, radio, and print media played up these broad social dangers said to be posed, or represented, by the voile, *and* if we appreciate the important social and philosophical issues raised by the voile. Perhaps in no other country does applied philosophy intertwine with media campaigns to the extent it does in France. Perhaps also nowhere else are print and televised media as intertwined through overlapping directorships and gatekeepers as in France.[1]

Each of the next three chapters examines the ways in which these linkages were made in public life. The three fears are deeply interrelated, but they draw on distinct strands of French self-understanding. Communalism (*communautarisme*) means the closing in of ethnically defined communities on themselves, a *repli communautaire* (literally, a "folding-in"), and the refusal of integration. Communalism threatens the processes of direct communication between the state and citizens that underlie French political philosophy. It separates citizens by valuing their affiliation to communities over their collective participation in the nation. Once safely distant in "Anglo-Saxon societies," communalism now appeared closer to home, in the poor suburbs of Paris and Lyon and in small communities taken over by Islamists. It threatened to pervert the public schools, those crucibles for molding citizens out of assorted humans, by introducing religious identity, marked by the voile, to divide children against themselves.

Islamism (*islamisme*) has become a usefully ambiguous term for some French social scientists and journalists. It is used to refer to movements that advocate creating Islamic states as well as to those that merely promote public manifestations of Islam. What both references share is a negative feature, the denial of a European notion that religion properly belongs in the private sphere. The ambiguity permits writers to draw on fears of totalitarian Islamist regimes abroad in order to condemn French Muslim associations that advocate a public presence for Islam in France. Such writers allude to past battles between Republicans and conservative Catholics when they gloss Islamism as a species of *intégrisme*, the term adopted by those who, at the turn of the twentieth century, would preserve Catholicism in its "integrity" against the threat of modernity. *Islamisme, intégrisme,* and *communautarisme* are nearly always used in a pejorative manner.

Finally, sexism and violence against women appear in recent arguments and writings as one of the principal dangers posed by Islamism. Physical abuse of women and misogynist attitudes in the poor suburbs are among the most alarming sign of the degradation of social life. These acts threaten the gains made by women in their fight for respect—and the precariousness of these gains makes the threat to them all the more worrisome. Feminists mobilized public opinion against the voile by linking communalism and Islamism to the oppression of women in France and throughout the world.

Of course, French social analysts, politicians, and public intellectuals know that the social and political problems found in France's poor neighborhoods are due in large part to French failures to welcome Muslim immigrants and their descendants. The world became aware during the riots in late 2005 of how deeply ran the resentments and anger created in the poor suburbs by these policy failures. Politicians who have advocated the law also have recognized that unemployment and discrimination have been the major causes of the problems. But recognizing political failures by no means hampered politicians' efforts to blame voile-wearing for exacerbating social problems. They charged the voile with marking some people as different, announcing the wearer's religion in public space, and limiting the freedom and autonomy of women. Stating formally, publicly, and through a law that the voile has no place in the "Republican sanctuary," as Chirac referred to the public school, might just reset the Republic on the right path toward integrating immigrants, privatizing religion, and giving women equal public and social rights. Or so went the arguments put forth in the period leading up to the new law.

Many observers in France have reached conclusions similar to those reached here. In attempting to explain the Stasi Commission's recommendation of a law against religious signs, *Le Monde*'s editor explained that tensions rising from the international situation and the processes of integrating Muslim immigrants into the society have "triply challenged our society." He mentioned the difficulties of civil servants who face new conflicts, women "who legitimately feel assaulted by actions that place in question a principle of equality acquired at great cost" and that "symbolize a great reversal of the feminist cause. Finally, the values of antiracism of the Republic are attacked head-on by disturbing signs of a new anti-Semitism carried by radical Islamism."[2]

COMMUNALISM VERSUS THE REPUBLIC

Now to the first argument, that the voile exacerbates communalism. This claim refers to the postulate of French political philosophy that citizens must all subscribe to the same values in the public sphere. As Interior Minister Nicolas Sarkozy declared in May 2003, "freedom is the rule in the private sphere; republican conformity is the rule in the public sphere."[3] To willingly conform, citizens must interact with each other or must participate in institutions that teach shared habits and values. Social "mixing" (*mixité*) leads people to see each other as fellow citizens rather than as tokens of particular ethnic, racial, or gendered types of person. Social mixing effaces particularistic identities and gives individuals a Republican sameness, a social anonymity in the public sphere.[4]

In his speech on December 17, 2003, President Chirac drew on this postulate to justify a new law against religious signs in schools. He invoked the "common values" of France (social justice, equality), its diversity of regions and religions, and the contributions made to France by immigrants. But he warned of the threat to France posed by the sharp divide separating the "difficult neighborhoods" from the rest of the country. The correct response is "not in an infinite closing-in [*repli*] or in communalism, but in affirming our desire to live together," he said, echoing Ernst Renan's famous definition of nationalism. He emphasized the importance of the public school as a "Republican sanctuary" in which must be preserved the equality of boys and girls and their mixité in all subjects, "lest they be exposed to the evil winds that divide, separate, and pit some against others."[5]

If President Chirac linked the isolation of poor neighborhoods to the lack of gender mixité in schools, symbolized and exacerbated by the headscarf, his prime minister, Jean-Pierre Raffarin, attacked "identity-oriented behaviors" (*comportements identitaires*) in the schools, a phrase that all understood as referring to ways of presenting oneself as Muslim. In the speech that laid out the government's position on the proposed law to the National Assembly in February 2004, Raffarin proclaimed that "rejecting communalism is a specific characteristic of France [*spécificité française*]; it places the general interest above particular interests." Moreover, he continued, "the major sign of communalism in the schools, the most symbolic, is wearing religious signs."[6]

The link between the headscarf and communalism was shared by politicians across the political spectrum. In his response to Raffarin's speech to the Assembly, the Socialist Party spokesperson, Jean-Marc Ayrault, though eager to stake out his party's distinctive position, nonetheless agreed completely with the prime minister on this point and pointed to the voile as the feature of Islam that invites communalism. Indeed, Ayrault went further than had Raffarin, demanding that we "preserve mixité in all our public spaces. We all know that communalist excesses extend to spheres of public life beyond the school." He cited the incidents mentioned in the Stasi Commission report where women refused emergency room services from a male employee, a judge was criticized because he was Jewish, and pupils contested the way a teacher taught history involving Muslims and Jews.

The Left does tend to be more sharply and broadly opposed to communalism than the Right. In his response to Raffarin, Ayrault went from his attack on communalism in the schools to an attack on Sarkozy for his announced intention to appoint a "Muslim prefect" in the name of positive discrimination. Sarkozy's statement had led to an outcry that the minister was promoting communalism by appointing someone on the basis of his particular ethnic identity, and Ayrault repeated the denunciation here. "When someone is appointed because he is Jewish, Muslim, or Christian," said Ayrault, "this act is not in accord with laïcité; the principles of laïcité that forbid evaluating a citizen in terms of his affiliations are not respected."

Communalism was not invented by self-seeking politicians. In some French neighborhoods, failing schools and poor job prospects do indeed lead some adolescents to turn inward or to seek alternative forms of "integration" than those of the Republic.[7] But anticommunalism is a club used to attack a broad range of behaviors and policies, far beyond such phenomena, and including any proposal that would pick out one group over another rather than simply applying to all individuals in France. Policies that channel funds to certain neighborhoods can be denounced as contrary to Republicanism and dangerously letting in the "American model." The prominent sociologist Dominique Schnapper, a member of the Constitutional Council, blames even the meager efforts by the French state to give preferences in certain state jobs to people from poorer neighborhoods or to grant special funding to poor school districts as "indirectly participating in the rise of communalism" by taking account of the particular characteristics of those neighborhoods.[8] Any politician's mention of the "Muslim community" or a "Corsican people" is similarly attacked as betraying the ideal of the Republic.[9]

Muslim leaders who agree with the idea behind the antiscarf law (if not the law itself) also have invoked the specter of communalism. The CFCM president and Paris Mosque leader, Dalil Boubakeur, warned the members of the Stasi Commission that emphasizing religious identity in public would "open the door to demands for a separate religious status, and to communalism, something the Republic rejects because it integrates individuals and does not recognize communities."[10] The Stasi Commission was sympathetic: one member, Alain Touraine, said that "seeing that the rise in communalism leads to terrorism was the principle preoccupation not only of the Stasi Commission but also of the Muslim organizations."[11]

The "Jacobin" Strain in French Republicanism

Although these charges concern communalism based on religion, the French fears that communities will shut themselves off from the Republic extend beyond religion and reach at least back to debates held shortly after the 1789 Revolution. The central "Jacobin" impulse of the Revolution insisted on the primacy of the political domain as the space where citizens experienced their common values and interests. Legislators abolished intermediate corporate bodies, such as guilds and religious groups, which had regulated much of social life under the old order. These bodies had stood between the state and citizens. As the architect of a 1791 law, Isaac-René-Guy Le Chapelier, proclaimed: "No one is allowed to inspire in citizens an intermediate interest, to separate them from common elements [*la chose publique*] through a spirit of corporations."[12] The laws abolished religious organizations (*congrégations*) along with other public bodies, as organizations that might compete with the state in molding its citizenry.

In the eyes of Revolutionary leaders and Republican thinkers alike, guilds and religious orders shared three objectionable features. They were communalist, separating their members from others in the society and giving them illusions of superiority. They constrained their members, preventing them from enjoying the freedom that the state had fought to bring them. Finally, they laid claim to authority independent of the state, forgetting that in Republican theory, the state was part of civil society. They were attacked as erecting "states within the state."[13]

These criticisms are much the same as those leveled against Muslim groups: that they constitute a closed order, that they constrain Muslims both by requiring them to follow certain rules (requiring girls to wear scarves) and by keeping them from participating in emancipation through immersion in state institutions, and that they follow a different authority than that of the French state—encapsulated in the Muslim Brotherhood slogan "the Qur'ân is our constitution," attributed (rightly or wrongly) to the leadership of the UOIF.

In 1789 as today, French politicians and philosophers recognized the rights of citizens to associate as private individuals, but reserved public roles to the state. Rousseau himself, the enemy of all intermediate bodies, applauded the flourishing of private social gatherings, cafes, and everything that would lead citizens to form social circles, as long as they did not take on a public role and thereby weaken the unity of citizens. The 1789 Declaration of Human Rights guaranteed the right to "free communication of thoughts and opinions," and the constitution of the year III (1795) allowed citizens to gather in private societies. But the same constitution forbade the members of such societies from scheduling public meetings, corresponding with other societies, and wearing distinctive signs of their affiliation in public—a ban echoed in the March 2004 law forbidding religious signs in public schools.

In practice, politicians soon realized that the state needed to rely on private associations, and devised ways to accord them some form of public recognition. Shortly after the Revolution, politicians pointed out that the old guilds had upheld standards of quality in produce and wine, and began to selectively reestablish them. During the 1870s and 1880s, politicians advocated legalizing trade unions in order to control workers' actions and reduce the number of wildcat strikes. In terms strikingly similar to those used to promote the creation of a semi-public Islamic body, Léon Gambetta in 1881 called for businessmen to recognize these unions as a way to create spaces that will "bring forth free communication, free deliberation, which are, nearly always, the openings toward agreement."[14]

Just as successive interior ministers were to see the creation of state bodies to regulate Islam as the way to "bring Islam out of the basement," so too were their nineteenth-century counterparts eager to create legitimate "privileged interlocutors" between the state and the mass of undisciplined workers. Centralized control was best exercised by way of intermediate associations, recognized by the state and co-opting the dangerous elements of society. Associations were given general legal recognition by the law of 1901, but only as the effects of contracts among private individuals and without the status of moral persons. Although the law provides for a type of association recognized by the state as being "of public utility," courts have been reluctant to expand this category.[15]

In the late 1990s, new demands for recognition arose from a number of kinds of groups: ethnic, linguistic, and regional as well as religious. Candidates faced pressures to pay attention to the demands of communities defined by countries of origin. An analysis in *Le Monde* prior to the 2002 elections pointed out the "paradox" that everyone denies that communities vote as a bloc, but many people vote according to politicians' responsiveness to their community's needs—for their own schools and teaching of their languages in schools—and their positions on French foreign policy toward their country of origin: Kurds look at positions on Kurdistan, Algerians at overall Middle East policy, Armenians at positions on secession of Karabakh, and so forth.[16] Was it acceptable to enter into politics in the name of ethnically defined communities, to affirm at the same time, in the words of *Le Monde*, "their engagement as citizens and their attachment to their particular identity characteristics"?

At the same time that communities were forming electoral blocs, France was promoting administrative decentralization and faced demands for the promotion of minority languages. These two processes were intertwined: some Corsicans and Bretons demanded recognition of their languages and their status as a "people" at the same time that their regions negotiated the delegation of certain powers. Were these groups distinct "peoples" on the basis of heritage, language, and common residence, as some demanded, or were they merely citizens who happened to abide in the same regions, as most politicians claimed? Could one agree with the philosopher Patrick Savidan that "ethno-cultural demands should not be considered as acts of self-isolation"?[17]

Any social groups claiming special rights run up against the Jacobin heritage of French political culture. When private religious groups seek to act publicly, they incur double suspicion. First, they compete with the state for the loyalties of their members, and thus promote communalism. But they are also suspected of going further and promoting constraints on their members that have divine sanction and thus higher authority than that of the state. Hence the great French fascination with cults (*sectes*) and with the Masons. The former are the subject of frequent special investigations by Parliament and the press; the latter are legal and powerful, but equally covered by the press. Both fascinations are due to the fear that each kind of group has constituted a "state within the state," an association that constrains its members to put the interests of their organization above the general interest.

Communalism Enters Public Schools, or The Lost Territories of the Republic

The voile affaire gave a wide array of politicians and public intellectuals an occasion to once again vilify communalism. The viewing and reading public encountered one exposé after another about the breakdown of mixité and mutual respect in schools, hospitals, and towns. The shock value of these exposés helped increase magazine sales and television audiences, and made a few books instant best-sellers.

Schools were the first focus of these exposés. Many in France place great hope in, and are repeatedly disappointed by, the public schools. Perhaps too much is expected from them: they are supposed to create French citizens, erase social inequalities, make everyone accept the same values, and serve as "the only space allowing each individual to live in total freedom of conscience."[18]

One important instrument in raising the level of alarm was a small book, the kind one can read in the subway, which appeared in September 2002 with the title *The Lost Territories of the Republic*, edited by a teacher named Georges Bensoussan who writes under the pseudonym Emmanuel Brenner.[19] The book features testimonies by middle and high school teachers about acts of communalism committed by Muslim students in poor districts in and around Paris. The teachers combine accounts of clearly offensive acts (such as insulting Jewish students), acts that might attest to sheer ignorance (such as contesting a teacher's version of the Shoah), and acts that offend only within the specific logic of laïcité in the French school (such as breaking the Ramadan fast on school grounds). The offenders are Muslims, and the authors blame "Arab Muslim culture" for these communalist actions. This culture, they argue, refuses mixité and therefore refuses integration into the Republic.

The Lost Territories appeared just months after public attention turned to the rising number of anti-Semitic acts occurring in France, including desecrations of cemeteries and verbal assaults on Jewish children (a rise that was followed a year or so later by a rise in anti-Muslim acts). Although some of the most flagrant acts turned out to be committed by neo-Nazi groups, the initial tendency was to blame Muslims for all such crimes, and this book fed that tendency.

Brenner and his colleagues also claimed that there had been a general "communalist closing-in" (*repli communautaire*). They list various indexes of this process, including the growth in the number of places for Islamic worship, the call by the UOIF secretary general, Fouad Alaoui, for Muslims not to vote for politicians who supported a ban on scarves in schools, and the sympathies of some young Muslims for radical Islamic groups elsewhere in the world. In their analysis, practicing one's religion, playing the French game of electoral politics, and supporting Islamic movements are all evidence of communalist tendencies.[20]

President Chirac read *The Lost Territories*, cited it publicly during 2003, and worked the title into at least one of his speeches. The book is said to have had a strong influence on his decision to advocate a law against scarves in schools.[21] The importance of the book lies not only in the many examples it provided of objectionable behavior by pupils, but also because it effectively shifted the argument against the voile. As we saw in chapter 4, objections to scarves in schools on the grounds of laïcité had run up against the constitutional guarantee of the girls' right to express their religious beliefs. The State Council had guaranteed the right to wear Islamic headscarves as long as the wearers did not proselytize or cause disorder. In practice, school heads had to show that girls either had tried to convert classmates or had done something specific to disrupt the normal functioning of the school. It was difficult to prove either of these contentions, and girls who had been expelled and then sued the school nearly always won their cases.

The authors of *Lost Territories* offered a new argument that promised to be more successful, namely, that the presence on French soil of Muslim culture leads to the disintegration of order in the schools, because it introduces a communalism that divides students among themselves and pits students against teachers. Regardless of what else a pupil does, in the very act of wearing a sign of her religion she divides and disrupts. Because (according to the State Council) the imperative of preserving order in the school allows constraints to be placed on religious expression, the voile can thus be banned generically, without having to demonstrate specific instances of disorder. (Presumably any other sign of Muslim culture also could be banned with the same justification.)

During 2003, politicians and public intellectuals regularly denounced communalism in the schools. In February, Education Minister Luc Ferry held a press conference to denounce the tendency of pupils to "close themselves off in pseudo-communities." In March, the weekly *L'Express* ran a cover story on teachers who feared turning their backs on their students to write on the blackboard. Raffarin and Sarkozy together appeared at the opening ceremony of the newly elected CFCM in May, where Raffarin linked the voile to communalism and mentioned cases of pupils refusing to take an oral exam from someone of the opposite sex and challenging the content of the curriculum.[22] As we saw in chapter 5, the educators who testified before the Stasi Commission agreed that the visible Muslim presence in public schools posed a communalist danger (even if they did not all support the law).

One of the more effective denouncers of communalism in the public schools was a school inspector, Alan Seksig. In his testimony to the Stasi Commission he began with a series of "facts" from the world of public school teaching. Seksig considered these stories to be so self-evidently shocking that he did not feel the need to provide commentary or argument. He told of a colleague who told of a teacher at his school who had asked him to point out the direction of Mecca. It turned out that a female student was standing in the hall wearing a headscarf. She had been expelled elsewhere but accepted there. She wished to pray and needed to know the right direction. Seksig's colleague gave the teacher a little lesson in laïcité then and there. He next told of a primary school principal, herself Jewish, who had wished her Jewish students a good Jewish new year at an assembly. "You can be assured that these are not isolated events," he told the commissioners. Then he told them a third story, also without commentary:

One Friday two years ago the principal councilor of education in a Paris-region high school heard noises and went to investigate. He came to a classroom, looked in, and found a dozen young men eating pizza and drinking cola. He asked them what they were doing and they replied that they were breaking the fast. "How is this?" he replied. "It is 5:45 in the afternoon. If you are here you are in class, and if you are not in class you are at home, the place for festivities." "But sir," they said, "We asked our teacher and he said it was alright." So the councilor looked for the teacher, who was a new teacher of mathematics. The teacher said that a group of boys had come to him at the end of the day and said, "We have had nothing to eat all day and have to eat." What could he do? He did not want to spend hours giving them a lesson about laïcité, so he told them they could go ahead and eat.

Seksig reflected on the origins of these self-evident problems. "Everything starts from the first day of school. On the first day of a nursery school, the principal asked the teachers to inquire of the parents as to which of the children would be eating in the cafeteria and who would not be eating there, and who could eat pork and who could not—and that was the first day of school! This topic became the main subject of discussion among the pupils, and at three years of age! You can imagine what that does to the pupils: 'Oh, you eat pork, and I don't.' We no longer know where we stand with laïcité in the schools."

Seksig pointed to the overemphasis on difference during the Mitterrand years as one of the culprits.

I was a teacher in Belleville [an area in Paris with a high percentage of immigrants] during the 1970s, and we said to parents from other countries: "You have to speak French at home if you want your children to succeed at school." Over time we changed our tune. The Council of Europe and our Ministry encouraged an intercultural pedagogy, with teaching of languages and cultures of origin. Now we say: "If you wish your children to succeed and to feel at ease, speak their language of origin at home; otherwise we will have schizophrenic children who fall through the cracks."

We have slipped toward the obligation to promote difference and membership in a community. At Belleville we created an association that put on a musical comedy with a song that went: "Come see Belleville, when you change houses you change country, we are not of this country, we all come from over there." I began to ask myself about this. Mitterrand visited this school. This is far from our objective; we are all from here even if we experience different influences.

Although other teachers' testimonies about their inability to resolve the problems brought on by communalism probably moved members of the Stasi Commission more than did Seksig's second- or thirdhand accounts, he provided the clearest analysis from within the educational establishment of the causes of problems in the schools. Overemphasizing the legitimacy of cultural differences, he claimed, had weakened the Republican bonds among students and led some teachers to forget the importance of laïcité in the schools.

Seksig's testimony also provided the opening clips on a television program that aired on France 5 on December 7, 2003, just at the end of the Stasi Commission hearings. Titled *Egalité, Laïcité, Anxiété*, it was structured as a commentary on the hearings. The producers selected several key witnesses, showed a few seconds of the witness's testimony before the Commission, and then followed the witness into his or her daily life, deepening the specific argument for a law against the voile. In the case of Seksig, we see the first two stories he told the Commission, and then we see him at work, presiding over a meeting of kindergarten school-teachers in Pantin, a northeastern suburb of Paris. He speaks about the practice of drawing up lists of the students who do and do not eat pork. He reminds the assembled teachers how such lists have been used "in history," a reference to the practice under Vichy and the Nazi occupation of posting lists of Jews. We then hear some tales from teachers of problems. One tells of young children who beat up another pupil for making fun of Muslims; the children said, "We had to apply sharî'a," she reports. Another teacher reports that students systematically miss Saturday morning classes "for religious reasons" (that they were Jewish is not made explicit). Seksig concludes the meeting (and this segment of the television program) by declaring that all ostentatious religious signs should be banned from schools, because they are aggressive and lead to conflicts and confrontations in school. This framing of the problem made it clear that Muslims create the problems but that a broad statement was important because Jews, too, forget their obligations under laïcité.[23]

In 2004, exposés on communalism in schools continued to refer back to Stasi Commission testimony. In March, the principal of Paris's third-arrondisement Turgot High School, Thérèse Duplaix (see chapter 5), worked with France 3 staff to create a documentary that shows her, in the words of *Le Monde*'s review of the program, in daily combat "against communalism, for laïcité." The program combines her Commission testimony with scenes designed to horrify the audience, from anti-Semitic insults in the playground to a young girl's attempts to transmit the Prophet Muhammad's message to her classmate. (*Le Monde* also qualifies as "stupefying" a scene where a Jewish father tries to have his daughter excused for the Sabbath.) After the film appeared, teachers and students met in assembly to denounce its "dishonesty" and recalled that the principal once had refused to allow a plaque to be erected to commemorate Jewish pupils deported from the school, on the grounds that it would be "communalist."[24]

Burkas at the Hospital

Although the schools remained the central focus of the debates around the law, late in 2003 a second site of struggle emerged in the press: the public hospitals. In October, the Stasi Commission had taken testimony from Claude Dagorn, director of a hospital in Montreuil, east of Paris, and a midwife from the hospital, Christine Picot. Although their testimony attracted little attention at the time, it soon became the basis for a broad media alert about new dangers to the Republic and particularly to immigrant women.

In his Stasi testimony, Dagorn focused on problems involving hospital employees who wore signs of their religion and who, because they were all public servants, violated laïcité. He mentioned seven cases involving Islamic scarves, although he admitted that it was often hard to tell "when you have a *voile islamique* before you" because many women working at the hospital covered their hair, and often were required to do so. Dagorn had been able to resolve each of the seven cases in one way or another; he gave the impression of an administrator who tries to negotiate, keep the peace, and yet preserve the principle of laïcité. Indeed, his flexible approach led the Commission's reporter, Remy Schwartz, to pose the rhetorical question of why Dagorn negotiated with public servants over the issue of religious signs when the law clearly forbids them.

Mme. Picot gave a slightly different impression of the situation by focusing on the problems posed by Muslim patients who refused treatment by a male doctor or who by their very appearance brought religion into the hospital. She described a woman who arrived at the hospital in a burka as "a bit disgusting." However, she, too, shows some flexibility; she arranges for private rooms, or, if possible, a female doctor for a female Muslim patient. She was more alarmed when a woman was afraid to ask for treatment by a male doctor because she feared her husband's reaction. "Behind these religious signs we see backsliding regarding the condition of women," she concluded.

The television program *Egalité, Laïcité, Anxiété* shows Dagorn and Picot at work and interviews their colleagues and some Muslim patients. An anesthesiologist at the hospital seconds their report that husbands sometimes speak for women and refuse epidurals given by a male, or refuse epidurals because they are unfamiliar. He recounts that in one instance, once the husband was out of the room the woman asked for an epidural. Later he learned that the husband had beaten her for contravening his orders. Several Muslims in waiting rooms are asked their opinions on the subject of choosing doctors by gender. One young couple agrees that what counts is expertise, but the man then adds that if you have a choice it is better for her to have a female doctor. Another Muslim man echoes this thought, explaining that in cases of necessity you take whoever there is, but then we hear a third man, in halting French, explain that women provoke men and that the voile is required in Islam. The exchanges display the merit of seeking more than one opinion, but have the overall effect of confirming suspicions that Muslim men are telling their wives what to do. Picot concludes by trying to bring the issue back to the legal proposal at hand, the law concerning the schools, by saying, somewhat cryptically (and along the lines of many National Assembly deputies' speeches): "By treating the problem of laïcité at school we will give a response, so women can find a means to express their religious convictions while also maintaining the law; we are not in an Islamic republic in France."

The brief appearance by Dagorn and Picot before the Stasi Commission had been on October 21. Their revelations were not immediately amplified by the media, but they led *Le Monde* to undertake its own investigations in Saint-Denis and Lyon, which it reported in its issue of December 7–8, just a few days before the Stasi report was due on the president's desk and the same day as the broadcast of *Egalité, Laïcité, Anxiété*. Much of *Le Monde*'s report concerned the wearing of headscarves by hospital personnel, echoing Dagorn's testimony. The public and the other media apparently cared little about that issue, however, despite the fact that it was the only revelation that reflected a possible violation of the laws and regulations concerning laïcité. The report also had found incidents of women refusing to be treated by male medical personnel, and it was this problem of mixité and access to urgent health care that jumped out of the report into the public eye and was repeated for months thereafter. As the author of the report in *Le Monde* noted, "the question goes well beyond that of the foulard as a distinctive sign: it concerns the condition of women and especially impediments to medical care."[25]

By December 2003, the hospital had become a major area of concerns over communalism in France. The Stasi report mentioned the disruptions caused by "political–religious pressure groups" and in his December 17th speech, President Chirac pointed to "new and growing difficulties" in applying laïcité "in the world of work, in public services, and in particular in the school and the hospital."[26] The president framed the hospital problems in terms of the "laïcité and neutrality of public services," but cases where hospital employees wore headscarves were few and easily resolved, as Dagorn had shown and as the Commission admitted in its report. The incidents that pushed sentiment toward legislation were about an incompatibility between communalist Islam and French Republicanism. They involved patients whose attitudes or requests offended the sensibilities of the staff, usually because these incidents translated a view of gender relations or separation between men and women that the staff found incompatible with French values. Although sometimes problems were said to "disturb the functioning of the hospital," in the words of the Stasi Commission, few incidents of physical disturbance were cited.[27] The disturbance was moral and aesthetic.

Now, women in France as in the United States commonly ask to be treated by women doctors. Moreover, the Public Health Code guarantees the patient's right to choose his or her doctor and, as the president of the Commission of Hospital Doctors pointed out, any limitations on this choice would run contrary to the law.[28] And yet a number of hospital administrators were troubled that it might be for religious reasons that this choice is exercised, and that the manner of exercising the choice implied the inequality of women rather than simple modesty. One administrator declared, "As a woman, it shocks me to see people refusing male doctors for religious reasons." We can unpack her complaint into two propositions. The first is that the right to choose one's doctor was intended to allow people to opt for the best medical treatment, so the law is perverted because the choice is made on nonmedical grounds. This proposition may reflect the debates around the law but glides over the commonly accepted norms of allowing same-sex consultation, especially of OBGYNs. The second proposition is that Muslim women choose female doctors on grounds that are part of a theology that denies the equality of women. Presumably, if a Protestant woman requested a female doctor, this second part of the objection would not be felt in the same way.

President Chirac argued that a law was needed to prevent patients from demanding doctors of the same sex.[29] One step toward limiting the practice of making such demands was taken in February 2005, when the new "Guide to the Rights and Duties of the French Citizen," to be distributed to immigrants, was prepared. The guide specifies that "it is not possible for a client to chose or refuse the person who takes care of him in a government service, in a hospital, etc."[30] It is not yet clear that this article is consistent with the law.

Hospital incidents became *affaires* because they indicated a growing dissonance between French values and the values of some Muslims living in France. The problem was not one of laïcité in the narrow sense of preserving the neutrality of the public service, but laïcité in the broader sense of keeping religious signs out of public space.

A close friend unintentionally verified this analysis in 2004 as we listened together to a radio interview with Isabelle Lévy about her recent book on religion in the hospital. Lévy described the rules for providing halal and kosher food in the hospital. My friend said that these practices irritated her. "They can say to the nurse, 'I don't eat mushrooms, or pork, etc.,' but why must they say, 'I am a Muslim'? That fact belongs in the private realm, not out in public."

A French Town Succumbs to Communalism

During 2003–2004, people living in France also learned about public space in towns being lost to communalism. Articles and television programs described urban sectors where many women wore headscarves, halal food was served, and people prayed in makeshift prayer halls, and decried these public spaces as lost to the Republic and to laïcité. *L'Express* revisited Creil, where the 1989 middle-school headscarf affair had occurred, to depict a market area where one in five women wear a headscarf, "as if laïcité, here, had given up its claims."[31] Muslims prayed behind "self-proclaimed imams," *L'Express* reported, as if imams were supposed to be appointed by the state. Officials contributed to communalism when they allowed halal food to be served on youth camping trips.

Perhaps the single most detailed such account of urban communalism was in a television exposé, *Trappes at Prayer Time* (*Trappes à l'heure de la prière*), in which we learn of entire towns falling to communalism. The program aired during prime time on France 2, February 12, 2004, after the debates at the National Assembly and before those at the Senate. The program concerned the behind-closed-doors lives of Islamists in what once had been a French town—and one near Versailles at that! It appeared on *Envoyé Spécial*, France's major investigative journalism series. Begun in 1990, *Envoyé Spécial* resembles *60 Minutes*. The moderator, Françoise Joly, opened the program by explaining that it took seven months to make the program although the town is only thirty miles from Paris. Trappes is neglected, left to misery and unemployment, she explained, and now has succumbed to a "hard-core" (*pur et dur*) Islam. The inhabitants have developed "a view of France increasingly tempted by what is called communalism."

Trappes had made the news over the previous year because of the relative size of its Muslim population—about one-quarter of the town's thirty thousand inhabitants—and because of the political skill exhibited by the Union of Muslims of Trappes (UMT). During 2003, the UMT's leader, Jaouad Alkhaliki, had succeeded in playing off rivals for the mayor's seat against one another and obtaining promises of aid for a mosque in the center of town and for the construction of a slaughterhouse, important for providing halal animals for Muslim feast-days. More than any other municipality in France, Trappes underscored the growing political might of organized Muslims.

For *Trappes at Prayer Time*, Frédéric Brunquell was both the investigator and the narrator. He arrives in town on the day of prayer at the end of the Muslim month of Ramadan. The congregational prayer, for four thousand Muslims, is held in the town gym, and men belonging to the UMT guard access and direct traffic. They let him into the building only on condition that he leave before the end of the prayer. He drives off with two other men in his car, who (their voices disguised) are heard to say "They made us pray in basements, now in the gym, since the 1960s. . . . We are going to pay them back in kind. . . . Trappes is going to explode." Right off, we are frightened.

Revealing "Hard-Core" Islam

Brunquell tells us that life has become harder and Islam has, as well. He tries to film in the projects but Muslim men forbid him. He now poses the basic question in voice-over: "Who is pulling Trappes Muslims toward fundamentalism?" He finds a guide for this "foreign country": Papi is a native French man who runs a theater school. He is an ordinary guy. They visit the retail area, and Papi explains that "before, everyone mixed together; today, business has changed. You cannot find a beer, and the charcuterie has become a Muslim butchery." Papi is easygoing, sometimes tongue-tied, and friendly with everyone. He complains that now there is "no diversity"; the communalist closing-off (*repli communautaire*) destroys that. The basic opposition between mixité (now lost) and communalism (the new reality) is clear.

Next we see Jaouad Alkhaliki, the UMT president (always referred to in the film as "Jaouad"), placing the cornerstone for the new mosque and Qur'ânic center. Jaouad is a computer specialist who came from Strasbourg, "on a mission" to develop the center. Jaouad speaks on camera of peace, but Brunquell informs us that four years previously, Jaouad had organized a demonstration to demand approval from the mayor for the center: "an Islam of peace moves forward with radical methods." We see UMT members demonstrating (in the same manner as do French trade unions, interest groups, and associations) for their construction permit. We see them praying in front of the mayor's office, and hear the narrator say, "That day, the Trappes Muslims' Union defied the Republic." To pray in public and to mobilize religion to obtain political goods evidently is to step out of bounds.

Brunquell now takes us to the Islamic bookstore in town, where Ibrahim, a French convert to Islam has been selling books and "everything to veil the Muslim woman" since he opened the store in 2003. Brunquell informs us that he is a member of the Tabligh Jama'ah, the group responsible for 80 percent of French conversions, which "preaches a return to hard-core Islam." He lets us listen to Ibrahim describing the rules and prohibitions attached to Islam, recommending a book to a Muslim visitor, and showing us books that instruct the convert about how to pray. (The Tabligh is indeed focused on rules in an unelaborated way; many people pass through it to others forms of Islamic activity or education.) Ibrahim remarks that the idea held by many French people of Islam as only about rules and prohibitions ignores spirituality. Brunquell does not develop this point, but shows Ibrahim explaining that issues such as stoning women and polygamy "are important subjects; they require clarification and cannot be dealt with in a few minutes." He tries nonetheless to explain why God had allowed polygamy, mentioning the fate of children without fathers. In his flat-footed way, Ibrahim stands for a rather unimaginative "hard-core" Islam.

Islam against Mixité

Brunquell next focuses on communalism. Papi is shown in his theater school, and Brunquell explains that "women are the first victims of an Islam of protest" (*Islam revendicatif*) and that fewer women now come to the school. Papi says some do not even greet him: "that assaults me" (*cela m'agresse*), he complains. We will see this expression again; it conveys the sense that another's appearance or actions, even when not directed toward me, offend me to the point of visually assaulting me.

The narrator finds a woman who "has left theater for the voile": Miriam, who is the leader of the women of the UMT. She takes him on a tour of the housing projects, pointing out the run-down rooms, graffiti, and the lack of children's play equipment. She has two friends with her, sub-Saharan African women in headscarves. They are eager to show Brunquell around, and they speak in a deprecating manner of their housing. They move inside and join other women. As the call to prayer begins, a French convert to Islam, holding a baby, describes her sense of coming close to God through prayer. "At last I was as I am, and proud. At the moment of prayer, face to face with God, I feel a sense of exhilaration."

The narrator adds no comment but poses a new question in voice-over: "Is Islam swallowing up the projects [*la cité*] to forge an identity or to do good?" He decides that he needs to talk to people who are not part of the "hard core" to find the answer. (Previous references to spirituality have been ignored; all Muslims so far are part of the "hard core.") We witness the performance of a musical group of mixed religion and gender, and he interviews members of the group. "The men in the group monopolize the conversation and defend the voile"; they complain of girls being expelled from the public school because of the voile. The two girls have little to say. "What about Ni Putes Ni Soumises?" asks Brun-quell, mentioning the much-publicized group that works for an end to violence against women. A man protests, saying that the group's name is vulgar because "it implies that if you are not a member of the associa-tion you are either *putes* (whores) or *soumises* (submissive)!" "Do you wear miniskirts?" asks the narrator of the girls. One says that she dresses so as not to be bothered by guys in Trappes, and that once out of Trappes she can loosen up a bit.

Brunquell complains in the voice-over that "I won't get girls to talk freely here, I have to find a place that is neutral and secular," so he turns to the all-girls high school, where the voile is forbidden. The school head guards the door, and Brunquell praises him for his firmness on the matter. A man is explaining laïcité to the students. (Narrator: "At last, a moment of free speech.") A girl says that the voile "is more for protection than religion." "Before, men respected women, now there is no respect; women are [seen as] whores, to be led by men." ("They are courageous, these girls," says the narrator.) When a girl says, "You wear jogging clothes so you are like a guy, and thus are respected," Brunquell adds in a voice-over, which concludes the segment: "They are seventeen years old and people have stolen their femininity."

Now we move to a center for adult learning, with an immigrant in-structor. Those present are all older women from North Africa, all wear-ing scarves. Some speak Arabic to each other or a mixture of French and Arabic. Some are learning to write. One, urging another woman who is complaining of the voile law to adapt to France, tells her: "This is their country, not back in the home country [*le bled*]. Here, if you wear the voile you will have no work." Some of these women have been here twenty years and cannot read or write, explains the teacher; "it is the fault of all the governments to have left them here in a sort of ghetto." She adds that "even if they did not wear the foulard in their country, their neighbor here says wear it and they do." Communalism works on the older women because of their isolation.

The narrator says in the transition, "Their daughters look to mark their difference," and we are back to Miriam and her African friends. They explain, "We read books and understand, and we have become more practicing [*pratiquant*] than our parents. To be French is no longer some-one who drinks his beer . . . it is a plural society." (This remark is not followed up.) We follow the girls to a demonstration organized in Paris in December 2003 against the law on the voile. The UMT organizes buses to take Muslims to Paris. "But the men have screwed everything down tightly," explains Brunquell. "They have rented two buses, one for them and one for the women. It is they who set the rules." The head of the Qur'ân school, Bashir, is in charge of the group. He gives instructions to the forty women on their bus, saying that their participation should appear to be spontaneous: "Do not speak of the UMT, speak only as Muslims. No one speaks to journalists; there are sisters ready to speak to them. There is no UMT, only Muslims."

They arrive at the Place de la République, where the march will start, and one of the appointed spokeswomen tells a television reporter: "We are here to defend our freedom, our modesty." The group chants, "No to exclusion, yes to laïcité." In the middle of all this, Brunquell interviews Miriam on the voile. "She who wears the voile has to be perfect, must have reached a certain stage. I wear it because it corresponds to an obligation and because of modesty." Brunquell: "So you do not stay out late at night?" Miriam: "A woman who stays out late at night, it's not good for her image." Brunquell now sums up in voice-over: "Miriam, wearing the voile out of obligation, forbidden to stay out late at night, sings the Marseillaise with the others. The Republic, called on to help the closing off of women, a strange twisting of values."

Brunquell's summation might strike us as odd, because Miriam has just explained her daily behavior in terms of norms about modesty and reputation as she understands them, and not in terms of oppression or control by men. But Brunquell's overall argument is that in an Islamic communalist society, women are separated from men (lack of mixité) and also oppressed (deprived of choice). Her reference to "obligation" was to divine norms; she understands her dress as an obligation that comes from God. Brunquell interprets her statement as an indication that men dictate her behavior. The multivocality of "obligation" has become a frequent sign of the "double-talk" of Muslims who say, to other Muslims, that wearing hijâb is a divine injunction and obligation, and, to non-Muslims, that there is no compulsion in Islam and that it is up to women to decide what to do. This is "double-talk" if women's choice is a sham in the light of divine decree; it is the nature of living in any religion if one considers humans to have free will.

Brunquell's labeling of the overall process as "closing off" (*enfermement*) works well for his purposes, because it places the voile in an iconic relationship to Miriam's place in society: just as the voile closes the face to others' inspection, so has communalism closed her off to French society. Thus what she sees as celebrating the freedom to live her life according to God's commands by singing the Marseillaise, he sees as an ironic invoking of a symbol of freedom by a victim of enclosure.

In the next segment we hear from dissident Muslims, unhappy with "this politicization of Islam" (which in fact was the sort of demonstration typical in France). Those Muslims who come from sub-Saharan Africa (mainly from Senegal) live in a separate housing complex and have organized their own association, whose spokesman denounces the politicization of Islam by the Arabs. He advocates a "tolerant and respectful Islam": "We are Muslims, not Arabs."

From this apparently good and well-integrated Muslim we return to one of the representatives of the bad sort, poor Ibrahim, the convert who runs the Islamic bookstore, and who is shown saying that "Islam is a giant standing up; there is no family, whether French, Italian, or American that will not be touched by Islam, whether it is the daughter, the son, the parent." He is quite calm, but these words, coming after his earlier attempts to explain polygamy and the stoning of women, make Islam seem pretty threatening.

Islam thus does have a salvageable version, the one shown by the sub-Saharan Africans, who keep their Islam in the private sphere, as well as a "hard-core" version, which encompasses all forms that take public action. Ironically, the more closely Trappes Muslims imitated past generations of French social movements and political groups, the less well-integrated they are judged to be.[32]

The next clip reminds us of UMT president Jaouad's public and political presence. We see the same clip showed earlier in which he lays the mosque's cornerstone, but now it is shown in slow motion, creating an eerie effect. We can surmise why this editing decision was made from the voice-over: Jaouad had promised to accompany Brunquell but then had reneged on the promise. We are made to understand how Jauoad succeeded when we meet the mayor, a member of the Socialist Party, who, according to his Communist Party rival, owed his election to the UMT: "He sold his soul for a mosque." But there is a "resistance based on laïcité" by the teachers. We see an open meeting led by the school teachers for laïcité, who have invited the "extremist fighter" Michèle Tribalat from Paris. As we saw in chapter 4, Tribalat works at France's National Demography Institute (INED) and early on adopted a militant stand against headscarves in schools, but at the same time advocated the use of ethnicity categories in the census. In her major analyses of assimilation, she took public religiosity as an index of a lack of assimilation to France.[33] Her address that evening in Trappes, as Brunquell summarizes it, is along the same lines. She argues that complete integration is unlikely, that "Islam will not renounce those things that it must renounce to fit into Europe."

After the debate, people from the audience engage in heated discussion (not unusual after debates in France). French women say to others in headscarves, "It is not my clothes that make my faith. . . . You have to evolve." A young man, whose face is blurred so he cannot be identified, talks of how he grew up in Trappes and saw people fall victim to drugs, and that it was Islam's arrival that put an end to that, "and how do people then treat Islam? They beat up on it!"

Brunquell ends the program with the following passage: "For the UMT militants there is only one path, that of Islam for everyone, as the only rule for living. This model begins to replace that of the Republic wherever it has given up the terrain, everywhere that the absence and surrender of the political structure has transformed the *cité* [the civilized urban setting] into a ghetto."

During the discussion with the moderator, Françoise Joly, at the end of the program, Brunquell describes how communalism silences everyone and how people feel caught between racist French and fundamentalists. He praises the firmness of the school head against the voile. To the moderator's question about the law against religious signs, which recently had been passed at the Assembly, Brunquell responds: "The only place where the girls can speak freely is the lycée, and why? Because there are no religious signs, nothing to separate them, confront them."

Rethinking Trappes

The reaction to the program was unusually intense. The mayor said it gave a "false and incomplete" view of the town, the Communist former adjunct to the mayor protested that "social mixité does exist at Trappes," and Miriam, given such a central role in the documentary, regretted that they had trusted Brunquell.[34] Jaouad Alkhaliki himself had written an article on the Web site www.oumma.com prior to the broadcast in which he listed the many times that he and Brunquell had spoken, and an article on the same site after the showing of the documentary, in which he cried foul, claiming that Brunquell erred by omission in failing to show the work of his and other associations in rebuilding the city.[35]

The ceremony that accompanied laying the cornerstone for the new mosque was covered by a number of reporters, including the television team (also from France 2) that produces the Sunday morning program on Islam. A Muslim reporter on that team told me that he thought Brunquell could have taken an even more critical stance than he had. "I say that because, for example, he could have just massacred the bookstore owner because he was so naïve and said all kinds of things that horrify non-Muslim French." He thought that Brunquell had correctly reported facts but slanted them to build an image of secrecy and control. The film opens with security forces directing traffic and controlling access to the place for prayer on the feast of day of Aïd al-Kabîr. "He made this out to be something malicious, but it is normal when you have lots of people driving in and out that you control the traffic." The program suggests that Islam was one cause of the current sorry state of Trappes: we come away from Papi's brief tour of the commercial district thinking that Muslim halal food shops drove away the French businesses. But (according to the France 2 reporter) the commercial area had been deserted before the Muslims arrived: "There had been a music store there and kids had broken its windows; this had nothing to do with Islam."

Trappes at Prayer Time indeed presents us with a communalist package. The Islamists keep the outside world at bay with their security forces and their leader will not even meet with the journalist. When they pressure the mayor to grant permission for their mosque, they "defy the Republic." They may even plan to take it over by converting "someone in every family," as predicted by the bookseller (who in fact had no connection to the UMT). Brunquell used a common trope that the Republic has ceded terrain to Islamic rules, a figure often accompanied by the phrase *lawless sector* (*cité de non-droit*) to suggest an absence of norms and law in certain neighborhoods or towns. Even Brunquell's final word, *ghetto*, is chosen in an effort to emphasize the isolated nature of life in

Islamist Trappes by drawing a parallel, frightening to many in France, to the urban United States.[36]

Brunquell emphasizes patriarchy. The Muslim men keep their women covered up, and tell them to shut up and stay home. Only in the secular all-girls school can Muslim girls speak freely, and then they complain about disrespect from boys. The voile is only indirectly mentioned, but Brunquell twists Miriam's words to make it seem as if she is compelled to cover herself and avoid late-night spots. He makes much of gender separation, with the separate buses as the emblem, and this impression of a lack of mixité is amplified by his selection of all-male or all-female groups to interview.[37] He has little to say about the apparent paradox that so many women, supposedly oppressed, felt fine about being filmed for the program, which they knew would be watched carefully in Trappes.

Indeed, Brunquell's narrative is implicitly challenged by Miriam and others in the film. Miriam tells of how she discovered true Islam and became more practicing by reading—a theme we explored in chapter 4. Other women on the program speak of Islam in terms of spirituality, as does Ibrahim in the bookstore, but Brunquell never comments on these statements; they do not fit the overall argument—or perhaps they do for a French viewer opposed to all forms of religiosity who would find Muslims' talk of spirituality disconcertingly similar to Catholic views. Miriam and the other women might impress some viewers as agents of their own lives, but this is not the program's intended message—it is rather that they are the unwitting agents of their own closing-off. Although we do learn of boys' disrespect toward girls, we find little linkage between that disrespect and Islam, and indeed it seems to be through Islam that Miriam and her friends take active, public roles. She, alone among Muslims, speaks up against Michèle Tribalat. Brunquell can afford to allow certain actors' statements to be heard because he has the final say through his authoritative moments of voice-over, a general practice in French documentary television, used to push the evidence a bit beyond what might be plausible on camera (and, of course, not at all foreign to television elsewhere).[38]

Judging from press coverage of the evening and from reactions by non-Muslim friends, *Trappes at Prayer Time* was one of the more disturbing programs on French television shown during the period in question. Viewers learned of "hard-core" Muslims, living just outside of

Paris, building a misogynist community. I believe that the images of Miriam and friends were offensive to some simply because they were dressed in black Islamic dress, regardless of what they said. Unlike the talking heads and interview approach of *Egalité, Laïcité, Anxiété*, the Trappes program was a window into life here and now—and perhaps in your own neighborhood, behind those unmarked mosque walls![39]

The revelations about Trappes, about schools, about hospitals concerned not so much laïcité as a gulf between the values and everyday lives of some Muslims, on the one hand—the "hard core," but also many young Muslims—and French people, on the other. The diagnosis of "communalism" focuses on the internal cleavages in French society. But it also points to the external sources of those cleavages, in political "Islamism" that, born abroad, now has invaded France. The next chapter explores the ways that international developments support an argument that the voile is not about religion but about politics—and a politics entirely incompatible with France.

EIGHT

Islamism

IF, IN the eyes of most French commentators, communalism is ipso facto a bad thing because it divides people, the communalism of the poor suburbs is seen as doubly damaging to France because it is Islamic in content. In much French writing about Islam and society, the Islam of the poor suburbs is not religion but "Islamism," a political project to reshape public life around Islamic norms. Because it takes religion out of its proper, private domain, Islamism violates French political ideals and social norms.

Islamism implies not only a political project but also a single, globally distributed set of ideas and norms. Some French social scientific studies of Islam and politics have analyzed a wide variety of Islamic movements and thinkers as variants of "Islamism." These writers, and others in the less scientific media, consider themselves justified in looking to events in any one Muslim society as evidence for the general nature of Islamism— and for what may likely happen in France. In the case of headscarves, this logic allows one to take the activities of Islamic fashion police in Iran or demands made by terrorists in Algeria as evidence that the headscarf has a true meaning and that this true meaning is—anywhere, anytime— the enforced oppression of women. The critique of the voile as sexist— the subject of fuller treatment in chapter 9–depends on this methodological preparation, the construction of "Islamism" as a unified, political object of study.

If Islamism is political and global, then a number of policy recommendations follow. Public signs of Islam must be pushed back into the private sphere, in order to "send a message," as legislators often said in the February 2004 debates, that the Republic values its laïcité. France must take active steps to domesticate Islam, to separate French Islam from international Islamism. Finally, following this logic, Islamists' claims that they can create a public and political Islam in Europe and at the same time be good citizens of European countries amount to double-talk and should be denounced as such.

RELIGION, PRIVATE AND PUBLIC

The term *Islamism* (*islamisme*) appears more and more often as a way of talking about Islamic practices and institutions. In an issue of the intellectual review *Esprit*, the editor Olivier Mongin observes that *Islamism* now is used more frequently than *Islam* in his own publication.[1] The broad use of *Islamism* is due in part to the wide range of meanings attributed to the term and in part to affinities with French philosophical ideas about the properly private role of religion in modern society.

Some definitions of *Islamism* give it a very broad range of reference indeed, as when the *World Dictionary of Islamism*, published by the prestigious press Plon, included "all those who seek to Islamize their social, familial, or professional environment" in its definition of *Islamist*.[2] In this sense, any Muslim who urged his family members to pray, or asked that her daughter not eat pork at school, would be an "Islamist." Other uses of the term are much narrower. Although he contributed to the Plon dictionary, the political scientist Olivier Roy restricts his own use of the term to projects or groups seeking to transform society by way of the state.[3] Still other writers consider all projects to make society more Islamic to be Islamist.

In less scholarly circles, *Islamist* can become a way of designating Muslims whose politics you do not agree with. When in 1994 the interior minister, Charles Pasqua, sought to justify his house arrest of twenty-six Muslims, he said that Muslims could be divided into "on the one hand the *modérés* and on the other the *islamistes,* with whom no dialogue is possible."[4] The journalist Thomas Deltombe has analyzed the references to Islam on French television during the 1990s and concludes that *Islamism* became a catch-all for all that commentators thought was not "normal" religious activity. "We arrive at a situation where any visibility of Islam in public space is suspected of being an indication of 'Islamism.' "[5] Some journalists use the term as a synonym for terrorism, as when *Figaro*'s story about a young man arrested on his way to fight with insurgents in Iraq was titled "Itinerary of a Parisian Islamist."[6]

Islamist suggests associations of religion, political activity, and perhaps terrorism. The mere knowledge that someone is Muslim can trigger these associations. A French convert to Islam once explained to me that if he spoke publicly without mentioning his religion, then few assumptions were made about his opinions on various matters. However, "if I speak in public and I am introduced as a Muslim, then people want to know whether I am for or against the voile, and if I am for, then they assume that I am for burning young girls in staircases,[7] for excision, and so forth, as if it were all one package." To be "Muslim" implies, for many, all the components associated with "Islamist."

Uniting these diverse senses of *Islamism* is the assumption that it illegitimately takes Islam out of the interior world of faith and into the public space of social or political life, where it threatens peaceable relationships among persons. In this sense, Islamism is redolent of an older Catholic project of infusing society and the state with religion—and some of the fear of the former comes from the memory of the latter. French references to Islamism often qualify it as *intégriste*, using the word borrowed from Spanish early in the twentieth century to designate conservative and dogmatic Catholicism, the defense of "integral" Christianity against the project of "modernity." This use suggests that underneath the worry about radical Islam lie longer-term concerns about maintaining a public sphere free of religious interference, and about preserving freedom of choice in the religious sphere.

The "Exit from Religion"

Where did this idea that public Islamic behavior is illegitimate come from? Although it was in the popular media and in books written by nonexperts that the radical attacks on Muslims appeared, the idea that modern European forms of religion are, and should be, private has developed out of sophisticated analyses of modern history. To understand the intellectual bases for contemporary French concerns, I turn to the historian Marcel Gauchet, coeditor of the review *Le Débat*, who has set forth an approach to understanding modernity that preserves a place for religion in an individualized and private form.

Gauchet brings together the philosophy of laïcité with political theory to formulate a liberal version of Republicanism. He argues that France has experienced parallel transitions toward democratic individualism in the domains of religion and politics. For Gauchet, France became modern when, and insofar as, it experienced an "exit from religion" (his trademark phrase) consisting of three simultaneous changes: religion ceased to suffuse the public world, God retreated to a position of absent power, and the individual assumed the right to choose to believe or not believe.[8]

Parallel to this modern revolution in religion was an equally profound transformation of the state. Once thought of as appropriately despotic (whether in royal or Republican form), the state became a moderator of arrangements among individuals in civil society. For Gauchet (1998: 83–84), Rousseau is the author of the modern political vision, but his ideas required an entire century to be enacted into law. The French Revolution had recreated absolutism by abolishing the corporate bodies that once intervened between the state and the individual. Gauchet's Rousseau, however, foresaw a way to allow individuals to pursue distinct interests in civil society and yet ensure that they would recognize the overarching importance of the general interest. The key lay in the proper understanding of choice. If individuals were born into intervening institutions, as once was the case, then these institutions did indeed interfere with the proper functioning of the political order. However, if individuals freely chose their affiliations and attachments to churches, societies, and labor unions, then these bodies were nothing more than voluntary associations, the secondary product of individual choices, and were perfectly consistent with Republicanism.[9]

Only gradually did French intellectuals and politicians come to understand Rousseau's point and see that the Republican model of the state could coexist with intermediate associative bodies. In the law of 1901 on associations they allowed individuals to legally organize in order to pursue private activities, and in the law of 1905 they extended this possibility to religious groups. More precisely, the law of 1905 created the possibility for private associations to replace the unacceptable public church. For Gauchet, the law gave the church the only place that it could have in this conception of society, namely, that of one association alongside many others, in civil society, to which individuals could belong or refuse to belong.[10]

This essentially liberal analysis via Rousseau shows why free choice of one's affiliations is so important. If people choose to belong to an association and are always capable of retracting that choice, then they are relatively easily induced to follow the general interest as well—or, more precisely, they learn that the particular and the general come to the same thing, that they can best realize their individual goals through full participation in society. In effect, Gauchet has refigured Émile Durkheim's notion of organic solidarity through the lens of liberal political theory.

Not only does individual choice permit associations to thrive without threatening the Republic, choice also creates the very norms that give the Republic content. If society is governed by the logic of the market, then it is arbitration and deliberation that create social norms. But then individuals must regard their social norms as open to challenge and to change, and they must not subscribe to their norms in a dogmatic manner or they will not be able to participate fully and openly in democratic Republican politics. If they are obliged by their birth, or their God, or their Party, to obey certain rules, they will never be able to change them. Moreover, they will see the individuals next to them in social space not as other citizens who, like themselves, freely chose their affiliations, but as people who have refused to accept absolute truth.[11]

The implications of this analysis are far-reaching. Catholic *intégrisme* threatens this social order just as much as does the Islamic sort. *Intégrisme* places the rule of religion over the general interest of society. It says that negotiation is fruitless, because the answers to important social issues already are known in advance. It places God over the constitution. In the presence of an *intégrisme*, it is unlikely that social market processes will lead to shared norms. Communalism is an inevitable consequence. Therefore, Islamism must be denounced as antidemocratic as well as anti-Republican.

Islamism contrasts with modern forms of religion. Gauchet underscores the legitimacy of choosing to follow a religion. Indeed, Gauchet's work had the effect of legitimating religiosity by Catholics (and others) by showing how French people could be both fully involved in their religious tradition and fully members of modern European society.[12] Part of this reframing of religion involves considering outward manifestations of one's religiosity as a way of presenting part of one's social identity, just as one might manifest an ethnic or social class identity.[13] Because manifesting an identity is an act of choice, it is not threatening to others—but only so long as everyone understands everyone else's social identity manifestations to be just that, rather than expressions of absolute truth.

If we assume, as I do, that Gauchet's theoretical analyses render explicit certain French social intuitions, then his work helps to account for assumptions made about the headscarf. The reasoning involves two steps. First, observers would assume that if a Muslim woman wore a headscarf in public, she did so in order to communicate to those around her something about her religion. Nearly all non-Muslim French writers on the headscarves do indeed refer to them as "religious signs," and such was the language of the law of March 2004. Even the most charitable views of scarf-wearing—that wearers are freely choosing their attire, that they are not always oppressed by brothers or husbands—generally see it as part of an act of communicating an identity to others.

While this signification may not threaten some (for example, religious Catholics), it is received as a sort of public visual assault by others, an "aggression" against them. This reaction is due to the second assumption, that this message is not about a freely chosen identity for which some other identity could have been substituted, but rather an identity that is commanded by God, that signals the wearer's greater piety and purity than those of others around her. Gauchet helps us to understand that these strong reactions are based on the assumption that the headscarf wearer is making inappropriate public claims about the superiority of her values to those of other people. Rather than signifying only a choice of individual identity, the scarf sends a message that is out of place in modern society because it involves absolute truth claims. (I return to this issue in the next chapter.)

Some Muslims in headscarves, of course, insist that wearing scarves is not at all a "sign" of their religious affiliation but rather a part of their religious lives. They do not choose their clothing to broadcast their values but to live according to their understanding of God's will, even if they take account of others' reactions when deciding whether or not to wear the scarf. They object to the language of the March 2004 law because of this misrepresentation of what they doing as well as because it constrains Muslim women in their religious lives. Few non-Muslims in France seem to understand this objection, and Gauchet's work helps to explain why this would be the case, why observers would assume that people dress in order to signal features of their identities.

What Will It Take for Islam to Become European?

Let us travel back along the logical link from clothing to politics. Gauchet argues that modern societies have, and should have, private religions. Wearing religious signs in public is acceptable in such societies only if these signs are seen as, as well as in fact are, manifestations of individual, voluntary choice. If such is the case, then such signs would signify voluntary attachments in civil society, chosen by citizens. They would not threaten either the preeminence of the state or the emergence of the general will from everyday social interactions. Religion would be private and friendly to national interests or (in a current French idiom), it would be socially *citoyen*, meaning that it grows out of and contributes to the proper life of the citizen.

Islamism as commonly understood in France violates both the private character of religion and its quality of promoting social citizenship. It involves an effort to bring religion into social and potentially political life, and it instructs the Muslim to follow religious doctrine as absolute truth. Islamism is about obedience, not choice. It defines *Muslim* through birth or conversion, as a quasi-ethnic label, and not through the constantly revisited individual choice to believe or to behave in particular ways. Worse, Islamism is global and transnational, and thus particularly ill-equipped to become *citoyen*.

The philosopher and political scientist Olivier Roy has produced the clearest analysis of Islam in this quasi-ethnic, communalist form. One of the most perceptive analysts of Islam and politics both in Muslim-majority countries and "at home," Roy has been particularly important in refuting essentialist notions of Islam and thus attacking the pensée unique concerning Islamist dangers. He has carefully developed his own distinction between those forms of Islam that have adapted to Europe and those which have not, a distinction that draws on ideas akin to Gauchet's about the place of religion in public life.

Roy develops this analysis not with the term *Islamism* but through an analysis of "neofundamentalism." "Neofundamentalists" emphasize the

universal Muslim code and community, but often form "neoethnic" enclaves, either in local communities or as national bodies, such as the
UOIF and FNMF, that have negotiated a new form of communalism
with the state. Roy calls this particular sort of nationwide "imagined
community" an "inverted dhimmi," that is, as a Muslim minority in
France that is held together internally by a "soft" version of Islamic
norms. Roy joins politicians on the Left and the Right who find the
creation of the French Islamic Council a throwback to Napoleon's Concordat rather than an application of modern laïcité.[14]

Roy is critical of neoethnic Islam because it makes religion into the
stuff of identity politics. It says that anyone is Muslim who was born
Muslim or converted to Islam, regardless of his or her degree of belief or
practice. If followed to its logical conclusion, it would carve Europe up
into religiously or culturally defined communities. Most French people
would doubtless agree with Roy that this result would be a disaster for
Europe as well as for France. For him, the answer to this challenge lies
in the individualized and privatized versions of Islam. Not only do these
conform to principles of laïcité, they also have naturally developed as the
result of broad sociological processes of secularization. Given that Muslims in Europe have neither a political or legal apparatus to enforce norms
nor broad-based social pressures to practice their religion, being a Muslim
has naturally become a matter of individual choice, adherence, and ex-
ploration of spirituality.[15]

The "Double-Talk" of Tariq Ramadan

Roy insists on the primacy of sociological processes over theological
justifications. Indeed, he sees the two as often contradicting one another,
as when some Muslim spokesmen preach a neoethnic line that opposes
the inevitable social tide of individualization. Roy explores this problem
in the writings of Tariq Ramadan. Ramadan is a Swiss national who is
particularly active in France, but increasingly throughout Europe. He
drew broad attention from an educated Muslim public beginning in the
mid-1980s, when he began working with the Tawhid publishing com-
pany based in Lyon, and, through his speeches, books, and cassettes,
reached a large audience. He has been controversial for more than a
decade, in part because of his lineage; his grandfather was Hassan al-
Banna, founder of the Egyptian Muslim Brotherhood, and thus some

have assumed (in the face of Brotherhood leadership denials) that Ramadan must be allied with the Brotherhood. For Roy, Ramadan deploys a
European discourse of multiculturalism and/or individual citizenship-
plus-private religion (depending on the country), in which Europe encompasses the composite cultures/individuals. But when speaking to a
Muslim readership or audience, according to Roy, he emphasizes the
universal code of Islam, albeit in a softened version, that encompasses the
particular societies and cultures of Europe, Asia, the Middle East, and
elsewhere, and thus he contributes to the development of neoethnic understandings of Islam.[16]

Other writers about Islam in France have accused Ramadan of "double-talk" (*double discours*) on these grounds. Gilles Kepel (2004), for example, attempts to show that Ramadan is engaged in the process known
in Arabic as *tawria*, "dissimulation." The accusation of "double-talk" has
become a standard trope in French discussions of Islam. On a single page
of *Libération*, for example, two stories claimed double talk by Muslims.
One concerned the supposedly "anti-Semitic" remarks of Tariq Ramadan, when he used the phrase *French Jewish intellectuals*.[17] Although usually
it is Ramadan himself who is accused of double-talk, in this story it is
the antiglobalization movement that is accused of this sin for not having
denounced Ramadan as anti-Semitic. The second story, distinct but
clearly linked in the minds of the daily's editorial staff, concerned the
duplicity of the UOIF. The organization's general secretary, Fouad
Alaoui, had stated to the Stasi Commission that although the voile was
a "prescription," the decision to wear or not wear it was a matter of the
"individual freedom of the woman." However, continues the journalist,
in front of Muslim audiences UOIF spokespersons routinely say that
women must wear headscarves and omit the part about freedom, and
thus engage in double-talk.

Such accusations became more frequent after two controversies in the
fall of 2003. In October, Tariq Ramadan had tried to publish a critique
of the unquestioned support given to Israel by "certain French Jewish
intellectuals," the phrase mentioned above, which kept major dailies
from running the piece. When the article finally appeared on the Internet, it led to accusations of anti-Semitism.[18] Then on November 20,
Ramadan appeared on France 2's prime-time television program *Cent
minutes pour convaincre* as one in a series of public figures to debate with

Nicolas Sarkozy. During the exchange, he ducked Sarkozy's invitation to condemn the Islamic penalty of stoning women (which Tariq's brother, Hani Ramadan, recently had excused in a column in *Le Monde*). Ramadan responded by calling for a "moratorium" on such penalties, during which he and others could carry out "pedagogy" in the Muslim world to "change mentalities."

Le Monde picks up the story at that point: "The camera came to rest on the worried face of Mme. Sarkozy, seated in the audience. 'A moratorium? What does that mean? We are in 2003,' retorted the interior minister."[19] Sarkozy then urged Ramadan to prove that he was a "moderate" "by 'asking girls to take off their voiles in public places. . . . Otherwise it is the *double discours*,' concluded Sarkozy, before a speechless Ramadan."[20] In his later, written comments on the exchange, Ramadan pointed out that *Libération* had considered the double-talk proven by giving its article the title "Sarkozy Knocks Out Ramadan's Double-Talk."[21]

Many of these accusations might appear bizarre to the outside observer, as they are invariably made without reference to specific contradictions in Ramadan's statements. Indeed, Sarkozy's accusation is incoherent: it would have been double-talk to speak in a usual human-rights manner on television and then discuss the subtleties of Islamic jurisprudence in Muslim-only circles. Tariq Ramadan (like his brother before him) got into televised trouble precisely by refusing to renounce scripture, on the grounds that such is the only way one can retain credibility with interlocutors in Muslim-majority countries. In other words, Ramadan did not practice *enough* "double-talk" for French prime-time audiences.

One year later the disputes resurfaced. Under the title "The Man Who Wants to Install Islamism in France," *L'Express* of October 18, 2004, summarized the contents of a book, *Frère Tariq*, in which the "investigative reporter" Caroline Fourest (2005) listened to his cassettes and read his books looking for evidence of double-talk.[22] Although *L'Express* clearly looked for the juiciest evidence, the short quotations that supposedly prove double-talk are so clearly taken out of context as to be unconvincing. A second book, *Tariq Ramadan Dévoilé,* appeared at about the same time and makes similar accusations. It received less mainstream press attention, perhaps because it was written by a journalist for the publication *Lyon Mag* (Lionel Favort) after the publication had been successfully sued by Ramadan for defamation.

The networks sought to capitalize on the interest generated by the books. The Swiss station Télévision Suisse Romande (TSR) featured Favrot's book on its October 27, 2004, broadcast of the panel debate program *Infrared*, titled "Tariq Ramadan: Misunderstood or Dangerous?" which pitted Favrot against Ramadan. The program was marked by Favrot contrasting the "Islamist" Ramadan with other "Muslims," and Ramadan unsuccessfully challenging Favrot to produce proof of his charges. Favrot mentioned a major example of Ramadan's supposed double-talk also cited by Fourest and by *Le Monde*, which concerns the relative primacy of Islam and the French Constitution. Ramadan states frequently on television and in other mainstream public settings that Muslims should obey the laws and the constitution of the country where they live. Fourest, Favrot, and others cite a passage supposedly destined for Muslims in which Ramadan qualifies that statement with: "only when it is not in conflict with Islam" as evidence of his double-talk. When Favrot brought up this example on TSR, Ramadan stated that his qualifier concerned cases where states prevented Muslims from practicing their religion, and then asked him to read the sentence after that quoted in the books, which specifies that no European constitutions or laws impeded Muslims from worshipping.

Ramadan has been invited to appear on a number of shows but also has been made the subject of televised investigations. On December 2, 2004, France 2's *Envoyé Special* broadcast (the popular show that had aired *Trappes at Prayer Time*) concerned Tariq Ramadan. The investigative reporter was Mohamed Sifaoui, who had testified against Ramadan at the *Lyon Mag* trial concerning his "double-talk." Sifaoui had developed the program for TSR, but when TSR required him to include a response by Ramadan, he broke the contract.[23] Coverage of the France 2 broadcast by *Le Monde's* media journalist several days later was titled "The Double Language of the Very *Médiatique* [Media-Friendly] 'Frère Tariq,'" and quotes approvingly from Fourest.[24] The case had become self-confirming.

The analyses by Gauchet and Roy help explain how it is that for less sophisticated French (and francophone Swiss) readers and viewers, it would be obvious that Tariq Ramadan *must* be engaging in double-talk, and that they would not need to see specific examples of his contradictions. Europe as a modern project is incompatible with communalism and Islamism, but the project was only secured with the defeat of Catholic *intégrisme*, and it remains vulnerable. Proper thinking in France (and, mu-tatis mutandis, elsewhere in Europe) requires a strict delineation of the acceptable contours of religion and a rejection of neoethnic forms. To do otherwise is unthinkable and dangerous. In some sense, Ramadan's claims that one can be publicly and communally Muslim, and yet also be a good citizen who follows the rules of laïcité *had better be* double-talk or else the entire normative edifice claimed by early twenty-first-century France would look shakier than one might wish. One must, therefore, denounce Ramadan's efforts to combine what must not be combined.

Why Does It Matter?

French intellectuals hardly spoke with one voice during the early 2000s. Many of those who study Islam in France, including some of Muslim background, did publish articles and books denouncing simplistic notions of Islamism and criticizing an eventual law against scarves in schools. The sociologist Farhad Khosrokhavar denounced the proposed law as based on erroneous assumptions about the scarves (that they stand for patriarchy, that their meaning in Saudi Arabia is identical to their meaning in France) and likely to alienate many Muslims. The real ques-tion, he writes, is "how to create a social tie among groups who free themselves from the state's paternalist efforts at assimilation but also claim an identity as French people?"[25] Younger Muslim intellectuals such as Youcef Mammeri, of the al-Islah Mosque in Marseille, denounced the assumption that merely wearing the voile amounted to proselytism and complained that France had now defined a new "clothing crime."[26] Oliv-ier Roy may have been critical of scarf-wearing but pointed out that the effect of the law was to deepen sentiments of alienation among Muslims.[27] Roy also objected to the demonization of Tariq Ramadan in the media.[28]

Some Muslim scholars of Islam objected to allowing headscarves in France but made their cases in a way that took full account of available scholarship. Leïla Babès, for example, a professor of sociology of religions in Lilla, in her *The Veil Demystified* sets out fairly and at length the argu-ments made by others that wearing Islamic dress can be liberating for women in Muslim-majority countries, before countering these claims on the grounds that women in France already are guaranteed basic rights, and that wearing headscarves plays into the hands of those who would Islamize society, a project that would decrease women's rights. She also engaged in a scholarly debate with the advocate of a reinterpreted Islamic law, Tareq Oubrou.[29]

Other Muslim scholars opposed a new law but were critical of the notion that one must wear a headscarf to be a good Muslim. Dounia Bouzar, an educator and social worker and a one-time member of the CFCM, in her book of dialogue with Saïda Kada, *One Veiled, the Other Not*, argues that the voile, once proposed to protect women, is no longer needed in a society such as France and should be dispensed with.[30]

There were, then, real debates, through books, in conferences, and in the pages of *Le Monde* and *Libération*—though not in many other newspapers or magazines. But those urging caution and respect for the lives of the young women concerned were not easily heard above the tumult of alarmist publications, testimony, and television programs. The Stasi Commission chose not to interview the many sociologists who had studied the question, and the Commission's only Muslim, Mohammed Arkoun, seemed to contribute little to the proceedings. There was little real debate in the halls of the National Assembly; rather, denunciation of extremists was the order of the day. Nor were the few books that made a case against the law widely available in major bookstores. What one did see on the front tables in Parisian bookstores were books denouncing Islamism and the voile, often in hysterical tones: *A Voile over the Republic* warning about the "theo-terrorism" incarnated in headscarves, *The Republic and Islam between Fear and Blindness* criticizing the State Council for having allowed scarves in the schools in the first place, and *Islamist Totalitarianism Attacks Democracies*, joining many other titles about Islamism and terrorism.[31]

The rhetoric of Del Valle's *Islamist Totalitarianism* can stand for many of these popular books. It juxtaposes accounts of global terrorist movements with descriptions of Islamic organizations in Europe, always said to be "radical Islamist."[32] This "method" of confusing public Muslim activities with a global Islamic political project, sanctioned by these books from major publishing houses, permitted the journalist or the ordinary viewer to condemn movements supporting the wearing of headscarves in public schools because they brought dangerous ideas into France. One learned that, peaceful though they might seem, those girls in scarves reinforce the weight of such quasi-political bodies as the UOIF, their foreign counterparts such as the Muslim Brotherhood, and "Islamist" parties in

Muslim-majority lands. All have ideas and values that are incompatible with the principles of modern France.

These ideas and charges have effects on everyday ways of thinking about the legitimacy of religious behavior. They led some scholars and administrators to assume that too much Islamic religious practice indicated insufficient integration into French society. The clearest example of this approach is the study carried out by Michèle Tribalat of the National Institute for Demographic Studies, INED (Institut National d'Études Démographiques), which postulates that assimilation implies not only the privatization of religion but also a lessened intensity of religious practices: "in sum, a laïcisation of behavior" (Tribalat 1996: 254).

Prayer (*salât*) is one index of such a change for Tribalat, for whom reducing the number of times one prays indicates greater assimilation. Muslims and others in France often point to the regular performance of prayer as the dividing line between a "practicing" Muslim (*pratiquant*) and someone who is merely a "believing" Muslim (*croyant*), who might fast and eat only halal meat, but does not regularly pray. Designating someone as a *pratiquant* can carry with it tones of fanaticism, of thinking in insufficiently French ways.

The sense that Islamic religious practices are somehow ipso facto illegitimate affects Muslims, too, in the way they speak to others. One incident struck me early on in my research, when a man who had converted to Islam and had been very active in Islamic education and publicity described the strategy behind a new magazine (*La Medina*) as "aiming for the non-*pratiquants*" among Muslims. "The *pratiquants* see what we write about and dismiss it, but the others will read it," he explained to me in 2000. This man was in fact a regular observer of Islamic ritual duties, and frequently excused himself to pray during our conversations, as he did during the very one in which he made this statement! Nevertheless, he used the term *non-pratiquant* to indicate someone interested in participating in French social life.[33]

Protesting that one does not pray *regularly* can be a way of assuring a nervous public that one is unlikely to be a terrorist. In early 2003, a baggage handler at Charles de Gaulle airport was falsely accused of possessing arms and sympathizing with terrorists. (It turned out that his in-laws had planted ammunition in his trunk in revenge for what they thought was his role in their sister's—his wife's—death.) Adding to the suspicions were reports that he obliged his wife to wear a head covering, but suspicion was reduced by the report by the secret police (who seem to know much about each Muslim in France) that he did not perform his prayers regularly. Upon his release from jail, the *bagagiste* complained that "they made us out to be terrorists, whereas we are simple Muslims. We practice an *Islam de France*, indeed we do not always perform our prayers at the right time."[34] Not praying regularly, or more specifically not having the kind of "fanatical" spirit that would lead you to insist on praying regularly, indicates a willingness to fit in with French society.

Exhibiting signs of insufficient assimilation can have very practical consequences for immigrants seeking acceptance as citizens. Each year the French government refuses about one-third of the applicants for admission, and some of those refusals were of candidates who met the formal conditions for naturalization. The candidate must show "good morals" but they can also be rejected on the grounds of insufficient assimilation, whether in their dress, their language, their travel outside the country, or the positions they have taken on Islam.[35] The police verify whether a candidate for naturalization has assimilated, and in their inquiry sometimes ask about private habits. One lawyer from Morocco was asked how many times a week she ate couscous, how often she traveled to Morocco, of what nationality her friends were, and which newspapers she read. A Tunisian was asked why he had made the pilgrimage to Mecca twice.[36]

IMPORTING FOREIGN EVIDENCE: THE BOBIGNY DEBATE

The outside world has had multiple direct bearings on the French debates. *Salafisme* and *djihadisme* presumably come from afar even if they are nourished in France, but usually do not involve references to specific countries. The United States and Britain serve as convenient counterpoints to French laïcité, bad examples of where we might end up if we do not act now. But the most consequential foreign references are to Muslim-majority countries, taken as laboratories where the terrible consequences of unchecked Islamism for women's rights and civil peace can be seen more clearly than in France.

Some of these references are evocative. Images of women in burkas, often from Iran or Afghanistan, remind readers of glossy magazines that when Islamic law and customs dominate a country, women are the first victims. Even a single scarf can bring to mind a complex of negative features. When the Lyon businesswoman and activist Saïda Kada spoke to the Stasi Commission wearing a scarf, she focused her remarks on the practical consequences for high school students of passing a law that would exclude some Muslim girls. However, the first response to her testimony, from Jacqueline Costa-Lascoux (one of the more hard-line opponents of the voile) was a sort of free association on the meanings of the voile that she saw before her. After asking Kada whether the foulard was a "religious symbol" for her, Costa-Lascoux said: "The foulard is but a visible sign of many other things that we have considered here: you know well that behind that there are discussions on the condition of the Muslim woman, her personal legal status, for example; do you demand the application of the [Muslim] family code in France, inequality regarding witnessing, inequality in inheritance, or is the foulard just a sign of identity for you?"[37] If even Saïda Kada's white headscarf could elicit this response, one can imagine the reactions to images of burkas and all that they represented for some viewers.

The Closeness of the Colonial Past

The Muslim experiences that most frequently are brought to bear on France come from the former French territories of Tunisia, Morocco, and Algeria. These territories remain close to France in at least three ways. First, for many in France the traumas of the Algerian War remain alive, and recently have been revived with new revelations of torture and the complicity of François Mitterrand, as well as the ongoing legal battles over the indemnities due to the repatriated native Algerians who fought for France, the "harkis." Algeria has never stopped haunting the French imagination: the current confrontation with terrorism in France harkens back to the Battle of Algiers and the bombings in France by Algerian extremists in the 1990s.

Second, the former French territories are the countries of origin or reference for most of the Muslims living in France today. Some French men and women born in France of immigrant parents refer to themselves as "Algerians" or "Tunisians," and cheer for that side at football matches. Many people travel back and forth between one of those countries and France. These trans-Mediterranean dual residents may have French nationality or the nationality of one of the former colonies, but more important is the continued importance of the participation in private or public life in both countries.

Finally, as I described earlier, the French state has continued to treat French Muslims in terms of these origins, as persons under the guardianship of the Moroccan or Algerian consulate or association. The Ministry of the Interior deals directly with foreign powers regarding mosques located in France, and ensures the cooperation of those powers regarding the organization of Muslims in the CFCM. One suspects that at some level French Islam cannot but be foreign. Even those imams of foreign origin who have lived many years in France, speak French, and are deeply involved in local cultural or educational activities are lumped into the Interior Ministry's accounting of "foreign imams" who are supposedly at the root of Islam's problems in France.

North Africa in Bobigny

In February 2004, I found myself in the middle of these tensions in a public forum on Islam and women in the eastern Paris suburb of Bobigny. I came to be there completely by accident. One afternoon I came across an email message from the magazine La Medina advertising a public meeting that evening on the topic: "Does religion impede the liberation of women?" The subject sounded interesting, and I decided to attend. I arrived at Bobigny City Hall a bit early and found all doors locked. I saw La Medina's editor, Hakim El Ghissassi, and went over to find out more. He invited me to dinner before the meeting. A bit later he asked if I also would participate, as one invitee, the noted Muslim intellectual Tareq Oubrou from Bordeaux, had been unable to attend. I had no idea what I would say but agreed to do what I was told.

Bobigny grew up as a working-class suburb, and its leadership generally has been Communist, the party of the current mayor, Bernard Birsinger. I ate dinner with three members of the municipal government, all women and all committed to feminist causes. They explained that the problems affecting Muslim women in their city had to do with difficulties getting legal residence, and the continuation of practices that are forbidden in France but that take place in their home countries, including polygamy, forced marriage, and excision, always done when a girl is taken home "for vacation," and then excised, married, or both.

Laurence Blin, in charge of "intercultural relations" for the city, said that the proposed antiscarf law was idiotic, and that what drove it was the fact that France remains a Catholic country and has had problems accepting Jews, Protestants, and now especially Muslims. "People mix up 'Muslim,' 'Arab,' and 'immigrant,'" she explained. "I was at the Paris stadium for the soccer match between Algeria and France at which people ran onto the field and stopped the game. I talked with the young man next to me who said he was 'Algerian' and complained of how he was treated by 'the French.' But it turned out that it was his grandparents who had come from Algeria, that he had never been there, knew no Arabic. And as we were talking, a man came by and said, 'All of you should go back home.' It is the way others consider them that gives the young people this sense that they are not French."

The mayor not only was present for the dinner and the debate but, aided by several of his staff, had organized the event. Hakim had run a number of these events across France, and always left it up the mayor to choose from among a number of possible topics and to select the participants. In Bobigny, one of the mayor's assistants, José Pinto, had selected the speakers (see chapter 3).

We sat along a table in an amphitheater hall, with about one hundred people present, in appearance equally European and North African. The mayor opened the conference, saying that during the debate over the foulard "we are in the middle of a campaign of stereotypes," and that this serves the *intégristes*, including the American ones, George Bush and his church, as well as those in France. He recalled that the combat for women's liberation was a constant struggle, that only in the 1970s could French women open their own bank accounts, and that "for fundamentalists, women's liberation is the sign of the modernity that they reject; they seek to place women in a patriarchal context."

The four speakers (other than Hakim and me) were women who each came from a different Muslim country, and three of them drew on their "home country" experience to comment on current debates in France. Salima Deramchi, a doctor from Algeria, was the most forthright, perhaps, when she discussed the Algerian family code: "It is drawn from the shari'a and therefore it is not just culture, but religion. We all struggle against it. Religion should be personal, a matter of faith; I should not have to say what I think, whether I am a practicing Muslim. Politics ought to be separated from religion and it should uphold the equality of men and women." She continued, calling on the audience to support the antiscarf law: "You who live here, defend freedoms in France! We also fought for freedom, and look where it has led us! We now have *intégristes* who threaten us. Take care that you do not end up in the same way!"

In the discussion a man in the audience, president of the Bobigny Muslims' Cultural Associations, objected to Deramchi's argument: "Why should you be hostile toward the voile as long as public order is not disturbed?" She responded: "I am a citizen of the world. I am for a law that would forbid the voile. If you have freedom only on one side then you do not have freedom: why forbid a Muslim woman to marry a non-Muslim man? How can anyone object to that? It leaves women their choice on all sides, not just on one side."

Fanta Sangarre from Mali took a very different stance with respect to the relationship of the overseas to the domestic, attempting to remain entirely within the French context. She presides over a Bobigny association working to ensure that women's rights are respected, and in her talk she denounced the practices of excision and forced marriages. She did not mean to say that these practices were carried out because of Islam, but she unfortunately ended her speech by responding to the title of the conference and saying that "yes, religion does hold back women's liberation."

The moderator then allowed a few initial questions from the audience. It became apparent that for the most part the room was divided into two orientations. To my left were men and women who spoke up in defense of Islam against efforts to blame cultural practices that have historically, and perhaps unfortunately, been associated with it, such as excision. To the right sat a group of men and women who objected to religious claims being given public sanction, as in the case of the state-run CFCM. Some of their comments were directed against the social effects of religion; one woman cited a statement made by Élisabeth Badinter on television the previous night (in a program regarding the Stasi Commission's report) that "women have had to fight against all the religions to make progress," and one man objected to the very idea of holding a public debate about religion in public space, which he saw as violating the rules of laïcité.

Sangarre was followed by Azza Ghanmi, a Tunisian feminist who had been in Paris for six months. "I have followed the debates here over the voile for the last few months and have been puzzled and also revolted." She and her fellow Tunisians really understood Islam, she said, because in Tunisia Islam once ruled society, and when it did it promoted the unilateral repudiation of wives. President Bourguiba made it into a state religion. Today it is in conflict with human rights. In France the struggle for human rights has been against religion; for a long time it was against the Catholic Church. The only change has been that now when the Pope condemns birth control, he has no power over what happens in France. In the 1930s Tunisian women began to take off the traditional voile, and they continued to do so in the presence of Bourguiba. They did it to say: "We want to attend schools."

Hanane Harrath, the fourth speaker, was born in Morocco but has lived in Paris for twenty years, where she is writing a thesis on immigration. She directs the Society of Moroccans in France in Saint-Denis, working with women who have legal problems. She reported on the legal changes that were in process in Morocco to give greater rights to women, and pointed out that the inequalities in inheritance were the one area left unchanged. "In Muslim countries people always look to religious institutions for answers to questions, so religious texts become normative, looked to for answers to everything, without recognizing the evolution of society. We should not work on the texts but on the social system that we have inherited from those texts." She argued that religion was properly understood as a private matter, and she quoted scripture to that effect.

I talked about Indonesia and other matters, but the audience was waiting to comment on the presentations by the four women. Some of the audience complained that religion and social issues and causes were all being jumbled together. The most passionate exchange came when a young woman sitting high to the left in the audience said: "I am very shocked at what Mme Ghanmi said. I am Tunisian but was born here, in France, and I live as a perpetual immigrant, continue to be a target of racism and *communautarisme*; I denounce that! I am French; I have lived here nearly all my life. You have just come here, and you speak about what is happening there, that has nothing to do with our situation here in France. In Tunisia what they did is to take the voile off the head and put it over the mouth." She joined others in criticizing several of the speakers for speaking as experts on Islam. "I object to you when you cite verses and *hadith*, when you have no competence in that domain. It is people who have really studied the texts who have the right to quote them."

The woman who objected to generalizing from Tunisia to France (and to glossing over the problems in that "secularist" country) was Radia Louhichi, an active member of the collective One School for All, who led the group's chants in their demonstrations. She also exemplified the complexities, if not confusions, of identities by identifying herself first as "Tunisian" and then as "French." As another woman in the audience then said, to appreciative laughter, "We always mix up categories, so now I can be a *française d'origine algérienne musulmane non-pratiquante*" (French of Algerian origin, non-practicing Muslim).

Two exchanges highlighted the divisions among the audience. One occurred on the left, generally provoile, side of the hall. A female doctor in her forties spoke of her many discussions with patients in headscarves. "When I see veiled women I often ask them why they wear the voile, and they always explain that it was because they made a voyage to Mecca, or because of a specific set of events in their lives. But what bothers me is when I see the very young, what would be the third or fourth generation, with a foulard, or when I see women completely veiled, all over their bodies. [At this point, people seated near her, including the young woman who had spoken earlier and a man seated next to her, objected: "And? So what!"] My mother wore a traditional voile, this was part of tradition, but now I see aggressiveness. The school is different in any case, it is a problem when they come there in a voile." (The same neighbors exclaimed: "They must not be expelled!")

The second exchange took place on the right-hand side of the hall, generally concerned with upholding laïcité. An older man said: "I was shocked that we were talking about Islam because we are in a public space." He explained that he was from Algeria and an atheist. "What freedom are we discussing? To be excised? To be struck? We should be promoting an opening-out to culture [*épanouissement*], but today walking with your head uncovered in Bobigny has become a crime!" ("It's not true! What are you talking about!" from the other side of the room; applause from his side of the room.)

The speakers all responded to the audience's complaints, Harrath and Ghanmi becoming visibly angry that they were criticized for quoting scripture without being experts. But the real issue was the relevance of these North African experiences for the French debates. The three speakers from the three North African countries had given strikingly similar speeches, each one arguing that France should ban scarves from schools and doing so on the basis of their respective experiences in their home country; Muslims in France supporting the right to wear scarves in schools had objected to this "foreign interference."

Staging the Foreign

I wondered how the speakers had been chosen, and I went to see José Pinto, the Bobigny mayor's assistant on religious affairs. Pinto told me that he had chosen the women from Tunisia and Algeria. He and other municipal councilors already knew them. "The public reacted sharply to Salima Deramchi, from Algeria, because she said that "we have democracy and freedom and look where it got us, with knives to our throats! Take care that freedom here [to wear the voile] does not lead to the same thing!" Some of the Muslims there that evening were Wahabis. They learn these ideas from people who come to Bobigny from time to time and give talks in foyers. The worst are the converts; some speak hatred toward France."[38]

The evening's organizer, Hakim El Ghissasi, later explained that the city officials already knew the speakers from Algeria and Tunisia through contacts with the organization Ni Putes Ni Soumises (Neither Whores Nor Doormats), which strongly opposes the scarves.[39] The two speakers were "feminist activists on the Far Left in their own countries, very much in the minority with respect to the Muslim populations in those countries." They had been recruited precisely to express strong antivoile positions based on North African experiences.

Hakim continued: "People here are very tired of those who come from other Muslim countries and say, "Here is what it is like in our country, you should do the same." People here react by saying, "We are here; in France it is not like it is back there." He summarized the Algerian speaker's message as: "We already tried freedom of religious expression in Algeria, and look where it got us! So, be careful or you will end up being dominated by *intégristes*, religion will control politics." He continued in his own words: "That is why the responses were to deny that Algeria had anything to say about France and to deny the speaker's approach that religion was only a matter of faith. She also said that governing through religious law was like Vichy and this shocked everyone; you cannot make that comparison."

After the debate, Hakim and I had both observed one man who approached the speaker from Algeria to say that her words had profoundly wounded him, that his wife wore the voile, and that this was her choice. The Algerian speaker said that her words need not wound him, and they went back and forth, and finally he said, "It does not matter," and walked off—no resolution being possible because the starting points for the two people were so different.

The day after speaking with Hakim, I spoke with Radia Louhichi. Radia is twenty-four and grew up in Bondy, a suburb northeast of Paris. I asked her to describe herself.

> French people think that to "integrate"—and how I hate that word—you must drink wine and be like them, you have to lose your traditions, your religion, your values, and take on theirs. Either you assimilate, thus Fedala Amara [the founder of Ni Putes Ni Soumises], or you are like Saïda Kada [the Lyon-area activist] and wear the foulard, and you are perpetually an immigrant and an *intégriste*.
>
> But excuse me, I have never drunk wine, it is not in my culture, and I am not about to! I am in-between, *moit-moit* [half-and-half]. I do not feel French; I never will be because others think me a perpetual immigrant or daughter of immigrants. But I am not completely Tunisian. I did say in the debate and do say that I am "of Tunisian origins" because I am bathed in Tunisian culture: we went there three times a year, spent summers there, I speak Tunisian Arabic perfectly.

Of Radia's sisters, three had been expelled from school for wearing headscarves, and after that they just quit school. Radia had a lot to say about the Bobigny conference. "What really got to me was that there were those two women, from Algeria and Tunisia, one had been here for only six months, and they were telling us what to do in France, that we had better pass the law to protect women!" I give her statement at length to give a flavor of one kind of reaction to these statements:

> This is not new. Long ago the Tunisian government began sending officials here to talk up the success of the Tunisian case. For the debate on the voile—

for it was that and not about laïcité—the French state needed to have foreign Muslim states speaking against the voile. If it had just been French people for and against the law, the arguments against the law were much stronger. The state needed to show how great a problem the voile presented, so they picked on Iran and Afghanistan because they are poor countries and because there are all kinds of problems of violence against women there. They could not use Dubai or Saudi Arabia because those countries are rich and we need their oil. These states [Iran and Afghanistan] have the burka and black clothing, and it makes people afraid.

The Algerian speaker was the worst; she said that if you allow the voile then Islamists will make your daughters wear it. The Tunisian and Algerian discourses were similar; the difference is in the history of the two countries. In Algeria there is the long history of war and violence, so people talk about that. There is violence in Tunisia but it is hidden, so no one talks about it and it is the great example. The day when there is violence in the streets, then the media will pay attention. The problem with Algeria is that the French have never resolved the revolution in their minds. French children do not learn about it in school.

They all spoke about "religion" and "Islam" as if they knew the Qur'ânic verses. The minute that the question for the evening was put that way, the results were predetermined, that Islam would be blamed for violence and discrimination against women. Why did the officials choose "religion" for the title? Perhaps it was to gain votes, or to see what residents thought, a way of testing opinion, or to provoke someone. Talking about excision, forced marriages, in terms of religion is absurd, but it takes responsibility away from French, who were the ones who brought people over here to work, with their own ideas and values and religion, and now do not want them to have those values. Our parents built this country, and they always were foreigners. They taught us to be discreet: "you are a foreigner, do not draw attention to yourself," which left the French people in peace because the workers did not complain. Now we are not like that, kids are not ashamed of their origins, fast in public during Ramadan; their parents would hide the fact they were fasting when they were at work.

Attributing problems to "religion" allows French people to avoid blaming themselves. The feminist associations in Bobigny were behind these speakers. I do not think that you can call yourself feminist if you are for excluding girls from schools! If someone is "feminist" then they can say anything they want; but where were they when women were raped and attacked?

As it happened, the Bobigny debate was filmed for later partial broadcast on France 2, as a half-hour installment in the Sunday morning series on Islam, *Vivre Islam*. The network gave the program the more innocuous title *Islam et Emancipation des Femmes* (*Islam and Women's Emancipation*) and showed it on February 11, 2004, edited to present a smoother and less controversial event than the one that had taken place. My friend Didier Bourg happened to produce this program, which I saw two weeks later. The producers omitted from their program nearly all references made that evening to France and the fierce debate over who had the right to speak about France. The selections made the program seem to be about the diversity of Islam, with brief reports from Algeria, Tunisia, Morocco, and (my part) Indonesia.

I asked Didier about how he chose what would be included in the program. He explained that in order to fit two hours of debate into a half-hour program, they had to cut radically and had to follow several principles. They had to give time to each of the speakers and had to show a number of different people posing questions. They needed to highlight issues that had to do with Islam rather than other topics (because the show is about Islam, after all) and make sure that the program had a theme. "We did not have any of the dialogue on the relevance of Tunisia for here, etc, because that was further from Islam."

They also had to take care not to show any women wearing headscarves. "We are the only program that deals with Islam that is forbidden to show women in foulards!" In 1999, the then interior minister, Jean-Pierre Chevènement, had seen a program that featured a young woman in a headscarf speaking very well about issues of sexuality and death. "You might have thought he would have welcomed these images because they showed that Islam was very open-minded, and it was when he was trying to create the Istichara [the Consultation, the forerunner to the CFCM]. But he took it as encouraging young women to wear headscarves. He called the director of the program and suggested they not do that." As a result, Islam appears on *Vivre Islam* as a faith, but people do not "look Muslim" unless they are shot in other countries. There, women "look Muslim," but not here in France.

Citing the experiences of Muslim-majority countries to condemn the scarves in France was not new. Right at the beginning of the head-scarf debates in 1989, some writers referred to international battles against Islamists as proof that France should ban headscarves. The philosopher Alain Finkielkraut warned that just as *bien-pensant* French intellectuals had made excuses for the excesses of Stalin, so too those who stood up for the Republic against Islamism were being accused of racism. And yet it is Muslims in France and elsewhere who oppose the scarves: "It is the Tunisian government, engaged in a courageous plan of secularizing culture and education, and the women of Algeria, Tunisia, or Jordan, attacked in the street when they wear European dress, who urge France to hold the line, so that *intégristes* may not claim to be inspired by the homeland of human rights in order to consolidate their totalitarian grip."[40]

At the second peak of headscarf fears in 1994, parallels were most often drawn with Algeria (see chapter 4). On December 4, 1994, *Le Monde* reported comments from French Muslim women about coverage of events by the major television networks. One woman pointed out that during their prime-time news programs, networks would place a report on scarves in schools "not toward the end with other reports on society but always just before or after a report on the FIS" (the Algerian Islamic movement). In 2003, the references had not significantly changed. Dalil Boubakeur, the head of the Paris Mosque, invoked the experience of his own Algeria in opposing the "politicizing" of the scarf issue. "The problem of the foulard is all the more striking given that in North Africa women are much less rigid in their behavior," he explained. "They are aware of the danger, having paid heavily through their suffering for the excesses of radical Islam, notably in Algeria and in Muslim countries."[41]

If political Islam or Islamism is a single set of objectives and values across the globe, then it becomes reasonable to draw from highly visible movements in Algeria or Afghanistan in order to illuminate less visible movements in Europe. Once this assumption is made, then it becomes still clearer that Tariq Ramadan must be engaging in double-talk when he advocates behavior that is both publicly Islamic and thoroughly European, that women in headscarves inevitably will lead to subjugated women in burkas, and that only a sharp slap from the Republic at public signs of Islamist identity has a chance of stemming the tide.

NINE

Sexism

MANY who ended up advocating a law against religious signs said they did so because they hoped it would protect women. On the Stasi Commission, advocates of a law were able to frame the question in those terms; Bernard Stasi himself declared that "the voile is objectively a sign of women's alienation."[1] One member of the Commission told me that "if even one girl were protected from pressure to wear the voile, the law would be worth it." Another, Jean Baubérot, complained publicly that supporters of the law succeeded in framing the issue in terms of shielding women, thus making it difficult for him to oppose the law lest he be seen as "an awful guy who tolerates an unacceptable situation of the submission of women."[2]

Proponents of a law made at least three distinct claims: schoolgirls were pressured by men and boys to wear the voile; the voile intrinsically attacked the dignity and the equal status of women; and, because it did so, it encouraged violence against women living in the poor suburbs. These claims strengthened the antiscarf movement in two major ways.

First, the sexism argument strongly appealed to French principles and emotions concerning the equality and dignity of women. Who could defend oppression of women?

Second, the argument about sexism moved the field of debate still further away from the constitutionally sensitive area of religion. Although arguments based on fears of communalism and Islamism also claimed that the voile was not about religion but politics, they took religion as their subject matter. The authors of the 2002 collection *The Lost Territories of the Republic* denounced "Arab-Muslim culture," and treatises on Islamism invariably criticized public forms of Islamic expression.

These arguments threatened to make it seem that the new law was aimed at Islamic religious thinking and practices—and of course some did support the law precisely because of their antipathy toward Islam. By emphasizing sexism as a reason for the law, its advocates made the issue not the religion of Islam, but the actions of certain Muslims that threatened human dignity.

But what precisely was the argument? Teachers and principals testifying to the Stasi Commission mentioned the voile unfavorably, but the practices that they most strongly denounced were anti-Semitic remarks, proselytizing, praying in school, arguing over history lessons, and general incivility. What was the scarf's role in encouraging oppression of women in school?

The most successful answer went as follows. The voile stands for the oppression of women and also acts as a direct mechanism for their oppression in France. Boys terrorize girls and the voile normalizes this state of affairs. Girls who refuse to wear the voile are told they should wear it and thus are oppressed even within the school. Foreign Islamists are manipulating girls, making them think that they need to wear the voile. Do away with the voile and you would do these girls a big favor. At last, a clear causal argument! And, in the end, it won the day.[3]

The Voile and Women's Dignity

Feminists were hardly the only public figures to make these claims, but they have been active on the scarf issue. With few exceptions, feminists who were active during the 1970s in the Mouvement de la libération des femmes (MLF, Women's Liberation Movement) opposed wearing the voile. Their opposition was clear early on, when, during the first *affaire* of 1989, most major feminist leaders and organizations denounced the scarves. The leading feminist politician at the time, Yvette Roudy of the Socialist Party, claimed that "the foulard is the sign of subservience, whether consensual or imposed, in fundamentalist Muslim society. . . . To accept wearing the voile is tantamount to saying 'yes' to women's inequality in French Muslim society." The Family Planning Movement (Mouvement pour le planning familial, one of the MLF's pillars) agreed:

"Women wearing the voile are a sign of sexist discrimination incompatible with a secularist and egalitarian education."[4]

Those who opposed expelling girls with scarves in 1989 often agreed on the major point that the scarf contradicted principles of women's freedom and equality. The statement published in *Politis* that opposed expelling the girls was preceded by an editorial remarking that the headscarf was a sign of feminine submission, and a petition in *Libération* in November urged the schools to keep the girls so as to integrate them but added that "the foulard is the sign of the oppression and constraining of Muslim women."[5]

Other leading activists for women on the Left joined the call for banning the scarves. The prominent civil rights lawyer Gisèle Halimi resigned from SOS-Racisme because the organization defended the girls' claims to remain in school and thus infringed on "women's dignity."[6] The state secretary for women's rights, Michèle André, combined several objections to the scarves when she said that "the Republican school must not submit to pressures from fathers and brothers; freedom can only exist in a climate of mutual tolerance, which requires respecting rules, traditions, and the culture of the host country."[7] In other words, wearing scarves signified an unwillingness to integrate or even to tolerate French values and came about through pressure from men on women. Adding to the focus on women as victims of insufficient integration were two other issues in the news at the same time: illegal excisions and polygamy, both involving mainly immigrants from West Africa and both mentioned in National Front anti-immigration campaigns.

The argument that headscarves violated the dignity of women began to be spoken by schoolteachers as well. One of the teachers who opposed admitting Alma and Lila Lévy to their school in Aubervilliers in 2003 stated, "We cannot let them think that they are making a statement about society by veiling. As a woman I cannot tolerate that." For her, at least, it was the gender implications rather than the legal issue of laïcité that was at stake. *Le Figaro* argued that the two sisters had started wearing the voile to protect themselves from boys.[8]

The authors of *The Lost Territories of the Republic* (2002) take this logic much further. One (female) lycée teacher describes how she and others felt challenged on a deeper level by Islamic attire. "The striking fact here is that girls and boys cover themselves with a kind of violence that makes one ill at ease. It seems that prior to the religious meaning of head coverings is the notion that the head ought to be covered because the body itself presents a problem. That is what one finds again and again, in pupils' refusal to attend swimming class, in their challenges to mixité, in the problems they raise on account of modesty [*pudeur*]. We even had to refuse their demand for separate toilets for girls and boys, so as to avoid an anti-Republican politics, even though the poor treatment suffered by girls justified it for their sexual protection."[9]

In this striking account, the field of combat is no longer the school but the girls' attitudes toward their own bodies. A measure that might strike an outsider as normal (building separate toilets), and that in this school would have protected girls from aggressions by boys, was considered to send the wrong message about Republican norms. Providing separate toilets would have meant accepting, even promoting, shame about one's body. It is this shame that lies behind wearing a headscarf and refusing to play sports with boys. It must be fought even at the cost of the girls' well-being. This trade-off reminds us of the logic of expelling scarf-wearers: send the girls terrorized by their Islamist community away from the Republican sanctuary that is supposed to save them and back into that community!

A Sense of Personal Assault

I encountered strong personal reactions to scarf-wearing from female friends of mine, and rarely from male friends. One woman shuddered as in late 2003 she expressed her sense that a woman she saw in the subway wearing black was forcing herself upon society, "with her expression all frozen." "*Cela m'agresse,*" she said: "it is an assault." She did not mind the colorful foulard tucked into a dress worn by a girl standing next to her; indeed, her hands fluttered down in two parallel lines as she described that second costume. In this and other instances I found that she would respond very negatively if the scarf flowed down the back of the neck, especially if it was black, but much more positively if the scarf resembled those worn by non-Muslim French women. I asked her to explain her sense of *aggresser.*

It was that they were throwing their difference right at me, that they had these principles, and were making me notice them. I am not bothered when someone has those principles, but I don't want them to force me to take notice of them [the principles]. We cannot pass a law preventing people from wearing what they want in the street, foulards, or any sort of clothing, but we can do so for public space. The street is where the public and private cross. But when they cross over into public space, then they should not exhibit these differences.

JB: What is public space?

That is difficult. We say the street is, but it is not where we can forbid different dress. But if a teacher were to wear a scarf to teach, I would complain. [Her husband thought the matter was overblown, that he had not suffered from being taught by nuns in habits.]

In other words, the emotions lead us to wish to ban the voile from public view entirely but the law does not permit it. At dinner with another group of friends during the same period, a teacher said that "high school girls wear the foulard to irritate the teachers [she drew herself up to imitate a girl daring the teacher]. They are showing off their Islam; that shocks me." (She mentioned that their children, at the nearby middle school, found the scarves worn by some of their classmates to be rather attractive.) Her husband, a social scientist, played down the independent role of scarves. He said that the fellow who built the house behind them, in an eastern suburb of Paris, always walked ahead of his wife, but that she did not wear a voile. "So if you made them take off the voile, you would not change anything. . . . You have to work on values first."

Some Muslim women who do not wear headscarves have spoken in similar ways, as when a high school student in a Paris suburb said of girls wearing scarves at her school that "I am no less Muslim than they are, and I resent that they wear it out of pride, to say 'we are better Muslims than you, we are good girls.'"[10] Even some who subsequently considered with sympathy the perspectives of the women in scarves reacted at first against them. Françoise Gaspard, who argued against the law on religious signs because she, with Farhad Khoskhavar, had discovered the multiple meanings accorded to scarves by their wearers, also admits that she has a strongly negative reaction when she sees women wearing them.[11] One can be Muslim, or support the right to wear scarves, but dislike the scarves themselves.

For some, the scarves brought up the question of the female body and its control. A French female colleague explained to me that she and others saw the voile question as "the first time that a major social change has taken place on the bodies of women." Another said "the scarf is not just religious; it involves the body, how you present yourself." As she spoke these words, she brought her hands down from the top of her head to cover her face and descend down her chest.

Comments about "shock" or "aggression" were frequently heard on television. In his speech in Tunis on December 5, 2003, President Chirac said that for the French, wearing the voile is "a kind of aggression difficult for them to accept."[12] But such comments were more often heard from women. One television program was typical: on a Sunday afternoon one week after Sarkozy's speech, three women were interviewed while seated by the river in Bordeaux. One, wearing a headscarf, sat facing two "French-looking" women. The girl said that the voile was her choice; the other two said that the voile "shocked" them because they were in a secular Republic, and they tried to undermine her claims that she, too, was French (having been born in France) by referring to their long genealogies as proof that they were *Française de souche* (of French stock) rather than merely *de papiers* (because of citizenship papers). One offered to fetch her genealogy.

Sometimes these reactions were shown in more subtle ways. In her testimony to the Stasi Commission, Thérèse Duplaix, the principal of the Turgot high school in Paris, describes a not very religious mother who came to see her: she wore jeans, with a low-cut blouse, and lots of jewelry—here the principal throws out her hands in an expansive manner, giving a sense of liberty and movement. At another moment, she describes a student who had been expelled but allowed to enter "just this once" to work with her supervisor for preparing for the baccalaureate, that she was dressed in "voile, very strict, very closed," and her hand came down in front of her to bring together the two sides of a garment, and her shoulder and head tightened inward, in a physical gesture indicating a rigid attitude.[13]

I found it intriguing that the witness sought to concisely convey something important about each woman by describing—through words and gestures—the relative sexually open or closed quality of her clothing. I began to notice how, beyond the headscarf issue, a French journalist often would describe the clothes, hair, or appearance of a woman in public life—particularly former justice minister Élisabeth Guigou's hair, it seemed. The attention to appearance is of course not limited to women. When in 2005 Bernard-Henri Lévy set out to be the second Tocqueville through a series of articles for the *Atlantic Monthly*, he frequently mentioned a feature of clothing to indicate his disdain for this or that American figure: slacks too short, suit too tight. But the connection between the correct physical appearance in public and personal dignity seemed to be even more important for women.[14]

VIOLENCE AND THE VOILE

Clothes and the voile have been invoked in debates about violence against women in the poor suburbs.[15] The most shocking incidents of this violence are collective rapes, which in the 2000s came to be known as *tournantes*. The public became aware of the tournantes through a 2000 film, *La Squale* (*The Shark*), and the 2002 best-selling account by Samira Bellil of her own rape in *Dans l'enfer des tournantes* (*In Gang-Rape Hell*). The same year, Bellil became the "godmother" of a new movement aimed at attacking this violence, called Ni Putes Ni Soumises (Neither Whores Nor Doormats, NPNS). In October 2002, a man burned to death a young woman named Sohane in a poor housing project. The first anniversary of this event was heavily covered by the national news media, and NPNS made it central to its campaigns. It also coincided with the Stasi Commission's hearings and entered into the debates concerning the law on scarves.

The film, the book, and the activist movement served to keep *tournantes* in the news during 2001–2003, with little attention paid to them before or after that period. Judging from media accounts, the rapes were invented by young men of North African background at the end of the 1990s. But in fact collective rape dates back at least to the 1960s, to activities by nonimmigrant gangs, and the incidence of these rapes has not increased over the past twenty years. According to the sociologist Laurent Mucchielli, what changed recently were not the practices but the claims made about them: specifically, attributing them to Arab-Muslim culture rather than to urban social problems.[16]

The media campaign around Sohane helped propel NPNS to national prominence. NPNS had begun life in the form of a manifesto published in January 2002 on a Web site connected to SOS-Racisme and then printed in *Le Nouvel Observateur*—both institutions close to the Socialist Party. The movement had caught the media's full attention in March 2003, when a cortege of "women from the projects" marched into Paris after traveling across France. That October, the group's founder, Fadela Amara, published a book (also called *Ni Putes Ni Soumises*) recounting the difficulties faced by women in the projects or in the eighteenth and nineteenth arrondissements of Paris, where many Muslims live. The book was released to coincide with the anniversary of Sohane's death.[17]

After first opposing a law against scarves in schools on the grounds that it would set off a backlash, by late November 2003 NPNS supported it, arguing now that the scarf was one element of a misogynist mind-set that had to be changed. Fadela Amara and most of the visible leaders of the movement were children of North African immigrants. Even if they did not come from the "troubled" neighborhoods of which they spoke, they met the political need to have an "authentic" female voice against the scarves. Even as she continued to be strongly supported by the Left, Amara and NPNS were given space and funds by the government of the Right. All the major politicians gave her a warm, public reception. At the same time as they were debating the headscarf law, in early 2004, the Parliament gave a prize to her book (which had been coauthored with a journalist from *Le Monde*).

The attention paid to NPNS—free space, automobiles, book prize— would never have happened had the women simply demonstrated for women's rights. What they did was to fashion an image of themselves as the socially "good" version of the children of immigrants, a reprise of the Beurs: unveiled women who speak up for their rights, accompanied by secular, gentle Arab men. What they attacked was their negative image: the situation of the veiled woman, a silent victim who can speak only thanks to her unveiled sisters, and the violent young Arab, whose natural instincts are to gang-rape his female counterparts.[18] The NPNS declaration conveyed a sense of the psychosocial backwardness of young North African, Muslim men, and in this way it converged with the politicians' arguments about communalism and Islamism to imply that Arab culture and Islamic folkways simply had not yet developed to the point where they would be on the same level as those of Europeans. The French could help the Arabs by passing laws that would ban their unwelcome accoutrements, starting with the voile.

For politicians the NPNS analysis was a pure gift. NPNS explained the problem of violence in terms of sexism in the underdeveloped portions of urban France rather than as the result of policies of labor migration and residential segregation. Problems of labor and discrimination would require imaginative, expensive policies; Arab sexism called for denunciation—and a law affecting Muslim women.

Now, despite the NPNS focus on poor suburbs, violence against women is by no means confined to those parts of France. Most such violence is domestic, and, although there are no firm statistics on domestic violence, an attempt by *Libération* to track down all cases for two months in 2004 found that twenty-seven of twenty-nine cases were perpetrated by men of "nonimmigrant" background (and only one of the two "immigrants" was of "Arab-Muslim culture"). Furthermore, media accounts tended to attribute violence by young men in poor suburbs to their "culture," but those involving other French people to "passion" or "blind love." In other words, "native" French men hit women because of too much French culture; "immigrants" do so because of not enough French culture.[19]

Some women disagreed with the NPNS position, but they received neither media attention nor book prizes. Christine Delphy, a feminist scholar associated with the journal *Nouvelles Questions Feministes*, argued that the arguments for the law were part of a historical movement of exclusion and repression. For Delphy (2005), the law represses those who would protest their second-class, neocolonized status, a position that led her to sign the 2005 petition that labeled the children and grandchildren of the former colonized subjects of France as *les indigènes de la République* (the autochthones of the Republic). The same Muslims who were told to integrate on Republican terms in Algeria, and again in France, she argued, protest this oppression by demanding that they be publicly accepted as Muslims and as full citizens of France. For Delphy, this demand (which is also that of Tariq Ramadan) is as unacceptable to those who govern France today as it was for those who kept Algerian Muslims in their second-class status of *les indigènes*, people in a second-class legal and political status as autochthonous, underdeveloped peoples. In response, those in power in France label the upstarts as either "bad boys" or "oppressed women," and explain the deficiencies of both in terms of their underdeveloped "Arab-Muslim culture."[20]

WOMEN'S MOVEMENTS DIVIDED

The distance between NPNS and Delphy illustrates the degree to which the scarf question has divided the loose coalition of groups supporting women's rights. On one side, NPNS objects to the participation of women in headscarves in joint demonstrations. On the other, a federation (*collectif*) of groups opposed to the law had developed during the 2003 debates under the heading "One School for All" (Une École pour tou(te)s), the federation that organized the February 2004 demonstration described in chapter 6 (and to which Delphy belongs). The federation's stance is entirely negative: they oppose expelling anyone from school but take no stand on the appropriateness of scarves on Muslim girls. They make the same arguments that had been made in 1989 by some on the Left against expulsions. Then, as now, the journal *Politis* is a forum for this position, along with the Web site Les Mots sont Importants (LMSI, Words Count).

Since 2003, the various associations that often demonstrate together for women's rights and against racism—SOS-Racisme, MRAP,[21] Planning Familial, and others—have engaged in a subtle dance: now joining with, now avoiding groups who object to expelling girls in scarves. NPNS was the most forthright in stating that it would not march together with such groups. In France, the decision to march together in or stay apart from a demonstration is a highly visible index of the current state of play of such alliances. Furthermore, and particularly on the Left, a group that is divided over participation usually will abstain, allowing supporters of the demonstration to make clear their support in other, less public ways.[22]

The divisions among groups supporting women's rights came to a head in March 2005, during preparations for the annual march of women's rights organizations on International Women's Day, March 8. The organizing body removed the One School for All movement from the list of marchers, but said that it would tolerate their presence. NPNS decided to withdraw from the march on the grounds that it had been captured by "Islamists," including women from the UOIF. In its manifesto, NPNS charged that mixité was now threatened in the public sphere and that people now justified violence against women—forced marriages, polygamy, excision—in the name of "free choice."[23] The Family Planning movement joined NPNS in an alternative demonstration on March 6, two days before the official celebration of International Women's Day. Thousands turned out. Their banner read: *Laïcité, Egalité, Mixité.* One school principal said that she chose this demonstration over the official one "because *Egalité, Fraternité* is written on the door to the school. I want the school to retain its neutrality. Let a girl who wishes to wear a skirt wear a skirt!" She added that she feared a "moralizing discourse" that might place gains in contraception and abortion in danger. In other words, she feared that the gains made at the expense of the Catholic Church might be threatened by a lax attitude toward demands made by Muslims.[24]

NPNS had succeeded in setting the agenda. The Women's Day organizing committee responded to NPNS's criticisms by saying that they, too, opposed the voile as an "instrument of oppression of women" but that their projects went beyond those issues to the broader questions of social and economic rights.[25] On the day of the march, when One School for All marchers, including women in headscarves, joined the march, several marchers left the cortege. One was the Green Party deputy Martine Billard: "On March 8th, don't ask me to defend their right to wear the voile."[26] Elsewhere, women in headscarves reported being shouted down or even visible attacked by non-scarf-wearing women prior to marches. The strongest denouncers of scarves remained those women who most ardently fought for women's rights.[27]

Feminism's Quandaries

Why were French feminists so strongly divided on the issue of the headscarves, and why did NPNS manage to set the terms of the debate? Let me advance some hypotheses. One is suggested by Joan Scott's (1996) phrase: French feminists have had "only paradoxes to offer." Throughout the nineteenth and twentieth centuries, leaders of the women's rights movement in France have framed their demands and the debate in good Republican terms. They have argued for equality for all citizens, not that men and women differ in an essential way nor that women as a class should have collective rights. The recent issue of electoral parity, or requiring parties to reserve places for women on their electoral lists, sorely tested this approach, for it amounted to a quota system. Parity advocates argued, successfully, that quotas were necessary to overcome a history of discrimination and thus to ensure universal representation. Feminist care to preserve a universalistic approach added to the difficulty in accepting as legitimate other kinds of public difference, especially when those differences had a direct bearing on gender ideas.[28]

But claims to universalism made during the parity debates are essentially "paradoxical," because invoking "women" as a political category in order to achieve equality highlights difference, thereby creating a space for a wide range of arguments about the meaning of femininity. Feminism's opponents were able to urge a naturalized image of femininity and to abjure the identity of the sexless feminist (a caricature supported by feminist proclamations that lesbianism was the better feminist position).

Two sociologists recently have argued that the success of feminism's opponents in casting the issue in these terms led to the emergence of a third term in the dialectic.[29] For them, "neo-feminism" celebrates both the feminine body and women's political achievements. Women do and should realize their autonomy through their femininity. In its "*Elle* magazine form" (Chollet 2004), neofeminism champions the free choice of women in lifestyle, appearance, and sexuality. This consumerist orientation retains the advances of legal equality in political space but urges women to celebrate their femininity in their personal lives, a category that includes careers, clothing, and sexuality.[30]

This form of neofeminism rejoins the distinctive French Republican form of liberal political philosophy in its valuing of political equality and social conformity in public life. Indeed, in its Republican version, but not its Anglo-American counterpart, modern political liberalism requires social conformity to gain and retain political equality. As Marcel Gauchet argues (see chapter 7), religion left the public sphere at the threshold of modernity so that citizens could enjoy anonymity with respect to their religious faith and practices. In public life, they resemble one another because they do not compare their religions. But how can they exist as sexed beings in the public sphere if they should interact only as citizens? Here we see again Scott's "paradoxes." The solution is the same as the solution for the electoral parity issue: to regard the universal citizen as male or female, and to take note of the difference. Men may be masculine and women feminine and remain equal as citizens.[31]

The cost of this solution is eternal vigilance, lest the dignity of the individual woman be assaulted through the institutions of male domination in work or in politics. Indeed, to harass someone sexually in France is felt first and foremost to be an assault on that individual's dignity (rather than, say, a violation of workplace norms).[32] Presenting oneself as a sexual being not only is allowed under this set of norms, it is part of the French compromise. To put this hypothesis provocatively, advertising through female bodies is the price of the "neofeminist" synthesis, the proclaiming of women's autonomy through the celebration of the female body.

If this first hypothesis is valid, it may help to account for the strong female reactions against images of women in Islamic headscarves. The voile suggests a different set of ideas about women's beauty and women's roles. It challenges the happy assumption that women all want femininity of a certain sort. Most tellingly, it raises the specter of rule by men, implying that these women might not mind being in a second-class role, and thus it touches a deep worry of many French women. Even before 1989, French feminists had criticized their colleagues in antiracism movements on the grounds that they failed to take patriarchal domination as seriously as they did imperialism and racism. The voile crystallized this problem: here was a social group that outdid Frenchmen in dominating their women.[33]

We already came across the idea that "the voile stole femininity" when discussing the film about Trappes in chapter 7. Loubna Méliane of NPNS fielded questions on a Le Monde chat forum during the week of October 23, 2003. To the question "Why is the voile for you an attack on freedom?" she responded: "It is above all an attack not on freedom but rather on femininity. Better to wear a miniskirt and assume one's femininity than to hide oneself behind a veil to avoid having people look at you. . . . Laïcité is the neutrality of public space." Méliane continues, arguing that laïcité does not allow girls to wear the voile in the public sphere (work, school, and so on); as citizens they know full well that the voile cannot be accepted in the workplace.

Moreover, and here we turn to a second hypotheses, male domination of women in the name of Islam evokes the all-too-recent domination of women by the Catholic Church. The struggles for women's rights to decide on matters of abortion and contraception, the two major components of the MLF's collective memory, were fought against the Church. The Church also ordered women to cover themselves in the name of piety. These images continue to be advanced by some in the Church and on the Far Right, making real the fear advanced by the participant in the March 2005 march quoted earlier that laxity toward women in head-scarves might weaken advances made against the Catholic Church.[34]

This vigilance led the lawyer Gisèle Halimi to write in *Le Monde* on May 19, 2005, in the midst of the French debate on the proposed new European Constitution, that the clause urging "open, transparent, and regular dialogue with the Churches" was worrisome, "because it could attack our Republican pillar, *la laïcité*. . . . The word is banned, whereas the terms *religions*, *Churches*, and *religious liberty* occupy the public square [*ont droit de cité*]. This unilateral reference to the Churches is a danger for women, for they all have contributed to patriarchy and to the subjection of women."[35]

That the feminist legacy in France is fragile is further supported by the great success of Élisabeth Badinter's critique of feminism in *Fausse Route* (*Wrong Way*). Badinter, one of the strongest original opponents of scarves in schools, attacks French feminism for unduly blaming (French) men for women's problems and for exaggerating women's handicaps. She has also singled out religion as the major impediment to women's rights, and emphasizes the importance of mixité, the working together of men and women, as one of France's key strengths.

Now, lack of gender mixité is one of the charges leveled against Islam as well as against certain currents of feminism. In his December 2003 speech advocating a law against religious signs in schools, President Chirac mentioned the importance of mixité, especially in sports. The objections against reserving certain time slots for women at public swimming pools were in part based on laïcité—that the Muslim and Jewish women concerned had religious reasons for making the request and those reasons made the requests inadmissible. But gender segregation itself was and is seen as damaging to living life together, *la vie commune*, in the Republic. When men and women sit separately at Muslim gatherings, they raise both fears at the same time: not enough laïcité and no mixité. (Objections to separate seating at UOIF functions led the leadership to allow mixed seating for the first time at its 2005 annual assembly at Le Bourget.)[36]

The free mixing of men and women is thus a sore point both for some feminists and for some Muslims. It is thus interesting to see how feminists have responded to Badinter. (The level of emotion is such that many have tried to avoid public debate entirely.) One of Badinter's main critics is Gisèle Halimi (2003), who defends French feminism against charges of being anti-men. She insists on the "specific quality of French feminism" that is its embrace of mixité, in contrast to American sex-separatism. This defense may explain why some feminists so strongly condemn Islamic projects of gender segregation (at swimming pools, for example). By so doing, they confirm their own commitment, suspected and challenged by antifeminists, to a brand of feminism that embraces Republican mixité as its proof that it is properly universalistic.

"WHERE HAVE THE FEMINISTS GONE?"

The idea that somehow wearing a headscarf is related to violence and to feminism's fragilities may seem abstract. Let me consider the narrative strategies deployed by one television attempt to make the connection. On December 8th, 2003, a few days before the Stasi Commission was to submit its report, the French-German station Arte, on the program *De Quoi J'me Mêle?*, presented two linked features. The overall program, presented by Daniel Leconte, was called *Où sont passées les féministes?* (*Where Have the Feminists Gone?*), and consisted of two distinct films: *Quand les filles mettent les voiles* (*When Girls Put On the Voile*) and *Profession: Féministe*. Between the two films was a panel discussion filmed in the studio.[37] The montage itself—voile plus feminism equals feminists' failure—implied that the problem of the feminists' legacy was related to the problem of scarves in the suburbs. The program is interesting both for its failure to make the connection and for what it does find.

Daniel Leconte begins by noting how shocked the producers were years earlier when they shot footage in one of the "zones outside the law" in Marseille, and realized that there were no women in public places. "At the same time, in France, feminists spoke of other things." Here is the link: France is divided into two spheres, the lawless zones abandoned by the Republic (as in Trappes), where women are kept indoors or veiled, and "France," the Republic, where women made "immense progress" in gaining the rights to abortions, contraception, and electoral parity. (Compare Sarkozy's proclamation that by visiting UOIF headquarters he "brought the Republic" to Muslims.)

Leconte continues: "And then, at the moment when these things seemed acquired, there surged forth a reality from another age. Sohane, seventeen years old, was burned in Vitry, women took on the voile to protect themselves, said some, or as a sign of religious affiliation, said others: go figure it out." And we move to the first of the evening's two films. It begins with the anniversary of Sohane's death on October 4, 2003. The filmmaker interviews Sohane's sister: "You have to go unnoticed in the projects if you are pretty." (There are photos of Mecca behind her). Two women, one in a voile, lay a wreath on the plaque commemorating her in Vitry; we learn that it had been vandalized twice. Her father tells us that Sohane was buried in Algeria, that "she is protected there." The film is dedicated to her. And then you see the title, *When Girls Wear Voiles*, and the credit that the film was made by Leila Djitli, brought up in one such project.

COPING THROUGH CLOTHING

Leila returns to her former home, recalling memories of boys and girls getting along, wanting to understand how Sohane's drama was possible. She describes the neighborhood as degraded, and then she sees a startling sight: "The appearance of three girls wearing *le voile*, unthinkable a few years earlier, reinforces the feeling of abandonment." An older woman (a friend of her grandmother) explains that one of the three girls in question started wearing the voile and the others followed: "It's fashion." Leila goes to see a second older woman, who serves her tea in an elaborately Moroccan interior. This woman, Fatima, explains that her head covering is not *le voile*: "I wear it because it goes well with my dress." They laugh. Her daughters are not in danger in the neighborhood. Sixteen and seventeen years old, they dress in jeans and shirts.

Now we are back to the first woman, an Algerian, who wears jeans and dances to North African music. Another friend complains that "all these young people who are into religion; it is because they are lost!" They complain about their sons telling them they cannot dress that way, in jeans and tight shirts. A younger woman says, "I have jeans on, and a little shirt that does not hide much—not that I want to—and my son says, "You cannot go out like that!" Down in the street, unruly boys are yelling. The women watch them and return to dancing. We switch back to the Moroccan woman, who has female friends over: they are having fun, relaxing, and complaining of how they keep quiet when they are around men.

Narrator: "I knew I would find the life of bygone days with these older women." Now she looks for girls of Sohane's age and finds them in a gym, "the only place, together with the school, where mixité is still respected." She speaks with some players on a handball team, who will serve as her "guides" for the rest of the film. They have their hair uncovered and reflect black, brown, and white origins. They win their game, and the guys from their project watching in the stands are ecstatic.

After much effort, Leila succeeds in inducing young men hanging out in front of "their" building to talk. She asks what they think of Sohane's story; they joke about it but say it could never happen there. The boys explain that things start to go downhill between girls and boys when they move from middle school to high school, because then they meet guys from other neighborhoods, and the trouble begins. "We won't be respected if the women are not respected."

The girls we met before pass by and have insults thrown at them by some guys, but apparently not the ones we have been talking with. (The director seems to want us to think that it is the same group.) Then we are back to the earlier group of boys. They explain that "ways of thinking have changed," that girls and boys do not go out together; that they have their secret loves but won't talk about them. Part of the problem is boredom: "99 percent of those in the neighborhoods have quit school," explains one boy, "and we are preoccupied with these little things."

Now the girls, standing by the road some distance away, discuss the boys. One girl does most of the talking for the rest of the film. She says: "Look how I dress," showing her baggy clothes: "If I went out in a skirt they would yell 'whore' at me." At this point we see two women pass by in the distance, one older and one younger, both wearing dark scarves. Leila asks the girls what they think of these women. "God willing [*In-sha'allah*] I will wear the hijâb, when I marry, or maybe before, depending on conditions, my state of mind, or what the school allows."

She then discusses her difficulties wearing a headscarf to school. "I put on a scarf [*foulard*] this morning, because I had not done my hair. A teacher said 'Take it off!' and I said 'Why?' Others in the classroom, not to be racist about it, they have their crosses, so you see they are Christians, but [my scarf] was not a marker of my religion, a way to say 'I am Muslim.' They made me take it off. They made another girl leave school because she wore the voile. She took her bac [school-leaving exam] this year and now she has failed, so there you are." One of the girls quotes her mother: "No school, no future."

These girls know the score and are coping with school, but little direct damage from the veil has been shown. The longest interview in the program is with Sabrina, twenty-two years old, living in a different neighborhood, who wants to become a pop star. We see her dancing and singing. "When I am out, people pass by in a car and they insult me, it does not matter how I am dressed." But then she adds: "When I go out I dress like a boy, in self-defense." She wears loose clothes and a cap, "to hide myself; I look like a bum." Leila asks her: "You hide your femininity?" "Yes, it's impossible to flirt." She then describes how she is criticized: "Everyone around me is into religion; they say 'you're not a Muslim' because of my songs."

Now we talk with older guys, the ones who had applauded at the handball game, and they describe a sudden change in the previous five years. One speaks of a "chasm" between boys and girls. "Girls try to avoid the guys. Today, if you wear a voile you are respected, but if you are in a miniskirt you're treated as a whore." Then they argued about whether the problem was with the younger guys or that the girls did not respect themselves. The program ends by replaying the scene where the older guys cheer on the girls at handball; we also see Sabrina dancing in her baggy clothes.

Notice that clothes are central to the film's argument that women in the poor suburbs are forced to "hide their femininity," but that the voile featured in the film's title plays a very small role in the film. No one wears Islamic dress for protection: the group of handball-playing girls and Sabrina wear baggy clothes, and most of them in fact have their hair loose. One boy says the voile gives a girl respect, and a girl expresses her hope that she will be able to wear the hijâb someday and discusses her teachers' objections when she wears any sort of scarf to school. And yet *Le Monde* summarizes the film's message as "wearing the voile guarantees respect in the projects"![38]

But in fact the film emphasizes intergenerational gulfs: the contrast between Leila's grandmother's generation—women from Morocco or Algeria who enjoy themselves, dance, and socialize with other women—and the current generation of young girls and boys, who are enjoying themselves less because they have so little hope for the future. They know that the school is the key to the future, even though most of them do not finish. Moreover, the older generation enjoyed its sexuality and sensuality as women; the new generation has to its conceal femininity to survive. What happened to feminism?

FEMINISMS OLD AND NEW

To find the answer, the narrator now tries to link the two parts of the evening's program through a debate involving two leading feminists from elsewhere and a representative of France's victims of male violence. The participants include the venerable leader of German feminism, Alice Schwartzer (who will figure in the next film), a leader of Québecois(e) feminism, Denise Bombardier, and Samira Bellil, the author of the bestseller on collective rape. Bellil begins with what I found to be a very perceptive and concise analysis of the problems among boys and girls in the poor suburbs. Boys of only fourteen or fifteen years of age are violent toward girls, "because sex and love and emotions are taboo." She gives an illuminating analysis of the system of social control in the suburbs, explaining that many consider it appropriate to correct everyone else, no longer only the members of their own families. She adds that it is not only Muslims who do this, "so do Stephane and Audrey." The narrator stops her at this point (though it would have been interesting to question the program's title, given Bellil's last comment), and gives the floor to Denise Bombardier. She says that she was most struck by the degradation in the condition of women; those in the previous generation "did not wear the voile, and wore skirts, real personages; we are backsliding." As she speaks shadowy images are projected behind them, including the receding images of two women entirely clad in hijâb, images that did not come from the film. Clothes become prime indexes of women's progress: from feminine skirts, we have retreated to masculine baggy clothes and the antifeminine voile.

Samira Bellil introduces the complaint that drives the second film, immediately to follow: feminism had nothing to say to women like her, in the poor suburbs. "No one knows anymore what 'les Plannings Familiaux' means," she complains. "I do not feel feminist; I got out of there on my own!" She explained that she belonged to NPNS and was not feminist because she was searching for "men who are good." "I don't need anyone in an office to tell me what I think; colonialism is over." Feminism appears as both anti-male and condescendingly bourgeois— and we are reminded of its fragilities.

Leconte poses the questions for the next film: "Now we address civil society. What has happened? Why did most feminists not see the social problems?" Note that we have not previously been "addressing civil society" because we were not really in "France"; we were in a space outside the Republic, a cité de non-droit. The new film is Profession: Féministe, directed and narrated by Sophie Jeaneau, a woman perhaps in her late twenties and whose mother left the Kabyle region of Algeria in 1967. Sophie reminds us of the milestones of the French feminist movement in the 1970s, and in particular the petition to legalize abortion by women who had been forced to have abortions outside the law, called 343 salopes pour l'avortement (343 Sluts for Abortion). Sophie asks whether the real battles for women today were not elsewhere. When Sohane was burned, she reminds us, NPNS refused to be called "feminist." Feminists accomplished nothing to remedy salary inequalities.

Sophie sets out to find "historic" feminists just before the anniversary of Sohane's burning on October 4, 2003. She visits Anne Zelensky at her home, and complains that Anne and the other historiques did not pass on the torch to the next generation. She interviews other feminists as well and finds them rigid. In Germany, she finds Alice Schwartzer, "the Beauvoir of Germany," who says that she considers NPNS to be the new French feminists. When Schwartzer saw NPNS on television, she wondered, "Where have my old friends gone? They should be proud of the daughters of the neighborhoods. If tomorrow there were a demonstration by Muslims, I would be with them in the front line." For Schwartzer, it seems, NPNS represents the interests of "Muslims" in France. Sophie is struck by sex-segregation in Germany: separate hotels and parking places. Only women are allowed to write for the magazine edited by Schwartzer.

Back in France, Sophie decides to interview Élisabeth Badinter, who had just published her critique of feminism, *Fausse Route*. But once she makes this decision, word gets around and various feminist organizations cancel their agreements to appear on the program. We conclude that they are afraid of debate; Badinter herself calls their refusal "Stalinist." Badinter criticizes feminists for their portrayal of women as victims, and asks: "What have they accomplished in the past fifteen years? Why do so many young women refuse the label *feminist*"?

We end the film with a visit by *les historiques* to the tomb of Simone de Beauvoir, where Sohane's sisters lay a commemorative plaque. No one from NPNS comes. Nor have the *historiques* ever attended demonstrations by NPNS. The two generations have nothing to say to one another; those who call themselves feminists have little to do with today's women's actions. We now better understand the sense of fragility attached to the legacy of feminism and the urgent sense that feminists ought to defend their position, one that combines the defense of the Republic with a demand for women's rights, against the new challenges—no longer from politicians or from the Catholic Church, but from an Islam that robs women of their femininity. Only if they run to catch up with their younger sisters will *les historiques* preserve their public credibility.

CAN VEILED WOMEN SPEAK FOR THEMSELVES?

In fact, *les historiques* did intervene in the debate over the voile, mainly on the side of NPNS. The same Anne Zelensky who had so vigorously defended herself to Sophie wrote, with Anne Vigerie, in *Le Monde* in May 2003, an article whose title proclaims their position: "Laïcistes Because Feminists." Although the term *laïciste* is usually employed to refer negatively to people carried away by their enthusiasm for laïcité, the two authors here embrace it in order to attack the wearing of the voile. They begin by acknowledging that women or girls who wear the "Islamic veil" do so in the name of their freedom to practice their religion. However, they add, "wearing the voile is not only a sign of belonging to a religion. It symbolizes the place of women in Islam as Islamism understands it. That place is in the shadow, downgraded and submitting to men. The fact that some women demand it does not change its meaning. We know that dominated people are the most fervent supporters of their domination."

They argue that laïcité presupposes a "neutral public space, free of any religious belief, where citizens develop under the same treatment, sharing common rights and duties, and a common good, all of which places them beyond discriminating differences." They call, in the end, for prohibiting the voile "in all places of teaching and of life together (*vie commune*) (school, university, business, government offices), and if attacks on women continue, forbidding the voile in the street."

Their article confronts two critical questions that arise once the debate has been reframed around women's rights rather than around the laïcité of the schoolroom: how broad should be the scope of a headscarf ban? And should one place any weight on the testimony of the girls in scarves themselves? The two questions are related. If the issue is keeping the schools free from outside pressures in order to allow pupils to learn in an atmosphere free of ideological pressures, then it makes sense to limit the ban on the scarves to the school grounds, or perhaps, as was the case in a number of schools, to the classroom. In class, all identities other than that of pupil in France are to be suppressed; in the rest of life, they may flourish, and freedom of religion requires that expressions of faith be permitted. Even if schoolgirls choose to wear the scarves, they still prevent the classroom from functioning as it should.

However, the argument that moves from communalism and Islamism to sexism takes the issue in a very different direction. Now the claim is that the voile is the symbol and instrument of broad, global forces that oppose French values, and that in particular oppress women. It no longer matters where the voile appears; it is equally noxious and dangerous in any public place—and why only in public places? It should be abolished everywhere that French people try to develop a life together, a *vie commune*. Such is Vigerie and Zelensky's argument, and their sentiments were shared by others. It was about this time, in May 2003, that one began to see banks, doctors' offices, and municipal offices refusing entry to women in headscarves, as well as cases where an ordinary person would ask a woman in a scarf to "leave this public place" on a bus or subway. The ambiguity of the French concept of "public," which means sometimes "having to do with the state" and sometimes "out in public view," was at work here, generating or reinforcing a variety of norms about what such women should or should not do. For Zelensky and Vigerie, and I suspect for many French feminists, the relevant meaning of "public" is that of *la vie commune*, a notion that includes the workplace as well as the government office.

In this broader view of the problem, how to treat the girls' own views becomes more difficult. In the narrower argument concerning the school, one that starts from the legal and perhaps the philosophical requirements of laïcité, the claim that scarf-wearing girls have freely chosen their garments need not be refuted, because good pedagogy require a scarfless classroom, whatever the pupils might think. In the broader argument that starts from the voile's socially corrosive force, however, statements by girls and women that they chose to wear headscarves must be addressed. What if they do not find the voile corrosive or oppressive at all?

Whose Voice Is Heard?

Where you start makes a great deal of difference. If you start from the subjectivity of a woman who wears a headscarf, then you are likely to understand its meaning to be that which she bestows on it as she positions herself with respect to her environment. You thus end up more likely to agree with the woman's own account, which will emphasize personal choice and commitment. This is how French sociologists studying the phenomena approached it, through interviews with young women who wore scarves. They ended up, not necessarily enthusiastic about scarf-wearing, but at least enthusiastic about paying attention to the attitudes and practices of the women concerned.

During the headscarf debates in France, from time to time someone would write a public statement from such a position of empathy with a

Muslim woman. A medical doctor, Anne Sobole, wrote in *Le Monde* describing her initial reactions to seeing women covered in black, the "burka" as she called it: "anger, horror, anguish, everything stirred together to forbid compassion." One day, a woman dressed in that manner showed up in her office for a consultation. Sobole had frequently dealt with young women in headscarves and had gotten to know some of them well. They wore their scarves for a mixture of reasons; one said she did it to meet guys, leading Sobole to recall how as a girl she had attended mass for the same reasons. The burka-wearer was a new experience for the doctor, but when she entered the consulting room, she took off her gloves and robe, and revealed underneath a low-slung pair of pants and a short tee-shirt. The doctor reflected: just as she herself had learned much from the nuns who taught her, she trusted that her own granddaughters would "find their identity among scarf, cross, *le piercing*, and plenty of other avenues more or less difficult, and then they, too, will know how to make their choice."[39]

This approach is "liberal" and appeals to Americans, and thus it is not surprising that this is also the way in which the American filmmaker Micah Fink constructed his film for Wide Angle, *Young, Muslim, and French*, shown on PBS stations in September 2004. Fink based his film on life at Lycée Joliot-Curie in the small town of Dammarie-Lès-Lys near Melun, south of Paris. He followed a schoolgirl who wore a scarf through her struggle with her school. He also showed a male Muslim teacher who spoke about intolerance in France. He interviewed the school principal as well (who happens to be a friend of mine), but we see her subjectivity next to that of the girl, and the liberal response that follows most easily from learning of these juxtaposed subjectivities is to say: let a hundred flowers bloom. It is hard to view the program without concluding: good Muslims (and reasonable principal), but intolerant French state.

The principal of the school, Ghislaine Hudson, had insisted that Fink interview a Muslim girl who chose not to wear a scarf was well as one who did. He decided against this course of action on the grounds that he needed to counter the dominant French line of thinking by giving the other side.[40] For principal Hudson, the larger issue was preserving the autonomy of the pupils: "The law does work to protect those who do not wish to follow others. We have one pupil, whose parents are from

Algeria and who recently moved here from another housing area. She is Muslim and religious but does not fast. She said that had they stayed there she would have had to fast because of the pressure. There is pressure within the school on girls. I want to make sure that people are free to decide on their own about dress, prayer, fasting, and so forth."[41]

If the American insistence on freedom of choice assumes the possibility of choosing, and thus sees the matter as a private one, the French emphasis on autonomy and dignity sees it as the state's obligation to take steps to create the conditions for meaningful choice. From an autonomy perspective, "choice" appears as a naively thin concept.[42]

TELEVISION STRATEGIES

If giving voice to young women in headscarves might lead viewers to see things from their point of view, one can perhaps better understand why French television viewers seldom had to trouble themselves over such a possibility. During the critical period for shaping public opinion, from approximately April 2003 through February 2004, one seldom heard young Muslim women in headscarves setting out their positions on French television. Two exceptions "prove" (in the older sense of "test") the rule. The Lévy sisters, expelled from their Aubervilliers lycée in fall 2003, appeared as foils for those who would defend the Republic (see the last section of this chapter). Lyon activist and businesswoman Saïda Kada did appear on talk shows, for two reasons. First, in early 2003 she published a book with a non-scarf-wearing French woman who had converted to Islam, Dounia Bouzar.[43] Bouzar was very critical of Tariq Ramadan and Islamic institutions in France, and this stance brought her public legitimacy. As a pair, they were a curiosity. Second, and only because Bernard Stasi happened to see her name on the book's cover, Kada had been summoned to appear before the Stasi Commission, and thus was doubly a curiosity.

Most Muslims who appeared and spoke on television programs concerning the voile or Islam more generally were either Muslim men who could serve as targets for the rest of the panelists (Tariq Ramadan, Dr. Abdallah, or various mosque leaders), or Muslim women or men opposed to the voile, including "moderate" authors (such as Malek Chebel or

Rachid Benzine), Socialist Party activists (such as Malik Boutih), or women from "Muslim countries" (such as Chadortt Djavann or Carmen bin Ladin). Each type of Muslim served a distinct purpose. "Target Muslims" usually appeared alone, and were the object of derision by everyone else. (This was also the role scripted for the Lévy sisters, as we shall see later). "Moderate" authors (the opposite is "Islamist") told the audience in heartfelt and gentle tones how to think correctly about Islam, that is, as a private, individual matter of faith. Socialist Party activists showed that Muslims can be hard-core secularists and advocated measures against discrimination without giving Muslims any special favors. Women from "Muslim countries" could speak with great authenticity about the oppression of women that occurs through the instrument of the voile.

Indeed, the most effective advocates of an antiscarf law were women who were seen as Muslim, and who could claim ties either to the poor suburbs or to Muslim-majority countries. In both cases, the argument was: I have been there and I know how damaging a certain kind of Islam ("fundamentalist" or "intégriste" or "radical" or "political") can be to women. Those women who came from Muslim-majority countries could add the claim, "I know how the veil is used to repress women." One striking cartoon published in Le Monde shows a woman in a "real" veil in a place that looks like Algeria, with a rifle held out across her face (see figure 6). For French readers the image conjugates terrorism, covered women, and North Africa, and specific memories of the Algerian War.

The link was made constantly by politicians. Laurent Fabius, for example, a major figure in the Socialist Party and a former prime minister, advocated the law on the grounds that the voile is the sign of the submission of women. "Think of those women in the cités who fight every day for their dignity. Think of those militants for freedom who, on the other bank of the Mediterranean, have paid with their lives for their refusal of the voile."[44] Another key public figure, the Republican Socialist Jean-Pierre Chevènement, declared that "the voile is the symbol of an inferior status for women."[45] President Chirac attacked, in the name of laïcité, "those who threaten those basic elements of a modern society that are the equality of the sexes and the dignity of women."[46] Two darlings of the talk-show circuit in fall—winter 2003–2004 were Chahdortt Djavann, a woman from Iran who had published a short essay titled Down

Figure 6. Editorial cartoon on the voile, *Le Monde*, January 19, 2004 (by permission of the artist, Nicolas Vial)

with Veils!, and Carmen bin Ladin, the sister-in-law of Osama, who had her own book. Both women made this argument.[47]

On television talk shows, these voices of "moderate Islam" were accompanied by non-Muslim experts (professors, businessmen and -women, politicians) who explained and advocated laïcité. Finally, there sometimes was a Muslim man who opposed the law, and who thus could become the focus of the attacks by the first two categories. Two examples will illustrate the types of framing devices used in these programs to make clear where the problems lie.

The France 2 program *Mots croisés*, which aired on December 15, 2003, and was moderated by Arlette Chabot, concerned the question: "The voile, do we need a law?" It opens by mentioning that Chirac would give his speech the next Wednesday, and shows an incident in a high school where a pupil rolls her headscarf into a bandana, leaving some of her hair uncovered, but we see the teacher, as cameras roll, sending her out of the classroom. All the guests save one support a law against religious signs. The only opponent is Amar Lasfar, the head of

the main mosque in the large northern industrial city of Lille. Other
guests include a high school principal, who provides commentary on the
reality in schools, a leader of Algerian women who explains that the voile
is "tied to the rise of political groups in Muslim countries, the closest to
France being Algeria," the Socialist leader Jean-Marc Ayrault, the "moderate" Muslim Malik Chebel, the hospital director Claude Dagorn, and
other public figures.

Second example: a special episode of France 3's *France-Europe-Express*
on the voile shown December 7, 2003, shortly before the Stasi Commission's report was to be issued. Christine Ockrent, Gilles Leclerc, and
Serge July are the moderators.[48] An opening film explains there have
been 1,256 "cases" this year (a highly inflated number) and shows Prime
Minister Raffarin saying that the voile places constraints on women and
is not just a matter of religion. On the evening's panel, the lone opponent
of a new law is Dr. Abdallah Milcent, the convert to Islam who supports
schoolgirls' efforts to wear the voile in Alsace. Other guests include the
UMP deputy and enthusiast for a new law François Baroin, Green Party
deputy Dominique Voynet, Commission member Jean Baubérot, Fadela
Amara, Chadortt Djavann, and Jean-Claude Santana, the teacher at La
Martinière-Duchère high school in Lyon who led the fight to keep girls
in foulards out of the school (as described in chapter 4). Abdallah is the
object of scorn from the others; the first question put to him is "Do you
heal women patients?" implying that as a Muslim he might refuse to see
them. He answers that he does, adding that he is an "ardent defender"
of laïcité, at which Amara and Djavann laugh. A few minutes later Baroin
says to Abdallah: "Now the masks have fallen and we know where you
and others with you stand."

The Lévy Sisters under the Microscope

Let us turn to one final television program, which will illustrate how
certain voices were deemed authoritative and others problematic. It also
shows how television producers, through their choice of guests, and the
moderator's decisions in the course of the program highlight the key
issues of communalism, Islamism, and sexism.

The school scandal that received the widest coverage in late 2003 was, of course, the case of the Lévy sisters in Aubervilliers. The fact that their decisions to wear Islamic dress to school was neither a family tradition (Jewish father, non-practicing Kabyle mother) nor a practice of long duration gave ammunition to those who saw headscarves as the product of international Islamism. The Lévy sisters made the talk-show circuit, especially after their book, *Des Filles comme les autres* (*Girls Just Like Others*), appeared at the beginning of 2004.

Let us consider their appearance February 19, 2004, on *Campus, le magazine de l'écrit*, a book-oriented talk show moderated by Guillaume Durand and shown regularly on France 2. The evening's themes were Islam and the new anti-Semitism. As with many such shows, there are a few regular participants who join the moderator in posing questions, and invited guests, some of whom would have appeared in other, similar shows during the same season. If someone writes a best-seller, or is known for one or another reason, then he or she becomes very much in demand for multiple appearances on talk shows. Three of this evening's guests were in that last category: the "moderate" Muslim author Malik Chebel, the strongly anti-Islamist author Martine Gozlane, and the very media-friendly Carmen bin Ladin, the ex-wife of Osama's brother.

The Lévy sisters already had been on the most famous talk show, *Tout le monde en parle*, hosted by Thierry Ardisson. This evening, moderator Duran lets them begin by explaining their decision to wear the voile; they state that the decision came from studying religious books, and not from any outside pressure. Lila: "We read the verse and then decided to wear the voile; but the four main scholars of Islam agree that it is required."

The moderator then turns to Malik Chebel, who although present as the author of a recent book is given the role of authority and asked to explain the meaning of the voile. He states that there are three kinds of voile or women who wear the voile. The first is "peaceful Islam . . . our mothers and grandmothers, in their countries, they have always worn the voile, they believe in God, it is the tie to God, I respect that in its context." Then there is "le voile marketing," which people wear when there is a camera. Finally, there is "le voile politique" worn by women in Afghanistan and Iran, who started wearing it all of a sudden in 1979. Bin Ladin adds "the imposed voile," and Chebel agrees: "Yes, political, not religious. I respect the first type, but I am against the voile in France because the voile here is used for political reasons; women wear it to transmit a political message." He then tells the Lévys that he is not at all aggressive, but he wonders why they are wearing it now, this year, letting it be understood that the explanation would lie in the politics surrounding Islam.

Before they can respond, Martine Gozlane (who had written a book called *Allah's Sex*) bursts forth to ratchet things up: "It is not a matter of being aggressive or not; the voile in itself is an aggression, principally against young women who do not wear the voile. I hear all my Algerian friends, Iranian friends, all these Afghans who explain what they underwent where femininity is considered to be a disease. . . . And I consider these lovely women in our country, France, who have struggled for the rights of woman, and I read in their book that women must obey their husbands. . . . I do not understand how, you, in Algeria there will be a presidential election, your Muslim sisters in Algeria are fighting so that the family law code will be abolished; in Morocco, all women are celebrating that the code will be softened. . . . In Iran tomorrow they will vote and they are in terror that the chador does not come down even further, and you [the Lévys] present this archaic image. I do not attack you but I consider that you are an aggression against all Muslim women who struggle, who are persecuted!"

The moderator gives the girls a chance to respond. Alma: "Our many friends who do not wear the voile are not attacked by young women who do." Moderator: "And what about men who criticize women who do not wear the voile?" Alma: "But the problem is with them, it is a problem of adolescence and has to be addressed, but it is not our fault, those who wear the voile."

After a further exchange, Lila turns to Gozlan: "When you say that you feel attacked by the voile, you have to justify it. You spoke of Algeria, Afghanistan, Iran, and Morocco, but two minutes before that you said that France has its own specific context. We are not trying to make France the same as Saudi Arabia." Gozlan: "But you know well that girls in the projects say they wear the voile for protection."

Then the moderator tried out a series of possible reasons for their wearing the voile, to which the Lévy sisters respond calmly. "Political demonstration?" "No." "Or one operated by remote by parents or others around you?" "No." "One has the impression with Malek Chebel that it is a voile marketing, that one leaves it in the hallway . . ." Lila: "When we started to wear the voile, I knew no one who wore the foulard; I did not know how it was considered." Moderator: "Do you plan to keep it for your life?" Lila: "Yes." Moderator: "Why? Good Lord! . . . [catching himself] and why 'Good Lord?' "! Alma: "Because it is our freedom of conscience, and I agree that what happens in the projects with girls who choose not to wear the foulard is terrible, but the solution is not to deny us our right to choose, but to guarantee everyone their rights."

Moderator: "What astonished me is that sexuality is depicted very negatively in the book, that the voile is a demonstration against Western society, which is hypersexualized." Lila: "Our opinion did not change when we put on the voile. I know that in Tunisia there are girls who wear the voile and who go out with boys." One of the regular commentators, Josyane Savigneau, then remarks that women's struggle in the West has been to be something other than a sex object, "but covering up and thinking that if you uncover you are prey for men, you become purely sexual objects once more." Alma denied ever having said that, and turned the argument back on her: "I would not say that you wear shorts because you are afraid to be the prey of men." Josyane: "When Tariq Ramadan was here, he said that his wife wears the voile out of modesty, and I'm sorry but having hair exposed is not immodest." Lila: "That is because you do not feel uncovered with your hair in the open but someone else can feel differently for herself." Bin Ladin: "You consider that when women wear skirts men automatically think of sex, and you wear the voile to keep men from having impure thoughts, so you are in a state of submission." Bin Ladin then describes her life in Saudi Arabia as a life of submission to men, "it is in the very nature of the voile." She then turns to Alma and Lila and questions them: "You are very young and do not understand what the voile means for you as women. You are not like the others even though you say you are. Do you do sports?" Alma: "Yes, my best grades were in sports." Bin Laden: "Do you take off the voile for sports?" Alma: "No." "And you wear shorts?" "No one wears shorts, boys or girls." "My daughter wears team uniforms when she plays sports." "No one wears shorts." Bin Ladin, trying another tack: "Now women who come to Europe and refuse to be treated by a male doctor, that's the problem!"

The Lévys' efforts to focus on their real motives and choices in the specific French context are parried at each instance by claims about the voile's objectively sexist and Islamist meaning, best seen through the struggle of "sisters" in Muslim-majority countries, and the doubtless naiveté of the girls, objects of manipulation. Another regular commentator, Marc Weitzmann, tries to interject an alternative perspective: "The problem is that we discuss the voile in Afghanistan or Saudi Arabia but forget the fact of choice; no one has forced them [the Lévys] to wear the voile; there is a French element here. There is a break here. . . . The maternal grandmother fought on the side of the FLN and the grandfather on the side of the French army. On the father's side, the family leaves in '57, left Tunisia, at the same time as many Jews who became French citizens. So the history here has more to do with the history of France and of decolonization than with the Islamic religion." Josyane Savigneau is quite unhappy with what she sees as a detour: "That is what men say now, that these are unusual cases that we should not concern ourselves with and do not have to do with all women."

After an unenlightening discussion of the stoning of women (which Alma says is terrible but if a woman chose it, then it would be her choice—"the worst sort of throw-back," comments Gozlan), the moderator asks "What has happened in France?" Chebel answers that this generation has become attached to the worst anachronisms of Islam but that the voile is not a real problem. "Well then, why do earlobes obsess the French? Why the law?" asks the moderator. Chebel answers: "Because it is a symptom of a larger problem, a return to religion, more and more aggressive, after centuries of Islam being peaceful." Gozlan: "Every time there is an advance for women, Islamists react against it, as in Egypt in the 1920s, when feminists took off their voiles—yes it happened that way, Mesdemoiselles, and now in France les 'beurettes' are showing signs of a wonderful integration, and so you see reaction, a new visibility of radical Islam, they bring out the voile. You say '[it is] your choice' but it is your choice in the context of a huge apparatus that encompasses you."[49]

Although the program shifts to anti-Semitism and the recently published *Inquiry into the New Anti-Semitism* by the France 2 journalist Sylvain Attal, we remain within the same framework. Attal argues that today's anti-Semitism is based on contesting the existence of Israel and is linked

to antiglobalization efforts. The discussion quickly turns to Tariq Ramadan and his use of the phrase *Jewish intellectuals*, and the presence of
the Muslim Brotherhood behind current anti-Semitic statements.
Carmen bin Ladin now gives a moving account of her efforts to get
back her daughters, and Gozlan remarks, "Muslims are the first victims
of Islamism."

The commentators then turn back to the Lévy sisters. Josyane Savigneau urges them to read *Reading Lolita in Teheran*, and promises that
they will discover things there they do not know: "The first victim is
literature." She mentions the petition in *Libération* signed by "hundreds
of people of Muslim origin declaiming three cancers in Islam: anti-Semi-
tisim, oppression of women, and homophobia."

The most striking aspect of this and many other programs that appeared during this period, roughly late 2003 to early 2004, is the asym-
metry of roles played by guests. Of course, hosts and commentators are
expected to provoke and pose questions. But the guests, all of them invited on the grounds that they had recently published books, were not
all positioned in the same way. The journalist Sylvain Attal appeared as
an expert, who informed us about anti-Semitism through his book and
on the program. The authors Malik Chebel, Martine Gozlan, and Carmen bin Laden were asked about their books, but much less than they
were asked to comment on (or simply intervened on their own to comment on) the persons and acts of the Lévy sisters. Alma and Lila, and
secondarily their book, were the main object of discussion. Their claims,
their choices, and their headscarves were the real text for the evening.
They were only allowed to speak as examples of the problem, the real
understanding of which was provided by the "experts."

Taken as a whole, the program shows the Lévys against the background of worldwide oppression of Muslim women (and of sexuality)
by Islamists through the mechanism of the voile. This oppression is then
linked to anti-Semitism and to the age-old struggle of women for their
rights, a struggle now threatened again by the voile. Marc Weitzmann's
effort to suggest a new context for thinking about the problem through
his references to decolonization is attacked as a typical male strategy to
avoid facing the dangers Islamism poses to all women. The former colonies are only a specific case with nothing to add of universal importance.
Were others to have picked up on Weitzmann's argument, they would

have discussed this history of decolonization, migration, and mixing of peoples, and the efforts to find new identities in this process. That argument might have made wearing the voile seem like an act of self-discovery, of forging an identity out of a confusing past, of the very modern, and French, act of finding in books and ideas one's own stance with respect to religion. But that sort of story was not on the program.

TEN

Conclusions

WHY DID France pass the law against religious signs in public schools? We have already brought together the elements of the explanation. The voile, for that was what the law was about, had become a symbol of mounting Islamism and decaying social life. Concern about the voile "tracked" anxieties about the fraying of the Republic and about political Islam. From 1989 to 2004, Islam came to be seen as an international threat *and* schoolgirls began to demand the right to wear headscarves. Violence in the poor suburbs seemed to grow, much of it directed against women, *and* Muslim boys challenged the right of teachers to teach and that of their sisters to go bareheaded.

These associations of fears had their peaks and valleys, as we saw. In 1989, 1993–1994, and 2002, the issues climbed to the top of public awareness. It was in 2003 that pressure to "do something" reached a tipping point. What changed? By then, the post-2001 fears of international terrorism had added to fears of Islamist violence in Algeria. A few key tracts on disorder in the schools and a rising number of reported anti-Semitic acts (themselves linked to the second Intifada) had raised the level of concern about tensions between communities. Nicolas Sarkozy seized the opportunity to refocus public attention on the voile, and politicians on the left and the right sought to outdo each other in defending laïcité.[1] Chirac signaled his approval for a new law, and the political die was cast. The Stasi Commission was forced to work quickly so that a law could be passed before the spring regional elections. In a sense, the timetable was set by the haunting fear that Le Pen's Far Right could repeat its April 2002 victories. In such a short period of time, banning the voile was the only way to show that politicians of the sensible center were responding to France's new enemies.

Why did it have to be a *law*? In an illustration of a particularly French passion for seeking statutory solutions to social ills, nearly all the deputies, schoolteachers, and public intellectuals who thought something needed to be done said it had to be via a new statute—not because a statute would be clearer than a ministerial directive, but because only a law would send a powerful message to Islamists. French political thinkers and actors long have conceived of laws as ways to teach the French people moral lessons. Rousseau had written that the legislator must instruct the people through laws and thereby transform each individual into "a part of a larger whole." The law concerns the abstract individual, the *citoyen*. Pierre Rosanvallon put it well: "A veritable utopia underlies the ardor of codifying: that of perfectly governing the world by remodeling it so that it becomes completely graspable because it has been abstracted."[2]

In the world as abstracted from social reality, the public school works by encouraging pupils to leave their particular forms of identity at the door and approach learning only as future citizens of France. Viewed in this way, it would be difficult to support allowing religious signs into the classroom. The Stasi Commission had proposed banning political signs as well, and many observers commented that Nike symbols had no place at school, either.

Whether either the school or the wider society really does work in this way is another matter. When girls of fourteen or seventeen try out, with all the fears and hesitations of that age, a new appearance, what does developmental psychology suggest is the best response? How do a girl's peers respond when she appears with her head covered? What are the various trajectories followed by girls who do continue to wear head-scarves through their schooling? By virtually ignoring the sociologies of education, of adolescence, and of religion in their deliberations, commissioners and deputies remained free to draw on an anecdote told by a friend, or the impassioned statement of a school principal or a minister, as their evidence of how the new plural France was getting on. Why did young women wear headscarves? A minister (Jean-Louis Borloo) responded, presumably drawing from anecdotes he had heard, that they did so in order to reject the Republic or because of pressure from Islamists. Women wearing scarves, or the many sociologists who had studied them, could have told other stories, about how taking on Islamic dress provided a way of life they found satisfying. No one story would have stood for the whole, but such is social life, appropriately grasped in its complexity. But elections were close, and complexity takes time.[3]

Of course, many supporters of the law were fully aware of the disjunction between social complexity and the abstraction underlying the law. Their response to critics of the law has been to underscore the law's role in protecting the individual. For one of the particularly influential members of the Stasi Commission, Patrick Weil, the law's virtue is that it protects girls who do not wish to wear headscarves from pressure to do so. Other members of the Commission justified their votes for the law on the same grounds.[4] Indeed, although its empirical base is unclear, this argument is perhaps the only one to withstand the many criticisms made of the law, including those made by others on the Commission.[5]

What does the history say about the role of the French *media*? Journalists on television and in print emphasized the dangers eating away at France, and sought to link them to the question of the voile, often in the most tenuous of ways. In late August 2004, a group of journalists looked back on how their newspapers and television stations treated the headscarf question during 2003–2004. They generally agreed that the question had been given too much attention by the media and that this attention often did not involve adequate in-depth study. Joël Roman, coeditor of the journal *Esprit*, offered the following analysis: "Journalism ought to calm things down and to show what is behind positions taken on the issue. For the debate on laïcité, juxtapositions with other profound debates, over problems of safety in the poor suburbs or Islamism, were very destructive. It is regrettable that we heard from people who presented caricatures, and not from a range of positions, which would have been more civic-minded."

If many of the other leading journalists present agreed—a television producer denounced the "binary character" of the reporting—one television reporter argued that the coverage "was impassioned and irrational because the debate itself was so. . . . The media should represent the reality of the debate even if it is irrational in certain aspects."[6] In other words, if people say silly things, take them seriously.

By privileging the speech of people who "caricatured" the debate, journalists and producers sent striking messages about Muslims in France. Attentive viewers and readers during 2003 would have derived a sociology of Muslims that consisted of several distinct types of people. They would have learned that women and girls who wore the voile were the objects of oppression, and that their actions were dictated, directly or indirectly, by men: older brothers, fathers, and shadowy imams. It was useless to ask them to speak, because they would simply parrot the words of their puppeteers. But women who refused (note: "refused") to wear the voile had the right to speak, because *they* had found their agency and could testify to the oppression that they once had felt and that their "sisters" continued to feel.

Viewers and readers also would have concluded that Muslim men came in three categories: Islamists, violent adolescents, and secularists. Islamists take rigid, radical positions incompatible with the Republic. We instantly know their game when they cite scripture as a guide to conduct. They include the leaders of the UOIF, whose bumbling responses make it clear that they belong to another place, if not another age, and converts such as Dr. Abdallah, who laughingly claims to be for laïcité. Because of their influence, the violent young men of the poor suburbs continue to live in a cloudy world governed by visions of a better life in an Islamic society, perhaps the Islam-governed *Khalifa*, and in the meantime insult Jews and kill girls who will not submit to gang-rape. They are animals, protected by their manipulative Islamist guides. Islamist and violent men are opposed, thankfully, by properly integrated secularist Muslims, those who might acknowledge that they are Muslim, and might even see themselves as the saviors of Islam—Malik Chebel comes to mind—but take the Republic as their sole guide for how to live together in public.

Of these types of Muslim men and women, only the bareheaded women and the secularist men are worth listening to for their opinions on society. Producers of a television exposé might feature some young men from the projects in order to scare us, and they might put some scarf-clad young women on the talk-show firing line to highlight their absurd self-conceptions. But we certainly would not ask their opinions about anything. Only the secularist Muslims earned the right to speak as authorities on talk-shows in 2003–2004. When the wrong kind of Muslim happened to slip through, as did Saïda Kada by appearing in front of the Stasi Commission, the response was to treat her presence as itself an example of the program, and to schedule right after her a roomful of attractive, secularist youngsters, extolling the Republic and advocating a law against scarves.

Finally, what does the law say about *France*? After the initial debates surrounding the 1989 headscarf affair, the sociologist Pierre Bourdieu posed the question in a way that, even if somewhat grandiose, is worth restating many years later: "In projecting on this minor event . . . of the voile great principles of freedom, laïcité, women's liberation, etc., the eternal pretenders to the title of master-thinkers have delivered, as in a projective test, their undisclosed positions on the problem of immigration, such that the explicit question—Should wearing the 'Islamic' voile be accepted at school?—hides the implicit question—Should immigrants of North African origin be accepted in France?"[7]

And that indeed is the immediate question posed by the voile. Although for a long time France has been a country of immigration, it now has become a country of visible differences.[8] The very neighborhoods decried as "communalist"—the poorer suburbs of Paris, Lille, or Lyon—in fact offer the most variegated mixtures of color, dress, and language. With these differences in appearance come differences in beliefs, norms, and practices that go far beyond those that resulted from Italian, Polish, and Portuguese immigration. Islam is part of this new challenge to France, but so are competing notions of masculinity and femininity, and new ideas about how one can be French but also part of a worldwide religious community—and part of a European social and political one as well.

But the debates and the anxieties extend beyond "the immigrant question" in ways that were perhaps less apparent when Bourdieu wrote those words. They go beyond racism or xenophobia (not that those are absent) to fears that the emergence of a public Islam challenges the particular institutions that guarantee life together in the Republic—a public space from which ethnic, religious, and other characteristics are erased, and the public schools that model for their pupils the erasure of differences and the collective embrace of the Republic.

These fears are real; the older model of the Republic *has* been challenged by demands that France recognize the capacity of citizens to be publicly different and yet equally French. This "multicultural challenge" is by no means specific to France, but it arises there in a particularly acute form. It takes narrower and broader forms. How much do immigrants have to give up? To what degree can newcomers retain their particular characteristics—their ways of appearing, ways of speaking, religious convictions—and yet construct the "common life" that is the basis of Republican society? Is "integration" only in one direction? Should laïcité mask differences or celebrate them?

The very term *integration* has come to mean quite different things to those who see themselves as the reference point and those who see themselves described as "the problem." French officials see integration as requiring merely that newcomers to France respect the terms of the Republican pact, by learning the language, rules, norms, and traditions that define France. What is wrong with requiring that immigrants consider men and women to be equal? That they respect the norms of laïcité for which so many in France have fought? Put this way, these demands seem legitimate. To have two wives, or to discriminate against women, or to challenge the norms defining the public school, contravene the laws of France and, often, basic Republican values.

But for those who are called on to "integrate," these demands pose two problems. First, many find that the ways French officials interpret and apply ideas of gender equality and laïcité are far from neutral with respect to different views on religion and family life. The vast majority of immigrants from Muslim countries encourage their daughters as well as their sons to advance through education, allow them to choose their marriage partners (and are monogamous), but some of them also demand that their children observe what they see as the demands of their religion.[9] When praying too often or wearing a headscarf (or a beard) become evidence that one has not sufficiently "integrated," then, for some, French norms of gender equality and laïcité have been defined too narrowly, or in ways that fail to take into account legitimate differences in religious institutions and practices.

Second, some Muslim immigrants find that the one-way direction of "integration" requires too little of those who drink wine and wear berets, and too much of those who prefer tea and headscarves. Calls for newcomers to integrate are not accompanied by calls for long-term residents to broaden their notions of what is acceptably French. It was those long-term residents (and their parents and grandparents) who brought those newcomers (or their parents or grandparents) to France to build, and rebuild, the country. For those people who have lived, worked, and paid taxes in France for years, a call that they "integrate" by buying new clothes and changing the way they view their religion seems ungrateful, if not offensive. For these reasons, the very term *integration* has become a barrier between officials (from the High Council on Integration down through the local immigration offices) and many Muslim public actors.[10]

The multicultural challenge to France also bears on its important efforts to recalibrate access to housing, jobs, and schools so as to better ensure equality of opportunity for all its residents. The riots that enflamed France in the fall of 2005 brought to the world's attention how far France has yet to go in fighting the high rates of unemployment and discrimination faced by residents of the poor suburbs, and made it even more urgent that France formulate adequate responses to the questions these problems pose. Must the state publicly recognize differences in order to provide equal opportunity? Does "positive discrimination" in favor of people from disadvantaged backgrounds, or even in favor of Muslims, contradict the spirit, if not the letter of the Republican pact? Would recording the race, ethnicity, or religion of its residents, currently not allowed, permit the state to better detect the effects of discrimination? Taking such measures would reverse long-standing policies of keeping this information out of the public sphere of official knowledge. It would acknowledge these components of identity as legitimate elements in globally assessing hiring practices and housing policies, rather than requiring proof of actual discrimination in a specific case.[11] It would legitimate the selection of an official with that person's ethnic background in mind. To take this policy route would be to make France's visible public differences into "speakable" differences, characteristics of citizens and residents of which the state should take account.

Most immigrants, Muslim or other, see the great strength of the Republic as being its promise to accept all those who wish to become part of France. The laws that underpin that promise seek to provide equal treatment, a common curriculum in public (and recognized private) schools, and support in learning the French language. In their public and private statements, most Muslim leaders who challenged the law on religious signs also made clear their wholehearted embrace of that promise and of those laws.

Muslims who demand the right to be visibly different defy older cultural notions of France, not the political and legal framework of the Republic. When Muslim women in headscarves say that it is with *these* clothes and *this* religion that they choose to abide by the rules of the Republic and the life together (*la vie commune*) that is France, they are challenging the conditions for belonging to the nation. This challenge creates anxieties about sociability and allegiance, but anxieties can lead to new self-understandings. The Republic is based not on a shared faith, but on a faith in the possibilities of sharing a life together, despite vast differences in appearance, history, and religious ideas. That faith is worth retaining. Properly understood, it liberates citizens to explore their differences, not to conceal them.

Notes

1. The phrase comes from Gallie (1964).

2. One may also seek to reinterpret it within the French framework, as I attempt in Bowen (2004b); see, in much the same vein, Roy (2005) and Gresh (2004).

3. For the development of this approach in an earlier study on Indonesia, see Bowen (2003a), and for closely related work on modes of justification, see the essays in Lamont and Thévenot (2000).

4. On the interconnections among writers and television producers, see Halimi (1997). Often a new *pensée unique* is created in the process of denouncing an old one, such as when the "New Philosophers" created their orthodoxy by denouncing that of the fellow travelers of the 1960s (Ross 2002).

5. See Bowen (2004a, 2004c) and my future volume on debates about and institutions of Islam in France.

6. See also the discussion in Lamont (1992) on interviews.

7. See Wertsch (2002).

8. Roy (2005) makes a similar point.

9. Gresh (2004) is probably the closest in spirit to the present work, but written for a French audience and from an internal, critical French perspective.

1. See Lebovics (1992) on the distinct idea of the French nation, and Revel (2003) on images of liberalism and of the United States in France. Republicanism is also developed as a political philosophy outside the French context, as in the works of Philip Pettit (1997).

2. For example, in the vociferous debates before the referendum on the European Constitution on May 29, 2005, nearly all French public figures based their positions on putatively common Republican principles of laïcité, state-run social protections, equal rights for women, and so forth. Their disagreements concerned the likely effects of the new constitution on these principles. See Favell (2001) for British/French contrasts in political philosophies, and Rosanvallon (2004) for an historical analysis of tensions within Republicanism.

3. Rousseau's *Social Contract* is the text of reference; see especially (in Rousseau 1968) book II, chapter 3, on the General Will, and, for French commentary, Kriegel (1998).

4. See Favell (2001). We can see Pierre Bourdieu as a native social theorist of the symbolic power attached to mastering cultural capital, especially poignant for a man from the provinces. See especially Bourdieu (1988).

5. Michel Foucault's emphasis on state vision and power described well the Republican political vision, especially as it became a modern and modernist vision. For more on contemporary French political thought, see the essays in Lilla (1994).

6. Weber (1976) describes the process of turning "peasants into Frenchmen" through schooling, railroads, and the press. See Ozouf (1963) and Curtis (2000) on the Church and the Republic on schooling. This key role of the public primary and, subsequently, secondary schools does not transfer to the universities; that distinction, along with the sense that the state perhaps has less of an obligation to protect young minds by the time they are eighteen, helps explain why it was never seriously proposed that the law on religious dress be extended to the universities.

7. Today, however, a majority of parents who place their children in religious private schools at some point do so not to give them religious instruction but because they believe that their children will be safer and better educated (Troger 2001: 41).

8. In her short *Michel Foucault Today* (2004), Kriegel defines Foucault's heritage against those on the Left who would claim it in the name of populism or socialism.

9. Kriegel 1998.

10. Guéry 2001: 46–47.

11. Nora 2001: xxxv, xxxix.

12. Rosanvallon 2004: 91.

13. Presumably, he is referring to the cost of following the Scientology program, not to a single book.

14. Sevaistre 2004; see Boussinesq (1994: 38) for the same point.

15. See Boyer (2005), Schwartz (2005: 88), and the Council's review of its decisions in Conseil d'État (2004).

16. The sociologist Françoise Gaspard did testify, but in her capacity as a public and political figure, not as a sociologist who did an early study of scarf-wearing girls (Gaspard and Khosrokavar 1995).

17. I suggest how this might work in Bowen (2004b).

18. Among the most recent works, Lalouette (2005) covers developments through 1905; Boyer (2004) focuses on Catholic reactions to the 1905 law; and Scot (2005) focuses on the law itself.

19. I draw on Baubérot (2000, 2004) for this section.

20. An analogous duality between centralized and associative views of political life is described by Rosanvallon (2004).

21. The phrase in quotation marks comes from Weber (1976).

22. Ozouf 1963.

23. For a recent, fascinating account of the close ties between the role of antireligious convictions in the rise of the social and biological sciences, see Hecht (2003).

24. In chapter 7, I return to the importance of the law of 1901.

25. Willaime 2005.

26. Baubérot (2000) has described the "three thresholds of laïcité."

27. See Rosanvallon (2004) and the discussion in chapter 7.

28. Constitution of 1946, article I of section I, "On Sovereignty"; Constitution of 1958, article 1 of the Preamble.

29. This embodiment is why a scandal arose in 2003 over the film *Être et Avoir*, about a sympathetic elementary teacher in rural France, when this putative emblem of the public school crassly demanded his fair share of the film's revenues!

30. See Poulat (2003: 365–381). It is because private schools serve a public interest that concern was expressed as to whether they would be affected by the law prohibiting religious dress in public schools. Early on, legislators reassured Catholic and Jewish schools "under contract" that they would not be affected by the law.

31. Gallie 1964.

CHAPTER THREE
REGULATING ISLAM

1. See Eickelman (1985) on Moroccan religious education; on the preponderance of Moroccan imams in France, see *Libération*, May 4, 2003.

2. Stora 2004.

3. *Le Point*, October 18, 2004.

4. On the history of the Paris Mosque that follows, I have relied on Kepel (1987); see also Bayoumi (2000).

5. Mosque-building was in the air: large-scale mosques were built at the exhibitions in Paris in 1867 and in Marseille in 1922, and permanent mosques were constructed in London in 1926 and in Berlin in 1924.

6. Le Pautremat 2003: 338. Assistance Publique, created in 1849, coordinates Paris-area hospitals dedicated to serving the needy. Today it is called Assistance Publique—Hôpitaux de Paris.

7. Kepel 1987: 72–74.

8. Alain Boyer (1992: 53) estimates that 100,000 Muslim soldiers were wounded or killed during the Great War.

9. *Le Monde*, December 31, 2003; and for reactions by other religious authorities in Egypt to this declaration, *Le Monde*, January 6, 2004.

10. For a detailed study of controversies surrounding mosque-building in Marseille and Rotterdam, see Maussen (2005).

11. Others see the creation of Muslim electoral blocks as counter to Republican principles; see chapter 8 for an example from the city of Trappes.

12. Haut Conseil à l'Intégration 2001.

13. Bobigny was not the first such case; the Adda'wa Mosque in Paris's nineteenth arrondissement, for example, also has two such associations. Because the region of Alsace and Lorraine was part of Germany in 1905, when the law on laïcité was passed, and rejoined France only after World War I, this area is under the legal regime that existed in 1870 when it was incorporated into Germany. This regime included the Concordat. Cities in this area thus can grant direct subsidies to religious groups. The Strasbourg city government, for example, has proposed to fund 10 percent of the costs of construction of the new city mosque.

14. On the cemetery's history, see D'Adler (2005).

15. Sevaistre 2005.

16. Napoleon's structure for Jews consisted of one central consistory and one consistory in each department. Each had the tasks of ensuring that rabbinical teachings did not deviate from the conclusions that had been reached by the Assembly of Notables in its negotiations with Napoleon's representatives two years earlier (Jaher 2002: 103–121). As with the French Islamic Council, the consistory structure reports to the Interior Ministry.

17. For a fuller account of this process, see Laurence (2005); for local processes attending the CFCM elections, see De Galembert and Belbah (2005).

18. On the controversy, see Bowen (2003b).

19. For more complete overviews of Muslim organizations and orientations in France, see an older but still indispensable work by Kepel (1987) and the more recent writings of Cesari (1994, 2004).

20. Haut Conseil à l'Intégration 2001: 36–39.

21. The CFCM's bureau, the central group, included only two of these "qualified persons," Dounia Bouzar and Soheib Bencheikh, both of whom work closely with the government.

22. In work in progress, I examine the landscape of French Muslim public intellectual life.

23. Internal report written by Vianney Sevaistre in May 2003, author's files.

24. El Ghissassi 2004.

25. *Le Figaro*, May 5, 2003.

26. "Boubakeur Explains Himself," *Le Matin* (an Algerian paper), April 22, 2003. The mosque leader claimed that he had been tricked by the French state, which had assured him that it would not let Algeria lose strength in the Council.

27. For details of the CFCM structure, composition, and elections, I refer to official documents of the CFCM, author's files.

28. *Le Figaro*, May 5, 2003.

29. My remarks to this effect in the June 18, 2005, issue of *Libération* seem to have touched a nerve; the current director of the Bureau des Cultes, Didier Leschi, told the *Libération* journalist that they were "totally wrong."

30. *Le Monde*, January 20, 2003.

31. See note 13 in this chapter.

32. *Libération*, May 4, 2003.

33. *Libération*, September 8, 2005.

34. The official statement came come from the UOIF on May 6, 2003; see also *Libération* of that date. Morocco's *Le Matin* of May 6 quoted extensively from Morocco's man on the CFCM, Mohammed Bechari of the FNMF, as agreeing with his rival Alaoui's complaints that "the CFCM suffers from the overly great presence of the interior minister."

35. *Libération*, September 8, 2005.

36. *Le Monde*, May 3, 2003.

37. The June 2005 elections, which followed the same procedures as those in 2003, saw a rise in the Paris Mosque's score and a corresponding drop in that of the UOIF, a result hailed by Sarkozy as evidence of "moderation" and perhaps a result of greater Algerian governmental pressure than two years earlier. The FNMF was the overall winner of the elections.

CHAPTER FOUR
SCARVES AND SCHOOLS

1. On the history of Algerian immigration, see MacMaster (1997), Silverstein (2004: 35–75), and Simon (2002). On the broader issues of immigration's effects on French national identity, see Bancel et al. (2003), Hargreaves (1995), and Noriel (1996). On changes in the legal and political structures regulating immigration, see Viet (1998).

2. Gresh (2004: 158) notes that polling data show that respondents who judged the presence of immigrants to be "useful" fell from 80 percent in 1974 to 35 percent in 1975!

3. Sayad (1999) gives a moving sociological account of the immigrant's plight; Boubeker (2003) does the same for the Beur generation.

4. On the Marseille project, see Maussen (2005).

5. In an avowed effort to drive Muslims out of his town, in August 1989 the mayor of Charvieu-Chavagneux, in the Isère region, ordered torn down buildings used for prayer by the local association. Two years later, he demanded that members of the local association leave another set of buildings loaned to them by the regional government (*Le Monde*, August 17, 1991).

6. Ahmed 1992: 52–56.

7. The major studies focusing on Muslim women are Boubekeur (2004), Gaspard and Khosrokhavar (1995), Guénif-Souilamas (2000), Venel (1999, 2004), and Weibel (2000). In addition, a number of studies examine the orientations of Muslim men and women and include analyses of dress: Cesari (1994, 1998), Flanquart (2003), Khosrokhavar (1997), and Tietze (2002).

8. Gaspard and Khosrokhavar 1995: 34–69. Gaspard was the (Socialist) mayor of Dreux—a town not far from Paris that became notorious for the victory of the National Front—and a leading feminist politician; Khosrokhavar, from Iran, was trained as a philosopher as well as a sociologist. Both teach in Paris.

9. Venel 1999; Cesari 1994.

10. Venel 1999: 52–55, 73.

11. Venel 1999: 71.

12. Compare her descriptions of quite similar motives and results of scarf-wearing for "accommodators" and "neocommunalists" (Venel 2004: 90–91, 232–233).

13. There undoubtedly are such cases, but despite claims by many in French public life that young girls are forced to wear the voile either by their families or to protect themselves, sociological studies show little evidence of this, nor have journalists looking to find such evidence been successful.

14. On that history, see MacMaster (1997); on current Kabyle-area associations in France, see Silverstein (2004); on the immigration of Algerians, see Simon (2002).

15. Kaplan 1995: 15–28.

16. *Témoignage Chrétien*, October 30–November 5, 1989. See Rochefort (2002) for a detailed analysis of media coverage.

17. Local politics have also determined in which cities these affairs erupt: the far-right mayor of Creil had opposed the "invasion" of France by immigrants and later he formed an association to "defend" France (Guénif-Souilamas 2005: 136–138).

18. *Le Figaro*, November 2, 1989.

19. Badinter et al. 1989; Brunerie-Kauffmann et al. 1989. These two letters set out what continue to be the two major positions taken by the political Left, in 2004 represented by, on the one hand, the Socialist Party (now joined by SOS-Racisme), which argued strongly for the 2004 antiscarf law, and, on the other hand, a coalition of antiexclusion movements grouped under the banner "One School for Everyone."

20. I take the account of these two 1993 cases from Kepel (1997: 220–227).

21. The State Council eventually confirmed the expulsions in 1995, on the grounds that the incident had disturbed public order—in other words, that the actions of other people justified expelling the girls. For the Council's analysis, see www.conseil-etat.fr/ce/jurispa/index_ju_aj9507.shtml, and for its overall analysis of its jurisprudence on the issue from 1989 through 2003, see Conseil d'État (2004).

22. *Le Nouvel Observateur*, February 24, 1994. Intriguingly, in 2004 Chénière opposed a new law, saying that the voile no longer stood for political Islam (*Le Nouvel Observateur*, January 29–February 4, 2004).

23. *Le Monde*, November 11, 2003.

24. *Le Monde*, September 22, 1994. Bayrou seems to have opposed the scarves as necessarily *ostentatoire* (ostentatious) and opposed to the principle of equality (Bedouelle and Costa 1998), but in the 2004 National Assembly debates, in his role as leader of an independent member of the majority Right coalition, he judged the proposed law *inutile* (useless).

25. *Libération*, April 1, 2002.

26. *Le Monde*, December 4, 1994.

27. *Le Figaro*, October 28, 1994.

28. *L'Express*, November 17, 1994.

29. Interview in the documentary film *Un racisme à peine voilé* (Host 2004).

30. Host 2004.

31. Rochefort 2002: 155.

32. The Council did not overrule the Bayrou directive, on the grounds that the order technically asked school principals to establish rules banning the scarves and as such did not directly harm pupils.

33. *Libération*, April 1, 2002.

34. *Le Monde*, May 9, 2003.

35. The head of the National Demography Institute, Michèle Tribalat, quit the Council over the issue of the voile, and wrote an open letter, published in *Libération* on May 6, 2003, in which she advocated a law against the voile in school. Gaye Petek, the president of Elele, an association that works for the integration of Turkish immigrants into French society, came out firmly for an antivoile law and continued to defend that position as a member of the Stasi Commission. Jeanne-Hélène Kaltenbach was a key figure in televised debates about the veil on television and in *Le Monde*. Tribalat and Kaltenbach then wrote a denunciation of the government's concessions to Muslims (Kaltenbach and Tribalat 2002).

36. *Libération*, April 1, 2002.

37. Intriguingly, Marseille and the south have contributed relatively little to national fears of Islam, except through the southern strength of the National Front.

38. *Libération*, March 13, 2003.

39. Fleming and Carreyrou 2003.

40. *Libération*, March 13, 2003; *Le Monde*, February 24, 2003, March 15, 2003. Chérifi's efforts to calm things down were met with disapproval by many opponents of the law with whom I spoke. Given that her advice to the girls—put your education first, look for compromises—was also that given by many respected Muslim teachers, I suspect that reactions by Arabic speakers were influenced by her own Kabyle-region origins and the notion that some from Kabylia, oppressed culturally and linguistically by the Algerian government, "settle scores" with Arabs in France.

41. Interview with Jean-Claude Santana, September 18, 2003, www .communautarisme.net.

CHAPTER FIVE
MOVING TOWARD A LAW

1. For Raffarin's declaration, see *Libération*, April 23, 2003.

2. *Libération*, February 21, 2003.

3. *L'Express*, September 18, 2003.

4. *Libération*, February 21, 2003.

5. I cite the official version of Sarkozy's speech from the Interior Ministry Web site, *www.interieur.gouv.fr/rubriques/c/c1_le_ministre/c17_discours_sarkozy/2003_04_22_islam-UOIF*, accessed January 2006.

6. The relevant distinction between the law of 1901 and the law of 1905 was explained in chapter 3.

7. Tévanian and Tissot 2002.

8. *Journal Official*, February 14, 1983.

9. *Le Parisien*, May 4, 2003.

10. The poll results can be consulted on the firm's Web site, www.bva.fr.

11. *Le Monde*, November 27, 2003.

12. *Le Monde*, May 2, 2003.

13. *Le Figaro*, April 30, 2003.

14. *Le Monde*, April 24, 2003; *Le Monde*, May 24, 2003.

15. *Le Monde*, May 2, 2003.

16. *Libération*, May 23, 2003.

17. *Le Monde*, July 2, 2003.

18. *L'Express*, April 30, 2003.

19. *Le Monde*, May 18, 2003.

20. *Libération*, May 20, 2003.

21. *Libération*, October 21, 2003.

22. *Le Parisien*, October 23, 2003.

23. *Le Monde*, May 19, 2003.

24. *Le Monde*, May 31, 2003.

25. *L'Express*, September 18, 2003.

26. *Le Figaro*, September 12, 2003; *Le Monde*, November 10, 2003.

27. *La Croix*, December 9, 2003.

28. *Le Figaro*, July 4, 2003.

29. *Le Figaro*, June 11, 2003.

30. *Le Monde,* December 2, 2003.

31. *Le Figaro*, December 2, 2003.

32. *Libération*, September 22, 2003.

33. *Le Monde*, September 24, 2003.

34. Information from *Le Monde* and from AFP (Agence France-Presse), September 24, 2003.

35. *Le Monde*, September 24, 2003.

36. Ibid.

37. *Le Monde*, October 16, 2003.

38. *Journal de dimanche*, October 12, 2003.

39. *Le Monde*, October 14, 2003.

40. *Le Figaro*, October 14, 2003.

41. *Le Monde*, October 14, 2003. In February 2004, the girls' expulsion was overturned on procedural grounds, but by then they were engaged in preparing for their baccalaureate exam by correspondence (*Libération*, January 15, 2004).

42. Whether significantly or not, the word *independent* later was dropped from the Commission's name.

43. As an indication of their initial diversity of background positions, Jacqueline Costa-Lascaux had argued early on for expelling girls in scarves (Rochefort 2002: 153), whereas Alain Touraine urged France to recognize cultural pluralism.

44. See the discussion of the Commission's work by two of its members in Baubérot et al. (2004) and by Weil (2004).

45. See also the analysis of the Stasi Commission's choices of witnesses and working methods in Gresh (2004).

46. Schwartz had made clear in previous writings that he thought the State Council's jurisprudence insufficient to deal with the problem, and that Muslim girls did face pressure to wear headscarves in schools, "in violation of their individual freedom" (2005: 93). He played an important role in shaping the Commission's deliberations. But most of the commissioners were experienced in governmental affairs and presumably could have made up their own minds. The weight of media and public pressure, generated not by the hearings themselves but by journalists' search for scoops, along with the resulting bandwagon effect among politicians, are at least equally important in explaining the outcome. For an account of the events that gives slightly more weight to the role of the State Council members than is given here, see Lorcerie (2005).

47. At least one member of the Commission, Ghislaine Hudson, had tried without success to get other Muslim women in headscarves to testify. The Commission may have heard other Muslim women in its closed hearings.

48. Three federations of educational unions asked the president to reaffirm existing laws and warned that a new law risked "stigmatizing a part of the population." The largest federation (the FSU), representing 44 percent of all public school teachers, supported the appeal, but the second most important such federation, the UNSA, representing 14 percent of teachers, abstained from taking part. In general, school principals were for the new law; teachers doubted its effectiveness (*Libération*, December 17, 2003; *Le Monde*, December 18, 2003).

49. *Le Monde*, September 9, 2003.

50. I draw here from the analysis of this segment of the hearings made by Erin Russell (2005).

51. *Le Monde*, February 2, 2004.

52. References are to the hearings, viewable as streaming video on the Public-Sénat Web site (www.publicsenat.fr) with time markers as follows (using the RealPlayer viewing option): Jocelyne Charruel from Lyon on September 12, 2003, at 1:33:42; Louis Arvaud from Paris on September 9, 2003, at 11:00; Thérèse Duplaix from Paris on October 14, 2003, at 1:12:55; and Philippe Piedvache from Lyon (from Santana's lycée) on September 12, 2003, at 1:20:12.

53. Duplaix's testimony was on October 14, 2003.

54. *Le Monde*, February 2, 2004.

55. *Le Monde*, December 17, 2003.

56. *Libération*, November 13, 2003.

57. *Libération*, November 21, 2003.

58. *Libération*, December 8, 2003.

59. During this period there appeared a total of 1,284 articles in *Le Monde*, *Libération*, and *Le Figaro* on the topic, compared to 478 articles on the next most covered domestic story, reforms in social security (Deltombe 2005: 344).

60. *Le Monde*, December 7–8, 2003.

61. Late October through November was the critical period: On October 22nd, Chirac suggested that a law would be possible. On the 28th, Alain Juppé said that it was inevitable. On November 12th, the Debré Mission advocated banning all visible religious and political signs from public schools, and the Socialists went on record in support of this proposition the same day. The UMP national council followed suit on the 28th, and by this point Sarkozy had publicly rallied to Juppé and Raffarin had hinted that a law was being prepared.

CHAPTER SIX
REPERCUSSIONS

1. *Le Parisien*, December 17, 2003.

2. *Le Monde*, December 18, 2003. *Le Monde*'s editorial committee was not unanimous on the issue, but the recognized expertise of Xavier Ternissien, the reporter on Islamic affairs, probably influenced the editorial outcome.

3. *Le Monde*, December 20, 2003.

4. *Le Monde*, January 19, 2004.

5. The march received subsidies from CEDETIM (Centre d'études et d'initiatives de solidarité internationale, Center for Research and Action for International Solidarity). Most Islamic organizations tried to keep away from Latrèche during this period. For example, the Collectif des musulmans de France gathered to protest the law in front of the National Assembly, three days before another such protest in which Latrèche was to take part.

6. The latter organization will be discussed in chapter 9: formed by daughters of North African immigrants, it is closely tied to the Socialist Party (as is SOS-Racisme) and enjoys government funding.

7. Émile Poulat (2003) takes the National Assembly as his prime example of this tension between two senses of *public.*

8. This comment was a slap at Nicolas Sarkozy for having urged the president to appoint a "Muslim prefect" and for supporting measures of "positive discrimination." This latter term is roughly equivalent to *affirmative action* in the United States.

9. The phrase *local law* (*droit local*) evokes customary laws of regions against which the early modern, centralizing French state sought to erect a single, uniform legal structure.

10. The European Court has jurisdiction over the forty-three member states of the Council of Europe, a much larger body than the European Union that includes Russia and Turkey.

11. In 1998, Costa had written that Parliament should pass a law but that the law should reflect a "more open laïcité" (Bedouelle and Costa 1998: 206).

12. As of 2006, Costa's prediction has proved to be correct. On June 29, 2004, the European Court on Human Rights upheld Turkey's rights to ban headscarves on university students. On November 19, the French Constitutional Council agreed that the new law was not in conflict with the European Charter (Décision no. 2004–505 DC). But article II-70 of the Charter of Basic Rights in the proposed European Constitution, which the French defeated in a referendum held on May 29, 2005, guaranteed "the right to manifest one's religion in public," a right that some warned would lead the Court to rule against the headscarf law. Former minister Roger-Gérard Schwartzenberg's article to that effect in *Le Monde* on May 26 led the newspaper's editor, Jean-Marie Colombani, to write a *front-page* editorial the next day branding this argument as "lies."

13. *Libération,* November 29, 2003.

14. Interview, Melun, October 2, 2004.

15. *Le Monde,* April 23, 2004.

16. *Le Monde,* July 1, 2004.

17. *Le Monde,* June 5, 2004.

18. I first saw it dated June 29 on the Web site www.oumma.com.

19. *Libération,* July 5, 2004.

20. *Libération,* July 6, 2004.

21. *Le Figaro,* September 3, 2004.

22. *Le Monde,* September 4, 2004.

23. *Le Monde*, September 3, 2004.

24. *La Croix*, September 1, 2004.

25. *Le Parisien*, September 20, 2004.

26. *Le Figaro*, September 20, 2004. This position was approximately that adopted by the principal Ghislaine Hudson, mentioned earlier in this chapter.

27. *Le Figaro*, September 3, 2004.

28. *Libération*, September 3, 2004.

29. *Le Monde*, October 2, 2004.

30. *L'Express*, September 6, 2004.

31. *Le Monde*, September 16, 2004.

32. *Le Monde*, September 26, 2004. For other, similar cases, see *Le Monde*, September 30, 2005, and *Libération*, November 19, 2005.

33. Ibid.

34. *Libération*, March 22 and 24, 2004.

35. *Libération*, September 30, 2004.

36. *Le Monde*, September 8, 2004.

37. *Le Figaro*, September 3, 2004. The argument was weak, of course, because everyone agrees that the turbans have religious meaning; whether they also have ethnic meaning is irrelevant. A few antilaw figures had argued that headscarves were "traditional" rather than "religious," but to no avail.

38. *Libération*, September 25–26, 2004.

39. *Le Canard Enchaîné*, September 29, 2004.

40. *Le Monde*, July 29, 2005.

41. *Le Monde*, October 9, 2005.

42. *Le Monde*, March 14, 2005.

43. Ibid.

CHAPTER SEVEN
COMMUNALISM

1. On the relationships of mutual admiration and support among editorial writers, television producers, and public intellectuals, see Halimi (1997); on the ways television hosts and producers blow up incidents into *affaires*, see Schneidermann (2003); on television more generally, see Bourdieu (1998).

2. *Le Monde*, December 12, 2003; also see Gresh (2004).

3. *Le Monde*, May 2, 2003.

4. Thus, the census should not record ethnic, racial, or religious characteristics. Although this requirement makes combating indirect discrimination difficult, another antidiscrimination tool, sending in résumés to potential em-

ployers without names and addresses, fits the idea of anonymity and thus has been welcomed.

5. Chirac emphasized the importance of mixité during classes in physical education, a curious emphasis made by others as well, perhaps better explained by the simple fact that some girls had refused to take part in mixed swimming classes than by any French idea that sports make citizens. (That would be more of an English claim.) The official text of Chirac's speech is available on the Web site of the presidency, at *www.elysee.fr*. The fear that certain neighborhoods in large cities were out of the control of the state is not new. During the Algerian war (1954–1962), the FLN (Front de Libération Nationale, the independence movement in Algeria) indeed took control of everyday life in certain slums, collecting funds, killing rival Algerian politicians, and carrying out divorce and marriage according to Islamic law (MacMaster 1997).

6. Speech to the National Assembly on February 3, 2004. This and other references to Assembly speeches are taken from the official record made available at the Assembly.

7. There is a telling anecdote about a young woman who speaks of her efforts to "integrate" into her local community of fellow Muslims and adds, "if necessary I could wear a headscarf" (Guénif-Souilamas 2000: 259).

8. *Libération*, May 7, 2003.

9. Of course, only references to politically charged communities elicit these responses; mentions of France's "Chinese community" pass without comment, as such a notion has no political associations.

10. Stasi Commission hearings, December 19, 2003.

11. Renaut and Touraine 2005: 32.

12. These references are taken from Rosanvallon (2004: 25–80).

13. Ibid.: 322.

14. Quoted in ibid.: 257.

15. Indeed, the status of foundations has remained singular in France: although they are private, each foundation is created by the state through the State Council.

16. *Le Monde*, April 17, 2002.

17. *Le Monde*, October 5, 2002.

18. The statement was made by a Paris middle school principal, Louise Arvaud, before the Stasi Commission, on September 9, 2003, at 1:14:01 on the streaming video counter. For an anthropological account of poor suburban life, including schools, see Lepoutre (2001); for problems of segregation and schooling, see two excellent sociological studies, Beaud (2002) and van Zanten (2001). On urban violence, see Beaud and Pialoux (2003).

19. Brenner 2002. Since the publication of *Lost Territories*, Bensoussan has criticized France for ignoring the responsibility of "young men of North African background" for most of the increasing numbers of anti-Semitic acts. Speaking at the Hebrew University of Jerusalem in November 2004 (where he was introduced as "a Polish Jew born in Central Asia"), he contended that the French people are largely silent on the issue because they cannot imagine that Arabs, victims of racism themselves, could be racists (*www.gafni.co.il/media/sicsa/171104/*).

20. Brenner 2002: 43–46. Ironically, in charging many young Muslim students with communalism, Brenner and his colleagues make generalizations of the sort strongly criticized by many staunch Republicans, who urge France not to single people out in terms of their ethnic backgrounds. For example, they cite (2002: 40) polling data that show the higher rates at which "youth of North African origin" say that Jews have too much influence in government or the media compared to respondents of long-term French origin. They then infer from these data that this category of people exhibit "anti-Semitism," because of the difference in means between the two groups. They certainly would deny that statements about the undue influence of Muslims in suburbs constitute "anti-Islamic" biases, but it is difficult to see the logical difference.

21. *Libération*, December 17, 2003.

22. *Le Parisien*, May 4, 2003.

23. The remaining segments of the program focused on communalist influences coming from the Muslim-majority world, the efforts of some secular Muslims to criticize these tendencies, and the hospital segment described in the next section.

24. *Le Monde Télévision*, March 20, 2004; *Le Monde*, April 5, 2004; *Le Figaro*, March 31, 2004.

25. *Le Monde*, December 7–8, 2003.

26. Stasi Commission 2003, section 4.2.2.3.

27. Stasi Commission 2003, section 3.2.1.2.

28. *Libération*, December 19, 2003.

29. Ibid.

30. *Le Monde*, April 12, 2005. A directive from the Ministry of Health, dated February 2, 2005, sets out an argument for the consistency of these norms with the law.

31. *L'Express*, April 30, 2003.

32. Rosanvallon (2004) points out that the French state recognized the specific right of trade unions to strike long before it recognized in law a general

right to associate, both because it hoped that the unions would prevent wildcat strikes and because it saw unions as representing quasi-natural social groups. Muslims demonstrating in the streets have no such "natural" existence and are seen as trying to create a political body that would put forward competing sources of authority. Hence, in the historical logic of France it makes sense to grant legitimacy to the one and withhold it from the other.

33. See her analyses of immigration and assimilation in Tribalat (1995) and Tribalat et al. (1996), and her denunciation of the state's capitulation to Muslim communalism in Kaltenbach and Tribalat (2002).

34. AFP, February 13, 2004; I thank Amel Boubekeur for the reference.

35. The two letters were posted on www.oumma.com on January 31, 2004, and February 16, 2004.

36. Löic Wacquant has sharply criticized this use of the term *ghetto* in France, and indeed any efforts to draw comparisons between French housing projects and U.S. ghettos. See, for example, his article at www.homme-moderne.org/societe/socio/wacquant/ghetto.html. Although the differences are important, recent work on social isolation in French suburbs (e.g., Beaud 2002) suggests that the comparisons may be more fruitful than Wacquant admits.

37. When the UMT leader told women participating in the Paris demonstration not to speak with journalists, Brunquell saw this as male domination, but the France 2 Muslim journalist's comment was that the leader "would have said the same thing to the men, because journalists always try to find someone who will say something stupid."

38. Schneiderman 2003: 73.

39. These fears escalated in March 2005 after a group of poor teens attacked lycée students demonstrating against proposed school reforms, and (some) cried out, "Dirty white!"—thereby completing the set of epithets already existing in France. Alarms were sounded that the teenagers were engaging in "ethnic wars," as in the special section titled "Who Wishes Ethnic Wars?" in *Marianne*, March 19–25, pp. 16–29. Many linked these alarms to what they saw as outrageously anti-Semitic remarks by the comedian Dieudonné and the general rise of anti-Semitism.

CHAPTER EIGHT
ISLAMISM

1. Mongin 2001: 78.
2. Sfeir 2002: ii.
3. Roy 2002: 29.
4. Interview on Europe 1, August 4, 1994.

5. Deltombe 2004.

6. *Le Figaro*, February 9, 2005. Of course, at the most vulgar level, different words function in approximately the same way: "Behind words that change—*intégrisme* in 1989, *islamisme* in 1994, *communautarisme* today—news reports continue to function according to the same schema" (Deltombe 2004: 28).

7. A reference to the murder of Sohane in 2002; see chapter 9.

8. Gauchet 1985. His essays in the political theory of religion should be read together with major French works in the sociology of religion by Hervieu-Léger (1999) and Willaime (2004), which converge on a Weberian analysis of "disenchantment" and individualization.

9. Gauchet's historical analysis parallels that by Rosanvallon discussed in chapter 7, but adds the religious and identity dimensions to the latter's more purely political argument.

10. Gauchet 1998: 42–45.

11. Ibid.: 85–88.

12. Danièle Hervieu-Léger, personal communication, October 1, 2005.

13. Gauchet 1998: 96–102.

14. Roy 1999: 57. In a similar vein, Jean-Marc Ayrault, the president of the Socialist group of deputies to the National Assembly, charged of Sarkozy's embrace of the UOIF, "This new 'Concordat' is a dangerous encouragement of *communautarisme*" (*Libération*, October 21, 2003).

15. Roy 1999: 77–103.

16. Ibid.: 97–100; Roy 2005: 15–18.

17. *Libération*, October 11–12, 2003.

18. *Le Monde*, November 11, 2003.

19. *Le Monde*, November 21, 2003.

20. *Libération*, November 21, 2003.

21. The reply is in *Libération*, November 25, 2003; the title appeared in the November 21st story. Compare Frégosi (1998) on Ramadan.

22. Similar exposés ran in major newsmagazines in early 2004 as well, just before the Assembly debates on the law (*Le Nouvel Observateur*, January 29–February 4, 2004; *Le Figaro*, January 31, 2004).

23. *Le Monde*, December 2, 2004.

24. *Le Monde*, December 4, 2004.

25. *Le Monde*, November 19, 2003.

26. *Libération*, December 12, 2003.

27. *Libération*, November 6, 2004.

28. Roy 2005.

29. Babès 2004; Babès and Oubrou 2002.

30. See Bouzar and Kada (2003), and, for her reflections on the controversies around her own position, Bouzar (2005).

31. The references are to Vianès (2004), Kaltenbach and Tribalat (2002), and Del Valle (2002).

32. Del Valle (2002: 253–254), for example, describes the association of halal sacrificers À Votre Service (AVS) as "close to the UOIF," "radical Islamist," and "a meeting place of Islamic fundamentalism" that uses violence and funds armed terrorist groups in Algeria. Unlike Del Valle, I have spent quite a lot of time at AVS headquarters and have yet to witness any such "tendencies"; I also doubt that the French secret police would have allowed an association matching Del Valle's description to continue to operate openly in Saint-Denis!

33. It is difficult to know the range of associations with the word *pratiquant*. On the one hand, one hears the use described here; it may be that the legacy of the word's use to describe a certain category of Catholics shades its meaning in these instances. On the other hand, when forced to choose between labeling oneself as *pratiquant* or merely *croyant*, believing, many Muslims choose the former. The survey conducted in late September 2001 by *Le Monde* and others of Muslims and non-Muslims in France asked Muslims to choose a label for themselves, from *believer* (42 percent), *believer and pratiquant* (36 percent), or *of Muslim origin* (16 percent). The "believer and practitioner" category was equal to its 1989 level, but up from an intervening survey taken in 1994. We do not know how various Muslim respondents interpreted the question, which was posed in a face-to-face interview, presumably by interviewers from a range of backgrounds, or whether any respondents might have labeled themselves as practitioners but not believers, if given the opportunity. However, *Le Monde* (October 5, 2001) interpreted the results as showing that Muslims in France are practicing their religion more, and are better able to do so collectively.

34. *Libération*, January 11, 2003.

35. Chattou and Belbah 2002. Some highly educated Muslim candidates have been rejected on those grounds (Dhaou Meskine, personal communication, May 2003). One man who at one time worked for the naturalization service told me of police files emphasizing a couple's overly Islamic dress, the man's beard, and their use of Arabic as criteria for designating them as insufficiently assimilated. The public records studiously avoid mentioning such details, each of which could be challenged in court.

36. Maschino 2002.

37. Stasi hearings, December 5, 2003, at 12:15 on the RealPlayer counter.

38. Interview, Bobigny, February 13, 2004.

39. Interview, Saint-Denis, February 13, 2004.

40. *Le Monde*, November 24, 1989.

41. *Le Figaro*, April 28, 2003.

CHAPTER NINE

SEXISM

1. *Ouest France*, October 31, 2003.

2. *Libération*, December 15, 2003.

3. Compare the similar account of the Commission's reasoning by one of the Stasi Commission members (Weil 2005).

4. *Le Monde*, October 25, 1989.

5. Langlois 1989; *Libération*, November 6, 1989.

6. *Le Quotidien de Paris*, November 2, 1989. Halimi and her group, Choisir, held a meeting "for the defense of laïcité and women's dignity" at the Mutualité on November 28, 1989 (Rochefort 2002: 153).

7. *Le Monde*, October 25, 1989.

8. *Le Figaro*, October 15, 2003.

9. Jacquard 2002: 194–195.

10. *Libération*, April 1, 2002.

11. Gaspard 2005: 111–117.

12. *Le Monde*, December 7–8, 2003.

13. Stasi Commission hearings, October 14, 2003, at 1:01 and 1:25 on the RealPlayer counter. I owe this contrast to Erin Russell.

14. *Atlantic Monthly*, May 2005. Olivier Roy (2005: 7) makes the intriguing point that Tariq Ramadan is often described as "attractive" or "seductive" to discredit his ideas, a usage found frequently in Kepel (2004).

15. This link will remind U.S. readers of attempts to blame rape victims for their choice of clothing.

16. Mucchielli (2005) and *Le Monde*, April 26, 2005. Mucchielli found himself the object of denunciations by Fadela Amara for "intellectual terrorism" because his findings undermined claims made by NPNS; see his contribution to www.oumma.com, May 31, 2005.

17. Amara 2003.

18. See the essay on these images by Guénif-Souilamas (2004).

19. *Libération*, October 25, 2004. See also the analysis by Mona Chollet in *Le Monde Diplomatique*, May 2005, pp. 12–13.

20. See also Macé and Guénif-Souilamas (2004). The movement's assembly in June 2005 (Les Assises des Indigènes de la République, June 25, 2005) called for "women's emancipation that does not criminalize our men."

21. The Mouvement contre la Racisme pour l'Amitié entre les Peuples (Movement against Racism and for Friendship among Peoples), founded in the 1960s.

22. Such was the case with MRAP on the scarf issue. MRAP was divided internally on the issue. They had objected to expelling the Lévy sisters in Aubervilliers (Laurent Lévy is a key MRAP lawyer and activist), but held off from joining antilaw protests.

23. From the tract *Appel pour un nouveau combat féministe* (*Call to a New Feminist Combat*), distributed in early March 2005, author's files.

24. *Libération*, March 7, 2005.

25. *Libération*, March 8, 2005.

26. *Le Monde*, March 10, 2005.

27. See the claims that women in headscarves were denounced and even spat on at the Marseille event, posted on http://saphirnet.net/, June 4, 2005.

28. See the interviews on this subject with a range of activist-scholars in Taraud (2005).

29. Macé and Guénif-Souilamas 2004; also see Rochefort (2002).

30. See Chollet (2004).

31. A result epitomized by the figure of Marianne, the image of the Republic who is modeled after a succession of beautiful French women. The values of the Republic include sexuality. NPNS, interestingly, proposed an alternative set of models who represented France's physiognomic diversity.

32. See the study by Saguy (2000).

33. Freedman 2001.

34. See Smith (2000). At the debate in Bobigny described in chapter 8, city councilor Laurence Blin confirmed this hypothesis: many women supported the antiscarf law, she said, because recent Catholic Church efforts to reverse women's progress (in the proposed law to suppress the right to an abortion) make them even more vigilant against anything else that would detract from their equality, including the headscarves. Caroline Ford (2002) shows how nineteenth-century anticlericalism circulated images of cloistered, covered, repressed women.

35. This alarmist piece is surprising in that "open dialogue with the Churches" is what the state does and always has done, but it indicates the sensitivity of a leading feminist to the issue of Church influence on the state.

36. *Le Monde*, March 29, 2005.

37. Apparently, the title of the program had been *Chiennes d'arrière-garde?* (*Rear-guard Bitches?*) until a lawsuit by one of the older feminists, Antoinette Fouque, forced the director to change the title and to remove certain scenes (*Le*

Monde, December 6, 2003). The phrase *mettre les voiles* also means "to scram" and there could have been a double-entendre here, but as the women in question are very present, I do not see it.

38. *Le Monde*, December 6, 2003. *Le Monde* (February 3, 2004) titled a review of a second showing of the program "The Roots of the Voile."

39. *Le Monde*, November 19, 2003.

40. Personal communication, October 2004.

41. Interview, Melun, October 2, 2004.

42. Compare Isaiah Berlin's distinction between negative and positive liberty, or, somewhat in the Republican tradition, Amartya Sen's emphasis on resources and capabilities. This distinction was central to the debate carried on in spring 2005 over the proposed new European Constitution, castigated as too "liberal" by many on the Left.

43. Bouzar and Kada 2003.

44. *Le Monde*, November 24, 2003.

45. *Le Parisien*, November 25, 2003.

46. AFP, October 21, 2003. In October 1989, sixteen feminist associations denounced the voile in the name of solidarity with feminists in Muslim countries (Rochefort 2002: 150).

47. Djavann's *Down with Veils!* (2003), a tract of forty pages, begins: "For ten years I wore the veil. It was the veil or death. I know what I am talking about."

48. As is often the case, television moderators also edit print media: Ockrent has been editor of *L'Express* and the director of the television station TF1, as well as a television newsperson and host, and July is the editor of *Libération*.

49. One gets a sense of Gozlan's cultural sensitivities from the excerpt from her book *Le Sexe d'Allah* (*Allah's Sex*) quoted by the moderator at that point: "In your book you say that in heaven the Christians float, the Jews feast, and the Muslims fornicate." Gozlan: "Well, I am not a theologian, but . . ." [camera on the Lévy sisters, stony-faced].

CHAPTER TEN
CONCLUSIONS

1. Ironically, or out of sheer political cleverness, Sarkozy waited until late fall 2003 before announcing his support for a new law, perhaps to distinguish himself from other politicians as the only one who took the concerns of religious-oriented people to heart.

2. Rousseau 1968: vol. 2, p. 8; Rosanvallon 2004: 96. For a parallel analysis of the abstract universalism of French ideas of gender, see Scott (2005).

3. In any case, many rejected the testimony of the girls in scarves as nothing but a stereotyped "it's my choice" that failed to take account of the oppression; see Commission member Jacqueline Costa-Lascoux's comments in Baubérot et al. (2004: 86).

4. Weil 2004. Weil rejects the arguments, particularly present in media campaigns, that the scarf should be banned because it carries the intrinsic meaning of the inequality of men and women, and because it brings private religious faith into the public sphere.

5. See, for example, Jean Baubérot's remarks in Baubérot et al. (2004: 49–78).

6. The occasion was the twenty-fifth Summer Institute on Communication at Hourtin; the session was number 831, held on August 26, 2004, and reported at www.crepac.com. See the examples of selection biases in television reporting on Islam in Gresh (2004) and Deltombe (2004).

7. Bourdieu 2002: 305.

8. See Simon (2004).

9. Although the evidence is only anecdotal, a number of colleagues who teach in Paris-region universities report that young women whose parents came from Algeria, some of whom wear headscarves, are among their most assiduous students.

10. Hakim El Ghissasi, who has worked with mayors throughout France to set up debates (one of which we learned about in chapter 8), told me that he would accept almost any suggested title from a mayor's office "except *integration*, which is a word that wounds."

11. See Calvès (2004) for a synthesis of the issues involved in "positive discrimination."

Glossary

banlieue — "suburb"; the poor outer cities that ring Paris and some other large cities

Beur — person (or man) of North African parentage born in France; generation of such persons coming of age in the 1980s (*la génération beure*)

CFCM — Conseil Français du Culte Musulman (French Council for the Muslim Religion), established by the French government in late 2002, with elections held in 2003 and 2005

cité — polis, public and political space; large housing complexes; projects in the banlieues

collège — middle school; an independent school at any secondary or higher level

communautarisme — "communalism," sticking together with one's own kind or forming distinct groups (always with reference to such putatively basic features as ethnicity, race, religion, and language and never with reference to class, lineage, occupation, and so forth)

Conseil d'État — State Council, once an advisory body to the king, now the highest administrative tribunal in France

CRCM — Conseil Régional du Culte Musulman (Regional Council for the Muslim Religion), regional assemblies under the aegis of the CFCM

culte — organized religion, consisting of a body of persons, place of worship, and well-defined worship rituals

FNMF — Fédération Nationale des Musulmans de France, National Federation of French Muslims, begun in 1985 and today associated with Morocco

foulard — headscarf; Islamic headscarf

Gallican Church — the Catholic Church under French state control

halal — permitted to Muslims

hijâb — "curtain" separating women and men; clothing that serves this function

intégrisme — (from Spanish) Catholic antimodernism; Islamic "fundamentalism," *islamisme*

islamisme — efforts or movements aiming at increasing the presence or role of Islam in social life, public life, or politics

Jacobin — political tendency to favor central state control over public life

laïcité — "secularity"; restrictions on the state set out by the law of 1905; laws or philosophies regarding the removal of religious content from public space

Law of 1901 — guaranteeing the right to form private associations

Law of 1905 — withdrawing state official recognition and financial support from religions, but guaranteeing the right of citizens to form private religious associations.

lycée — high school

Maghrebin (*Maghrébin*) — person of North African background.

mixité — "mixing," of men and women, or poorer and richer people

MRAP — Mouvement contre le Racisme et pour l'Amitié entre les Peuples (Movement against Racism and for Friendship among Peoples), founded in the 1960s

NPNS — Ni Putes Ni Soumises (Neither Whores nor Doormats), movement to fight violence against women in the poor outer cities, founded in 2002

pratiquant — "practitioner"; one who practices his or her religion; those who regularly do so

religion — faith and practice by individuals

Renseignements Généraux — French secret police, roughly equivalent to the FBI

salafi — the "pious ancestors"; those close to the Prophet Muhammad

salafisme — tendency to urge Muslims to imitate the Prophet or return to the social life of the time of the Prophet; more generally, equals *islamisme*

secte — cult, always used pejoratively

SOS-Racisme — antiracism association founded in 1984 by Harlém Désir

UOIF — Union des Organisations Islamiques de France, Union of French Islamic Organizations, founded in 1983

voile — veil; head coverings adopted by Muslim women

References

Abdallah, Dr. Thomas Milcent. 1995. *Le foulard islamique et la République française: Mode d'emploi.* Bobigny: Éditions Intégrité.

Abélès, Marc. 2000. *Un ethnologue á l'assemblée.* Paris: Odile Jacob.

Ahmed, Leila. 1992. *Women and Gender in Islam: Historical Roots of a Modern Debate.* New Haven, Conn.: Yale University Press.

Amara, Fadela, with the collaboration of Sylvia Zappi. 2003. *Ni putes ni soumises.* Paris: La Découverte.

Babès, Leïla. 2004. *Le voile démystifié.* Paris: Bayard.

Babès, Leïla, and Tareq Oubrou. 2002. *Loi d'Allah, loi des hommes: Liberté, égalité et femmes en islam.* Paris: Albin Michel.

Badinter, Élisabeth, Régis Debray, Alain Finkielkraut, Élisabeth de Fontenay, and Catherine Kintzler. 1989. "Profs, ne capitulons pas!" *Le Nouvel Observateur,* November 2–8.

Bancel, Nicolas, Pascal Blanchard, and Françoise Vergès. 2003. *La République coloniale: Essai sur une utopie.* Paris: Albin Michel.

Baubérot, Jean. 2000. *Histoire de la laïcité française.* Paris: Presses Universitaires de France.

———. 2004. *Laïcité 1905–2005, entre passion et raison.* Paris: Seuil.

Baubérot, Jean, Dounia Bouzar, and Jacqueline Costa-Lascoux. 2004. *Le voile, que cache-t-il?* Paris: Les éditions de l'atelier.

Bayoumi, M. 2000. "Shadows and Light: Colonial Modernity and the Grande Mosquée of Paris." *Yale Journal of Criticism* 13 (2): 267–292.

Beaud, Stéphane. 2002. *"80% au bac" . . . et après? Les enfants de la démocratisation scolaire.* Paris: La Découverte.

Beaud, Stéphane, and Michel Pialoux. 2003. *Violences urbaines, violence sociale: Genèse des nouvelles classes dangereuses.* Paris: Fayard.

Bedouelle, Guy, and Jean-Paul Costa. 1998. *Les laïcités à la française.* Paris: Presses Universitaires de France.

Bellil, Samira. 2003. *Dans l'enfer des tournantes.* Paris: Gallimard.

Ben Jelloun, Tahar. 1999. *French Hospitality*. New York: Columbia University Press.

Boubeker, Ahmad. 2003. *Les mondes de l'ethnicité*. Paris: Balland.

Boubekeur, Amel. 2004. *Le voile de la mariée*. Paris: L'Harmattan.

Bourdieu, Pierre. 1988. *Homo academicus*. Stanford, Calif.: Stanford University Press.

———. 1998. *On Television*. New York: New Press.

———. 2002. *Interventions politiques (1961–2001): Textes et contextes d'un mode d'intervention politique spécifique*. Marseille: Agone.

Boussinesq, Jean. 1994. *La laïcité française*. Paris: Seuil.

Bouzar, Dounia. 2005. *Ça suffit!* Paris: Denoël.

Bouzar, Dounia, and Saïda Kada. 2003. *L'une voilée, l'autre pas: Le témoignage de deux musulmanes françaises*. Paris: Albin Michel.

Bowen, John R. 2003a. *Islam, Law and Equality in Indonesia: An Anthropology of Public Reasoning*. Cambridge: Cambridge University Press.

———. 2003b. "Two Approaches to Rights and Religion in Contemporary France." In *Human Rights in Global Perspective*, ed. Richard Ashby Wilson and Jon P. Mitchell, pp. 33–53. London: Routledge.

———. 2004a. "Beyond Migration: Islam as a Transnational Public Space." *Journal of Ethnic and Migration Studies* 30 (5): 879–894.

———. 2004b. "Muslims and Citizens." *Boston Review*, February/March, pp. 31–35.

———. 2004c. "Pluralism and Normativity in French Islamic Reasoning." In *Remaking Muslim Politics*, ed. Robert Hefner, pp. 326–346. Princeton, N.J.: Princeton University Press.

Boyer, Alain. 1992. *L'institut musulman de la mosquée de Paris*. Paris: Centre des hautes études sur l'Afrique et l'Asie modernes: Diffusion, Documentation française.

———. 2004. *1905, la séparation Églises—État: De la guerre au dialogue*. Paris: Éditions Cana.

———. 2005. "Comment l'État laïque connaît-il les religions?" *Archives de sciences sociales des religions* 129: 37–50.

Brenner, Emmanuel (pseud.), ed. 2002. *Les territoires perdus de la République: Antisémitisme, racisme et sexisme en milieu scolaire*. Paris: Mille et une nuits.

Brunerie-Kauffmann, Joëlle, Harlem Désir, René Dumont, Gilles Perrault, and Alain Touraine. 1989. "Pour une laïcité ouverte." *Politis*, November 9–15.

Calvès, Gwénaële. 2004. *La discrimination positive*. Paris: Presses Universitaires de France.

Cesari, Jocelyne. 1994. *Être musulman en France: Associations, militants et mosquées*. Paris: Karthala.

———. 1998. *Musulmans et républicains: Les jeunes, l'islam et la France*. Brussels: Éditions Complexe.

———. 2004. *L'islam á l'épreuve de l'occident*. Paris: La Découverte.

Chattou, Zoubir, and Mustapha Belbah. 2002. *La double nationalité en question: Enjeux et motivations de la double appartenance*. Paris: Karthala.

Chollet, Mona. 2004. "Un féminisme mercenaire." *Périphéries*, November, www.peripheries.net/crnt58.htm.

Conseil d'État. 2004. *Rapport public 2004: Jurisprudence et avis de 2003; Un siècle de laïcité*. Études et documents, no. 55. Paris: La documentation française.

Curtis, Sarah. 2000. *Educating the Faithful: Religion, Schooling, and Society in Nineteenth-Century France*. DeKalb: Northern Illinois University Press.

D'Adler, Marie-Ange. 2005. *Le cimetière musulman de Bobigny: Lieu de mémoire d'un siècle d'immigration*. Paris: Autrement.

De Galembert, Claire, and Mustapha Belbah. 2005. "Le conseil français du culte musulman à l'épreuve des territoires." *French Politics, Culture and Society* 23 (1): 76–86.

Delphy, Christine. 2005. "Race, caste et genre en France." http://lmsi.net/article.php3?id_article=368, consulted June 15, 2005.

Deltombe, Thomas. 2004. "Partis-pris des médias français." *Le Monde Diplomatique*, March.

———. 2005. *L'Islam imaginaire: La construction médiatique de l'islamophobie en France, 1975–2005*. Paris: La Découverte.

Del Valle, Alexandre (pseud.). 2002. *Le totalitarisme islamiste à l'assaut des démocraties*. Paris: Éditions des Syrtes.

Eickelman, Dale F. 1985. *Knowledge and Power in Morocco: The Education of a Twentieth-Century Notable*. Princeton, N.J.: Princeton University Press.

El Ghissassi, Hakim. 2004 "Les secrets de Sarkozy dans la représentativité de l'islam de France." *Sezame*, October 8, www.sezame.info.

Favell, Adrian. 2001. *Philosophies of Integration: Immigration and the Idea of Citizenship in France and Britain*. New York: Palgrave.

Fetzer, Joel S., and J. Christopher Soper. 2005. *Muslims and the State in Britain, France, and Germany*. Cambridge: Cambridge University Press.

Flanquart, Hervé. 2003. *Croyances et valeurs chez les jeunes Maghrébins*. Brussels: Éditions Complexe.

Fleming, Charles, and John Carreyrou. 2003. "France's Head-Scarf Issue." *Wall Street Journal Europe*, December 12, 2003.

Ford, Caroline. 2002. *Divided House: Religion and Gender in Modern France*. Princeton, N.J.: Princeton University Press.

Fourest, Caroline. 2004. *Frère Tariq: Discours, stratégie et méthode de Tariq Ramadan*. Paris: Grasset.

Freedman, Jane. 2001 " 'L'affaire des Foulards': Problems of Defining a Feminist Antiracist Strategy in French Schools." In *Feminism and Antiracism: International Struggles for Justice*, ed. France Winddance Twine and Kathleen M. Blee, pp. 295–312. New York: NYU Press.

Frégosi, Franck. 1998. "Les contours discursifs d'une religiosité citoyenne: Laicité et identité islamique chez Tariq Ramadan." In *Paroles d'islam: Individus, sociétés et discours dans l'islam européen contemporain*, ed. Felice Dassetto, pp. 205–221. Paris: Maisonneuve & Larose.

Gallie, W. B. 1964. *Philosophy and the Historical Understanding*. London: Chatto & Windus.

Gaspard, Françoise. 2005. "Entretiens avec Françoise Gaspard." In *Les féminismes en questions: Élements pour une cartographie*, ed. Christelle Taraud, pp. 105–122. Paris: Éditions Amsterdam.

Gaspard, Françoise, and Farhad Khosrokhavar. 1995. *Le foulard et la République*. Paris: La Découverte.

Gauchet, Marcel. 1985. *Le désenchantement du monde: Une histoire politique de la religion*. Paris: Gallimard.

———. 1998. *La religion dans la démocratie: Parcours de la laïcité*. Paris: Gallimard.

Gresh, Alain. 2004. *L'islam, la République et le monde*. Paris: Fayard.

Guénif-Souilamas, Nacira. 2000. *Des beurettes aux descendantes d'immigrants nord-africains*. Paris: Bernard Grasset.

———. 2004. "Des nouveaux ennemis intimes: Le garçon arabe et la fille beu-rette." In *Les féministes et le garçon arabe*, by Éric Macé and Nacira Guénif-Souilamas, pp. 59–95. Paris: Éditions de l'aube.

———. 2005. "Entretiens avec Nacira Guénif-Souilamas." In *Les féminismes en questions: Élements pour une cartographie*, ed. Christelle Taraud, pp. 123–148. Paris: Éditions Amsterdam.

Guéry, Alain. 2001. "The State: The Tool of the Common Good." In *Rethinking France: Les lieux de mémoire*, ed. Pierre Nora, 1:1–52. Translated by Mary Trouille. Chicago: University of Chicago Press.

Halimi, Serge. 1997. *Les nouveaux chiens de garde*. Paris: Liber—Raisons d'Agir.

Hargreaves, Alec G. 1995. *Immigration, "Race" and Ethnicity in Contemporary France*. London: Routledge.

Haut Conseil à l'Intégration. 2001. *L'Islam dans la République*. Paris: La documentation française.

Hecht, Jennifer Michael. 2003. *The End of the Soul: Scientific Modernity, Atheism, and Anthropology in France*. New York: Columbia University Press.

Hervieu-Léger, Danièle. 2001. *La religion en miettes ou la question des sectes*. Paris: Calmann-Lévy.

Host, Jérôme, director. 2004. *Un racisme à peine voilé*. Documentary film. Paris: La Flèche Productions.

Jacquard, Élise. 2002. "Un cas de dés-école." In *Les Territoires perdus de la République: Antisémitisme, racisme et sexisme en milieu scolaire*, ed. Emmanuel Brenner, pp. 159–206. Paris: Mille et une nuits.

Jaher, Frederic Cople. 2002. *The Jews and the Nation: Revolution, Emancipation, State Formation, and the Liberal Paradigm in America and France*. Princeton, N.J.: Princeton University Press.

Kaltenbach, Jeanne-Hélène, and Michèle Tribalat. 2002. *La République et l'islam: Entre crainte et aveuglement*. Paris: Gallimard.

Kaplan, Steven L. 1995. *Farewell, Revolution: Disputed Legacies: France 1789/ 1989*. Ithaca, N.Y.: Cornell University Press.

Kastoryano, Riva. 2002. *Negotiating Identities: States and Immigrants in France and Germany*. Princeton, N.J.: Princeton University Press.

Kepel, Gilles. 1987. *Les banlieues de l'islam: Naissance d'une religion en France*. Paris: Seuil.

———. 1997. *Allah in the West: Islamic Movements in America and Europe*. Translated by Susan Milner. Stanford, Calif.: Stanford University Press.

———. 2004. *The War for Muslim Minds: Islam and the West*. Cambridge, Mass.: Belknap Press of Harvard University Press.

Khosrokhavar, Farhad. 1997. *L'islam des jeunes*. Paris: Flammarion.

Kriegel, Blandine. 1998. *La cité républicaine*. Paris: Galilée.

———. 2004. *Michel Foucault aujourd'hui*. Paris: Plon.

Lalouette, Jacqueline. 2005. *La séparation des Églises et de l'Etat: Genèse et développement d'une idée (1789–1905)*. Paris: Seuil.

Lamont, Michèle. 1992. *Money, Morals, and Manners: The Culture of the French and American Upper-Middle Class*. Chicago: University of Chicago Press.

Lamont, Michèle, and Laurent Thévenot. 2000. *Rethinking Comparative Cultural Sociology: Repertoires of Evaluation in France and the United States*. Cambridge: Cambridge University Press.

Langlois, Bernard. 1989. "Fichu fichu (bis)." *Politis*, November 9–15.

Laurence, Jonathan. 2005. "From the Élysée Salon to the Table of the Republic: State-Islam Relations and the Integration of Muslims in France." *French Politics, Culture and Society* 23 (1): 37–64.

Lebovics, Herman. 1992. *True France: The Wars over Cultural Identity, 1900– 1945*. Ithaca, N.Y.: Cornell University Press.

Le Pautrement, Pascal. 2003. *La politique musulmane de la France au XXème siècle*. Paris: Maisonneuve & Larose.

Lepoutre, David. 2001. *Coeur de banlieue: Codes, rites et langages*. Paris: Odile Jacob.

Lilla, Mark. 1994. *New French Thought: Political Philosophy*. Princeton, N.J.: Princeton University Press.

Lorcerie, Françoise. 2005. "À l'assaut de l'agenda public: La politisation du voile islamique en 2003–2004." In *La politisation du voile, en France, en Europe, et dans le monde arabe*, ed. Françoise Lorcerie, pp. 11–36. Paris: L'Harmattan.

Macé, Éric, and Nacira Guénif-Souilamas. 2004. *Les féministes et le garçon arabe*. Paris: Éditions de l'aube.

MacMaster, Neil. 1997. *Colonial Migrants and Racism: Algerians in France, 1900–62*. New York: St. Martin's Press.

Maschino, Maurice T. 2002. "Si vous mangez du couscous . . . " *Le Monde Diplomatique*, June 2002.

Maussen, M. 2005. "Constructing Mosques: Negotiating Islam and Cultural Diversity in The Netherlands and France (1900–2004)." Ph.D. diss., University of Amsterdam.

Mongin, Olivier. 2001. "Introduction." *Esprit* 8–9 (août—septembre): 78–81.

Mucchielli, Laurent. 2005. *Le scandale des "tournantes."* Paris: La Découverte.

Noiriel, Gérard. 1996. *The French Melting Pot: Immigration, Citizenship, and National Identity*. Translated by Geoffroy de Laforcade. Minneapolis: University of Minnesota Press.

Nora, Pierre. 2001. "Volume Introduction." In *Rethinking France: Les lieux de mémoire*, ed. Pierre Nora, 1:xxxv–xl. Translated by Mary Trouille. Chicago: University of Chicago Press.

Ozouf, Mona. 1963. *L'école, l'Église, et la République, 1871–1914*. Paris: Éditions Cana.

Pena-Ruiz, Henri. 2005. *Histoire de la laïcité: Genèse d'un idéal*. Paris: Gallimard.

Pettit, Philip. 1997. *Republicanism: A Theory of Freedom and Government*. Oxford: Oxford University Press.

Poulat, Émile. 2003. *Notre laïcité publique*. Paris: Berg Internationale.

Renaut, Alain, and Alain Touraine. 2005. *Un débat sur la laïcité*. Paris: Stock.

Revel, Jean François. 2003. *Anti-Americanism*. San Francisco: Encounter Books.

Rochefort, Florence. 2002. "Foulard, genre et laïcité en 1989." *Vingtième Siècle* 75 (July–September): 145–156.

Rosanvallon, Pierre. 2004. *Le modèle politique français*. Paris: Seuil.

Ross, Kristin. 2002. *May '68 and Its Afterlives*. Chicago: University of Chicago Press.

Rousseau, Jean-Jacques. 1968. *The Social Contract*. Trans. Maurice Cranston. London: Penguin. French original, 1762.

Roy, Olivier. 1999. *Vers un islam européen*. Paris: Esprit.

———. 2002. *L'islam mondialisé*. Paris: Éditions du Seuil.

———. 2005. *La laïcité face à l'islam.* Paris: Stock.

Russell, Erin. 2005. "Laïcité Unveiled: Conceptions of Religious Identity in French Schools." B.A. honors thesis, Department of Anthropology, Washington University in St. Louis.

Saguy, Abigail Cope. 2000. "Sexual Harassment in France and the United States: Activists and Public Figures Defend Their Definitions." In *Rethinking Comparative Cultural Sociology: Repertoires of Evaluation in France and the United States,* ed. Michèle Lamont and Laurent Thévenot, pp. 56–93. Cambridge: Cambridge University Press.

Sayad, Abdelmalek. 1999. *La double absence.* Paris: Seuil.

Scheidermann, Daniel. 2003. *Le cauchemar médiatique.* Paris: Denoël.

Schwartz, Rémy. 2005. "Le jurisprudence de la loi de 1905." In *La laïcité: Archives de philosophie du droit,* 48:85–94. Paris: Dalloz.

Scot, Jean-Paul. 2005. *L'Etat chez lui, l'Église chez elle: Comprendre la loi de 1905.* Paris: Seuil.

Scott, Joan Wallach. 1996. *Only Paradoxes to Offer.* Cambridge, Mass.: Harvard University Press.

———. 2005. *Parité! Sexual Equality and the Crisis of French Universalism.* Chicago: University of Chicago Press.

Sevaistre, Vianney. 2004. "Le Conseil Français du culte musulman: Genèse et enjeux." Paper delivered at the conference "L'État et les cultes en France," Aix-en-Provence, February 16.

———. 2005 "Les relations entre le Conseil Français du culte musulman et l'État: Quelle nature?" *French Politics, Culture and Society* 23 (1): 66–75.

Sfeir, Antoine. 2001. *Les réseaux d'Allah: Les filières islamistes en France et en Europe.* Paris: Plon.

———, ed. 2002. *Dictionnaire mondial de l'islamisme.* Paris: Plon.

Silverstein, Paul A. 2004. *Algeria in France: Transpolitics, Race, and Nation.* Bloomington: Indiana University Press.

Simon, Jacques. 2002. *L'immigration algérienne en France: De 1962 à nos jours.* Paris: L'Harmattan.

Simon, Patrick. 2004. "L'encombrante visibilité." *Libération,* January 23.

Smith, William B. 2000. "The Image and Role of Women Promoted by the Extreme Right and Catholic Integrists in Contemporary France." In *Women in Contemporary Culture: Roles and Identities in France and Spain,* ed. Lesley Twomey, pp. 47–62. Bristol, U.K.: Intellect.

Stora, Benjamin. 2004. *Histoire de l'Algérie coloniale (1830–1954).* Paris: La Découverte.

Taraud, Christelle, ed. 2005. *Les féminismes en questions: Élements pour une cartographie.* Paris: Éditions Amsterdam.

Tévanian, Pierre. 2005. *Le voile médiatique: Un faux débat: "L'affaire du foulard islamique."* Paris: Raisons d'agir.

Tévanian, Pierre, and Sylvie Tissot. 2002. *Dictionnaire de la lépenisation des esprits.* Paris: L'Esprit frappeur.

Tietze, Nikola. 2002. *Jeunes musulmans de France et d'Allemagne: Les constructions subjectives de l'identité.* Paris: L'Harmattan.

Tribalat, Michèle. 1995. *Faire France: Une grande enquête sur les immigrés et leurs enfants.* Paris: La Découverte.

Tribalat, Michèle, Patrick Simon, and Benoît Riandey. 1996. *De l'immigration à l'assimilation: Enquête sur les populations d'origine étrangère en France.* Paris: La Découverte.

Troger, Vincent. 2001. *L'École.* Paris: Le Cavalier Bleu.

Venel, Nancy. 1999. *Musulmanes françaises: Des pratiquantes voilées à l'université.* Paris: L'Harmattan.

———. 2004. *Musulmans et citoyens.* Paris: Presses Universitaires de France.

Vianès, Michèle. 2004. *Un voile sur la République.* Paris: Stock.

Viet, Vincent. 1998. *La France immigrée.* Paris: Fayard.

Weber, Eugen Joseph. 1976. *Peasants into Frenchmen: The Modernization of Rural France, 1870–1914.* Stanford, Calif.: Stanford University Press.

Weibel, Nadine B. 2000. *Par-delà le voile: Femmes d'islam en Europe.* Brussels: Éditions Complexe.

Weil, Patrick. 2004. "Lifting the Veil." *French Politics, Culture and Society* 22 (3): 142–149.

Wertsch, James V. 2002. *Voices of Collective Remembering.* Cambridge: Cambridge University Press.

Willaime, Jean-Paul. 2004. "The Cultural Turn in the Sociology of Religion in France." *Sociology of Religion* 65 (4): 373–389.

———. 2005. "1905 et la pratique d'une laïcité de la reconnaissance sociale des religions." *Archives de sciences sociales des religions* 129: 67–81.

Zanten, Agnès van. 2001. *L'école de la périphérie: Scolarité et ségrégation en banlieue.* Paris: Presses Universitaires de France.

Index

Throughout the book, I refer to certain organizations (UOIF, CFCM) by their French acronyms, and in each of those cases I have made the acronym the principal entry. See the glossary for definitions of key French terms and names.